An
Arrow
in the
Wall

POEMS TRANSLATED BY

W. H. Auden
Patricia Blake
Robert Bly
Diana Der Hovanessian
Vera Dunham
Lawrence Ferlinghetti
Nicholas Fersen
Jean Garrigue
Allen Ginsberg

Max Hayward
Stanley Kunitz
Inna Bogachinskaya Perlin
F. D. Reeve
William Jay Smith
Fred Starr
H. W. Tjalsma
Richard Wilbur

PROSE TRANSLATED BY

Antonina W. Bouis

·

An Arrow
in the
Wall

Selected Poetry and Prose

·

ANDREI VOZNESENSKY

Edited by
William Jay Smith *and* F. D. Reeve

HENRY HOLT AND COMPANY
New York

Published by Henry Holt and Company, Inc.,
521 Fifth Avenue, New York, New York 10175.
Distributed in Canada by Fitzhenry & Whiteside Limited,
195 Allstate Parkway, Markham, Ontario L3R 4T8.

Library of Congress Cataloging-in-Publication Data
Voznesenskiĭ, Andreĭ, 1933–
An arrow in the wall.
Text of poetry in Russian, parallel English translation.
Published simultaneously in Canada.
Includes bibliographical references.
1. Voznesenskiĭ, Andreĭ, 1933– —Translations,
English. I. Smith, William Jay, 1918– .
II. Reeve, F. D. (Franklin D.), 1928– .
III. Title.
PG3489.4.Z6A2234 1987   891.71′44   86-10301
ISBN 0-8050-0100-X

First Edition

Designed by Jeffrey L. Ward
Printed in the United States of America
1 3 5 7 9 10 8 6 4 2

ISBN 0-8050-0100-X

Acknowledgments

Some of the poems and both essays in this volume first appeared in Russian in Andrei Voznesensky, *Sobranie sochinenii*, vols. I, II, and III (Moscow, 1983, 1984). Volume I, copyright © Vstupitelnaya statya, Oformlenye, Izdatelstvo, "Hudozhestvennaya literatura," 1983; volumes II and III, Oformlenye hudozhnika, Bl. Medvedeva, copyright © Oformlenye, Izdatelstvo, "Hudozhestvennaya literatura," 1984. Reprinted by permission of VAAP-USSR Copyright Agency.

The translations in Part I are from *Antiworlds and the Fifth Ace: Poetry by Andrei Voznesensky*, a bilingual edition, edited by Patricia Blake and Max Hayward, with a foreword by W. H. Auden. Copyright © 1966, 1967 by Basic Books, Inc., Publishers. Copyright © 1963 by Encounter Ltd. Reprinted by permission of Basic Books, Inc.

The translations in Part II and of "Book Boom" in Part III are from *Nostalgia for the Present*, edited by Vera Dunham and Max Hayward, with forewords by Edward M. Kennedy and Arthur Miller, published by Doubleday and Company, Inc., 1978. Copyright © 1978 by Doubleday and Company, Inc. Reprinted by permission of Andrei Voznesensky.

The translation of "Autolithography" is included through the courtesy of Universal Limited Art Editions.

Содержание

I Антимиры

Гойя	2
Ахиллесово сердце	4
Мотогонки по вертикальной стене	6
Охота на зайца	10
Лобная баллада	16
Бьют женщину	20
Кассирша	24
Осень в Сигулде	28
Замерли	34
Первый лед	36
Стриптиз	38
Антимиры	40
Параболическая баллада	44

Contents

Introduction by William Jay Smith   xiii

I Antiworlds

I Am Goya   3
My Achilles Heart   5
Wall of Death   7
Hunting a Hare   11
The Skull Ballad   17
Someone Is Beating a Woman   21
The Cashier   25
Autumn in Sigulda   29
Dead Still   35
First Frost   37
Striptease   39
Antiworlds   41
Parabolic Ballad   45

Пожар в архитектурном институте 48

Баллада точки 52

Нью-йоркская птица 54

Итальянский гараж 58

Баллада-диссертация 60

Голова ли от ветра кружится? 64

Выйду ли к парку 66

Ты сегодня, 16-го, справляешь день
   рождения 68

Плач по двум нерожденным поэмам 74

Зов озера 80

II Ностальгия по настоящему

Ностальгия по настоящему 88

Частное кладбище 92

Сага 94

Васильки Шагала 96

Провинциальная хроника 100

Похороны Гоголя Николая Васильича 106

Автомат 110

Стрела в стене 114

Старая песня 118

Смерть Шукшина 120

Ироническая элегия, родившаяся в
   весьма скорбные минуты, когда не
   пишется 122

Морозный ипподром 126

Не забудь 132

Хор нимф 136

НТР 138

Исповедь 142

Июнь — 68 144

Забастовка стриптиза 148

Нью-йоркские значки 154

Молчальный звон 158

Fire in the Architectural Institute   49

Ballad of the Full Stop   53

New York Bird   55

Italian Garage   59

The Nose   61

Does a High Wind Make Me Reel?   65

Her Shoes   67

At Hotel Berlin   69

Lament for Two Unborn Poems   75

The Call of the Lake   81

II Nostalgia for the Present

Nostalgia for the Present   89

Family Graveyard   93

Saga   95

Chagall's Cornflowers   97

Provincial Scene   101

The Interment of Nikolai Vasilich Gogol   107

Phone Booth   111

An Arrow in the Wall   115

Old Song   119

On the Death of Shukshin   121

An Ironical Elegy Born in Those Most
Distressing Moments When One Cannot
Write   123

Winter at the Track   127

Do Not Forget   133

A Chorus of Nymphs   137

Technology   139

The Eternal Question   143

June '68   145

Striptease on Strike   149

American Buttons   155

Silent Tingling   159

Порнография духа   162
Скрымтымным   164

III Прибавьте тиражи … журавлям

Книжный бум   168
Почему два великих поэта   170
Автолитография   172
Мать   178
Мать   180
Водитель   184
Певец   186
Памяти Владимира Высоцкого   188
Яблокопад   190
Диалог   200
Чем больше от сердца отрываешь   206
Портрет   210
Беседа в Риме   212
Два стихотворения   214
Линкольну   216
Чеколек   218
Сон   220
Вечер в «Обществе слепых»   224
Скульптор свечей   228
Школьник   232
Вор воспоминаний   236
Человек породы сенбернар   240
Кабанья охота   244

Pornography of the Mind   163
Darkmotherscream   165

III "Release the Cranes"

Book Boom   169
The Great Confrontation   171
Autolithography   173
Mother   179
Elegy for My Mother   181
The Driver   185
The Singer   187
Epitaph for Vysotsky   189
Applefall   191
Dialogue   201
The More You Tear Off, the More You Keep   207
Portrait   211
A Conversation in Rome   213
Two Poems   215
At Ford's Theater   217
A Man Is Changing His Skin   219
A Dream   221
An Evening at the Society for the Blind   225
The Candle Sculptor   229
The Schoolboy   233
The Thief of Memories   237
A Saint Bernard of a Man   241
The Boar Hunt   245

IV Selected Prose

I Am Fourteen   255
O   287

Notes   325

•

Introduction

In the past fifteen years Andrei Voznesensky has firmly established himself not only as Russia's leading poet but as a writer of international reputation. In his own country, where his collected works appeared in 1983–84 in a three-volume edition, he has achieved the popularity of a film star. As many as 14,000 people have gathered in a sports stadium in Moscow to hear him read and 500,000 have subscribed to buy a single volume of his poems. His poetry has been translated into all the major languages and often by the world's major poets; he has packed auditoriums in London, Paris, New York, and Washington, and on college campuses throughout the United States.

The art critic John Russell has described his appearance in London in the sixties: "He read on the same bill as Laurence Olivier, Paul Scofield and Nicol Williamson. All were at their best. As manipulators of other men's words, the great mummers in question had no equal. But even so, it was Mr. Voznesensky whom people talked about on the way home. Reading his own work, he had seemed like a man possessed by language. Open vowels were stretched forever. Consonants had the ring of cavalry on cobblestones. Even silence had its heartbeat. It was on every count a prodigious performance."

A man of slight build, Voznesensky seems at first highly vulnerable and scarcely able to evoke such a response. On the platform he stands with his feet spread apart, like a boxer ready to dance in on his opponent, his wide gaze directed upward, his nose tilted back, bright blue eyes fixed on something far off in space, his right hand raised, thumb slightly extended as if hailing some heavenly bus. With this stance, the Hungarian poet Sándor Weöres said, Andrei Voznesensky is attempting to enlarge the scope of poetry. In his reading he sketches a kind of verbal parabola, beginning quietly, building up and ballooning out, then descending until at times the last few words are spoken separately in a staccato fashion, almost whispered into the microphone.

In the poem "Autumn in Sigulda," translated by W. H. Auden, the poet has said:

> *Voznesensky* may one day be graven
> In cold stone but, meanwhile, may
> I find haven
> On your warm cheek as *Andrei*.

It is this personal warmth and unusual vitality that communicates itself to his listeners. And if the reading of his poems is impressive, dazzling even, it is their substance, their originality and power, that in the end makes them memorable.

Andrei Voznesensky was born in Moscow on May 12, 1933. Part of his early childhood was spent in the ancient Russian city of Vladimir, where his first book, *Mosaic*, was published in 1960. During the war years, 1941 to 1944, he lived with his mother in Kurgan, in the Urals. His father, an engineer, helped evacuate factories from Leningrad during the siege. In some of the most moving pages of his memoir of Pasternak, included here, he tells of his father's arrival one day in Kurgan on leave, thin and unshaven, carrying in his canvas rucksack, along with a can of American pork and beans, a book of etchings by Goya. On the young boy who had first dreamed of being a painter, the book made a lasting impression. Goya was to be the subject of one of his early, and still most celebrated, poems.

Voznesensky enrolled as a student at the Architectural Institute in Moscow. Shortly before he was to graduate in 1957, a fire broke out, destroying an elaborate design project on which he had worked all year. "We were so tired," he said, "that we were glad that final examinations had to be postponed. But for me it was more than a fire. I believe in symbols. I understood that architecture was burned out in *me*. I became a poet." The event became the subject of his poem "Fire in the Architectural Institute."

Although the fire turned him to poetry, his interest in architecture has never left him. In some of the autobiographical pages of "O," also included here, he pays tribute to Pavlov, his teacher at the Institute, and describes his feeling of guilt at having abandoned what he calls the "most honest profession." He describes the monument that he wishes to erect to language. The project for such a metallic golden sphere, a "Poetarch," containing a hall for poetry readings and concerts, had been accepted with enthusiasm by Jack Lang, the French minister of culture, for the Paris Fair that was to have been held in 1989, but dropped when the fair was called off. Painting and architecture have played an important role throughout his poetry. His essentially visual imagination has even led him to several successful experiments with concrete poetry.

Voznesensky's formal education was at the Architectural Institute but his poetic apprenticeship was with his mentor Boris Pasternak, whose poems his mother had read to him early on. In his memoir, he tells how as a schoolboy he sent Pasternak some poems and the latter replied with an invitation to visit him. "I moved out to Peredelkino," Voznesensky says, "and stayed near him until his death.... He was my only master." Voznesensky was influenced as much by Pasternak's moral stance as by his poetry. He followed Pasternak's lead in reacting against the total corruption of language that had occurred during the Stalinist years. It was Voznesensky's espousal of the individual values that Pasternak had championed that made for his immense popularity with the members of his own generation in the early sixties. But that popularity made him immediate enemies among the cultural bureaucrats and literary hacks who felt threatened by anything that did not follow the party line.

An attack soon came from the very top. At a meeting between government members and representatives of the intelligentsia at the Kremlin on March 7, 1963, Khrushchev lost his temper and berated the young writers present in violent language. He shook his fist at Voznesensky, accusing him of formalism and of attempting to bring about a Hungarian Revolution in Russia. "Clear out of my country!" he shouted at him. For a long time afterwards Voznesensky was not allowed to publish anything, and he wandered about like a fugitive. The pain of this internal exile, which deepened his poetic resolve, underlies much of his best poetry, even that written many years later.

He may have been thinking of this lonely, painful time when he said not long ago: "There is a kind of drawn-out music in Russian speech that comes from the great distances on the Russian steppes. This cello-like note resounds in the lengths of our names — in our surnames and patronymics. Language is the music of thought; it is what our ancestors called the soul. . . . Russian is especially suited to the transmission of psychological states; the mood landscapes that it can evoke are unique and untranslatable."

To understand Voznesensky's popularity as a poet, one must appreciate the position that a poet occupies in Russia. The poet there is taken seriously and listened to in a way quite unknown in the West. His opinions are sought out and respected; he is revered as a guardian of culture. This was even truer in tsarist times. People all over the provinces, as well as in Moscow and St. Petersburg, knew by heart the poems of Alexander Blok, who was paid five gold rubles a line for them. When today the poet reads his work during prime time on television (after the regular evening news program), as Voznesensky has done, he reaches not thousands but millions of listeners. In 1984 Voznesensky published in the *Literary Gazette* an article titled "Builders of the Spirit," in which he spoke of cultural values past and present that were being shunted aside and of those who set out to defend them. He praised patrons of the arts like Pavel Mikhailovich Tretyakov, the merchant-founder of the Tretyakov Gallery in Moscow, who have given spiritual as well as financial support to the arts. These "pistons of the spiritual process, builders of the superstructure, the public activities of culture" he called "builders of the spirit." "Art is fragile," he said, "and it needs the support of these builders, who have always been hated by the barbarians of all ages."

Voznesensky received more than twenty-five hundred letters in response to his article. One man wrote from Chagall's birthplace Vitebsk to say that several buildings there had been saved as a result of the piece. In a follow-up article, "The Ecology of Culture,"

Voznesensky called these correspondents, these "blue and white swallows," today's patrons and cultural defenders. "It is not only the environment, the age-old forests and rivers that are endangered," he wrote, "the ecological dimming of our spiritual environment is much more dangerous.... The layer of atmosphere that protects us is as fragile and thin as a fingerprint on a glass. But even more defenseless is the layer of human culture."

Because of his special privileges and his ability to travel abroad, Voznesensky appears to some critics in the West a favorite of the regime. Eugene McCarthy, introducing the poet at Ford's Theater in Washington on a recent visit, answered that charge by saying that the Soviet authorities don't seem to know what to do with Voznesensky "because what he writes is the ultimate kind of propaganda—the truth." Voznesensky's reputation abroad has, of course, helped him considerably at home. His close association with powerful political and literary figures, his friendship with Senator Edward Kennedy, his private meetings with heads of state have all worked to strengthen his hand in Moscow. But although he does indeed enjoy certain privileges, he is certainly not immune to attack. It seems that the greater his reputation becomes, the more vicious the attacks. Nothing in recent years has equaled the condemnation of Khrushchev, but some of the critical savagery directed at him would have finished off writers of lesser tenacity and courage long ago.

When his poem "The Great Confrontation" appeared, it was bitterly condemned. Voznesensky was accused of showing himself to be an anti-Marxist with no working-class vision simply because he had chosen to equate the two great powers. The same critic said that because the poem to Chagall speaks of blue cornflowers and because blue is the color of Israel, Voznesensky had sold out to the Jews. The poet has also frequently been condemned for his connection with Georgia. One of his forebears was a Georgian nobleman, who, because of his anti-Russian activities, had his son taken from him and sent off to a seminary. When the son became a priest and married, his children took the name Voznesensky, which means literally "Ascension." His enemies have found his pride in his Georgian ancestry suspect and anti-Russian. Voznesensky helped design a monument erected in Moscow to honor the Georgians. It consists of a copper column made up of letters of the Georgian alphabet ingeniously stacked one on the other. His detractors have termed it "the tattooed prick."

One of the most vicious attacks on the poet in the West was that of Clive James in the *New York Review of Books* on August 16, 1979. The point that James made at great length was that since Voznesensky could not tell the direct political truth, he could not tell the truth about anything. He could operate only through hints and evasions. Because Voznesensky refused to do any of the honorable things left for him to do—to die, to go into exile, or to keep quiet—he was finished as a poet. Altough he might be treated as a star in his own country and abroad, he could still not, according to Clive James, attain any real stature. Just as vicious have been attacks from Russian émigré writers once closely associated with the poet and others whose departures from the Soviet Union were somewhat less heroic than they would have us believe. In their understandable bitterness at being themselves cut off from their native country and their native language, they appear to resent any writer left behind. They object to Voznesensky's enjoying benefits, as a member of the Writers' Union, which they themselves enjoyed. Sometimes using the same words that Clive James used, they say that Voznesensky is the victim of the horrible Soviet system, which has destroyed any talent that he had.

Andrei Voznesensky once said: "The poet is two people. One is an insignificant person, leading the most insignificant of lives. But behind him, like an echo, is the other person who writes poetry. Sometimes the two coexist. Sometimes they collide; this is why certain poets have had tragic ends. Often the real man has no idea what path or what action the other will take. That other man is the prophet who is in every poet. . . . When a man writes he feels his prophetic mission in the world. The task of the Russian poet today is to look deep inside man."

The poet's task, as Voznesensky sees it, is nowhere better defined than in two quatrains that first appeared in *Metropol*, the anthology of writings brought out privately in 1979 by some members of the Writers' Union after they had failed to gain official approval for its publication. He had originally used as titles the names of the poets Derzhavin (1743–1816), who held high office under the empire, and Yesenin, who committed suicide in 1925, but it is clear that the verses express Voznesensky's view of the poet's total moral commitment and of his look "deep inside man":

I

Over a dark and quiet empire
alone I fly—and envy you,
two-headed eagle who at least
have always yourself to talk to.

II

To hang bare light bulbs from a ceiling
simple cord will always serve;
it's only the poet who must hang
by his glaring white spinal nerve.

The poetry of Voznesensky speaks with a force and courage that
would be admirable anywhere under any circumstances. It is true that
in a country where censorship prevails his approach must frequently
be indirect. But who can doubt that in "Old Song," although he is
referring to Turkish janissaries, he is in reality writing eloquently of
his revulsion at the Soviet occupation of Czechoslovakia? And in
"The Driver" that the "Caesar" being hailed is, of course, Stalin? All
the same, it is well to remember what Auden said in introducing
Voznesensky twenty years ago to English readers: "Every word he
writes, even when he is criticizing, reveals a profound love for his
native land and its traditions. I wish to stress this strongly because,
given the existing climate, there is a danger that we shall misunder-
stand him by looking for ideological clues instead of reading his
poems as one would read any poet who is a fellow countryman."

We have tried in this volume to present Voznesensky as if he were one
of our fellow poets writing in English. Part I, "Antiworlds," includes
poems in which the poet's attention, like that of Goya in the opening
poem, is fixed on the horror of war and its consequences. Others are
concerned with his personal suffering and with the suffering around
him. There are also love poems and poems treating the role of the
artist and the artistic process. A number of poems, in a light ironic
vein, present a variety of views of the modern scene; some like
"Striptease" and "New York Bird" picture America in the sixties
through Russian eyes. Playing with the concept of anti-matter, the
poet examines in "Antiworlds" the question of identity and the
problem of communication.

In the title poem of Part II, "Nostalgia for the Present," the word "present" in the original has a double meaning. It means the "present" in time and also that which is real:

> I long not for art — I choke
> on my craving for reality.

Voznesensky develops, in poems of passion and insight, this craving for reality and this search for the genuine:

> In towers of skeletal steel, — an arrow!
> In pomposities one and all.
> Who says it's the electronic era?
> There's an arrow in the wall!

Voznesensky's arrow, which cuts through pomposity and falsehood, has a searing ironic edge, and nothing escapes it. Even when he cannot write, he observes the hundreds of his empty, unimpeded colleagues who can; and the arrow again hits its mark.

Part III, "Release the Cranes," includes examples of Voznesensky's recent work, for the most part previously unavailable in English, in which his search for the genuine is no less acute:

> It's rare in our polluted skies
> to hear the crane's lonely cries,
> while every bookstore's lined with stacks
> of monolithic published hacks.

The difficulty of the search is brought home to the poet when reading to the blind, guided by them across "their invisible Russia":

> Trying to read one's poems
> at the Society for the Blind
> is like trying to hide one's sins
> in the company of saints.

> They don't give a damn for a leather jacket
> and they scorn a show of hands
> and yet they bridle at
> any false or insolent sound.

Many of the new poems are looser in form but more probing in their psychological analysis than any that he has previously written. Two of them, "Applefall" and "Candle Sculptor," are concerned, in a highly original way, with creation. "Applefall," with a subtlety reminiscent of Wallace Stevens, is one of the finest poems Voznesensky has produced.

The two prose pieces in Part IV provide much of the background from which the poems have developed. "I Am Fourteen" gives an intimate, moving portrait of Voznesensky's mentor, Pasternak. Nowhere in modern literature is there a more telling tribute by an apprentice to his master. In speaking in detail of Pasternak's poetic credo, Voznesensky reveals his own point of departure and the basis of his own conception of poetry. This memoir was something of a sensation when it first appeared, providing as it did the first public mention of Pasternak's funeral. Although it made no mention of *Dr. Zhivago*, Voznesensky's Russian readers knew that when he describes Pasternak's lengthy Sunday readings from his new work, he means not new poems but passages from the novel in progress. "I Am Fourteen" is the one piece by Voznesensky that has not been attacked.

The same cannot be said of "O," which Voznesensky had difficulty getting published. When it first appeared in *New World*, the *Literary Gazette* carried an acid condemnation of it. The title itself is anathema to some critics. "O" means "about" in Russian and hence its frequent repetition in the original has a playful significance that cannot be conveyed in English. But Voznesensky has in mind also all that the letter *O* symbolizes in the way of geometry, sex, memory, as well as the supreme representation of harmony and the entrance to other spheres. He attempts in this piece, which is at times reminiscent of Mandelstam or Tsvetayeva, to record, in a kind of Fellini-like montage, actual events in a highly surrealistic manner. It is considered so far from the norm of contemporary Soviet prose that no favorable mention of it, or even reference to it, is permitted anywhere. "About" is not anything that anyone on the Russian literary scene is permitted to speak publicly about.

The visits to Picasso's house in the south of France before and after his death, as described in "O," prompted the poet to write "Applefall." The evening at the Vakhtangov Theater with Pasternak to see Lyubimov in Pasternak's translation of *Romeo and Juliet*, fully recorded in "I Am Fourteen," is the basis of the poem "Schoolboy."

The portrait of Vladimir Vysotsky in "O" makes Voznesensky's epitaph of the balladeer all the more poignant. The teenage murderer encountered in hell in "O" had already appeared in the poem "Provincial Scene." In these and other instances one can establish clear links between prose and poetry and see the poet's mind at work on his material.

Both prose selections contain memorable portrayals of Voznesensky's idols, Pasternak, Moore, Picasso, and Pavlov, but they present at the same time a carefully wrought self-portrait, more revealing than any the poet has previously given us. Some of the most affecting pages are of his boyhood in the courtyards of the Zamoskvorechie district of Moscow and of the war years with his mother in the Urals. The scene of his father's arrival there with the book on Goya in his rucksack makes his poem "I Am Goya" with its harsh, staccato invocation of the horrors of war all the more understandable as the poet's true beginning.

Just as in "Antiworlds" Voznesensky plays with the concept of "anti-matter," here in "O" he makes mocking and yet serious poetic use of the "black hole." In the hands of a lesser writer Voznesensky's characterization and personification of the black hole that suddenly one day sweeps into his room would seem coy and even downright silly. But Voznesensky knows how to turn it into a telling symbol, and while using it as a point of departure for sharp observations, how to extract from it every bit of black humor.

When Voznesensky showed W. H. Auden's translation of one of his poems to the Russian poet Chukovsky, himself a brilliant translator, the latter read it through with admiration and then commented, "One madman has understood another." And this may explain the success that Voznesensky's poems have met with in their English versions. Poets must translate poets; and even if they know little of the other's language, something of the fine frenzy of the original will somehow work its way through.

"As a fellow maker," W. H. Auden said, "I am struck first and foremost by Voznesensky's craftsmanship. Here, at least, is a poet who knows, whatever else it may be, a poem is a verbal artifact which must be as skillfully and solidly constructed as a table or a motorcycle." His poet-translators, working closely with their scholarly informants, have done their best to give in English a sense of the solid construction of these artifacts, despite the realization that, as

Auden puts it, Voznesensky's "metrical effects must make any translator despair." Another realization that makes him despair is the greater number of words he must use in English. Russian is an inflected language, employing no articles. The compact Russian originals swell out in English like Japanese paper flowers put into water, and the results can sometimes be more monstrous than beautiful. One can approximate in English the metrical line length of the original, although the Russian seems always more heavily stressed. But it is fortunate that English has stress; in an unstressed language like French, Voznesensky's poems come through far less well. Rhyme and assonance are natural and easy in Russian, and throughout his work Voznesensky has made good use of both. But in many of his recent poems he dispenses with rhyme entirely and uses assonance sparingly, thereby putting an even greater burden on his translator. What is free and well turned in the original may sound merely sloppy when translated.

This comprehensive volume of Voznesensky's poetry and prose represents in English, we believe, the full range and variety of his work. We trust that our selections will be read, as Auden cautioned, not for ideological clues but for what they have to say about the human condition. "It has long been my feeling," Voznesensky has said, "that the poetic strophe is a crystal, a model of the world, a structure of harmony, a method of thought penetrating to the essence of what is happening, a way of revealing the truth. Poetry knows no borders; it has no capitals and no provinces. Languages are many but poetry is one."

Our volume is directed to the English reader, but for the reader who has some Russian the original texts of all the poems are given on facing pages. Part V reprints the notes compiled by Max Hayward and Patricia Blake for *Antiworlds and the Fifth Ace* and by Max Hayward and Vera Dunham for *Nostalgia for the Present*. F. D. Reeve has annotated the new poems in Part III.

A word of explanation about the texts: All the cuts, rearrangements, and alterations in both the poetry and the prose have been made with the author's approval. The deletions in "I Am Fourteen," usually of Pasternak's verses, have been minimal. Because of space, we have been able to include less than half of "O," but have retained all the most important passages.

— *William Jay Smith*

I

Антимиры

·

I

Antiworlds

All translations in this section are taken from *Antiworlds and the Fifth Ace: Poetry by Andrei Voznesensky*, edited by Patricia Blake and Max Hayward (Basic Books, 1966, 1967).

ГОЙЯ

Я — Гойя!
Глазницы воронок мне выклевал ворог,
          слетая на поле нагое.

Я — Горе.

Я — голос
войны, городов головни
            на снегу сорок первого года.

Я — голод.
Я — горло
повешенной бабы, чье тело, как колокол,
           било над площадью голой...

Я — Гойя!

О, грозди
возмездья! Взвил залпом на Запад —
          я пепел незваного гостя!

И в мемориальное небо вбил крепкие
                  звезды —
как гвозди.

Я — Гойя.

I AM GOYA

I am Goya
of the bare field, by the enemy's beak gouged
till the craters of my eyes gape
I am grief

I am the tongue
of war, the embers of cities
on the snows of the year 1941
I am hunger

I am the gullet
of a woman hanged whose body like a bell
tolled over a blank square
I am Goya

O grapes of wrath!
I have hurled westward
                    the ashes of the uninvited guest!
and hammered stars into the unforgetting sky — like nails
I am Goya

translated by Stanley Kunitz

3

АХИЛЛЕСОВО СЕРДЦЕ

В дни неслыханно болевые
быть без сердца — мечта.
Чемпионы лупили навылет —
ни черта!

Продырявленный, точно решета,
утешаю ажиотаж:
«Поглазейте в меня, как в решетку, —
так шикарен пейзаж!»

Но неужто узнает ружье,
г д е,
             привязано нитью болезненной,
бьешься ты в миллиметре от лезвия,
ахиллесово

                    сердце

                              мое!!

Тсс, любимая, тише...
Нашумело меняя места,
я ношусь по России —

                              как птица
отвлекает огонь от гнезда.

Все болишь! Ночами пошаливаешь!
Беззащитно спасителен плюс.
Не касайтесь рукою шершавою —
от судороги валюсь.

Невозможно расправиться с нами.
Невозможнее — выносить.
Но еще невозможней —

                    что снайпер
перережет дрожащую нить!

MY ACHILLES HEART

In these days of unheard-of suffering
One is lucky indeed to have no heart:
Crack shots plug me again and again,
But have no luck.

Riddled with holes, I laugh
At the furious pack: "Tallyho, boys!
I am a lattice. Look through me.
Isn't the landscape lovely?"

But suppose a gun should locate,
Tied by an aching thread,
Beating a hairbreadth off target,
My Achilles heart.

Beware, my darling. Hush. Not a sound,
While I charge noisily
From place to place around Russia,
As a bird diverts the hunters from its nest.

Are you still in pain? Do you act up at night?
This defenseless extra is what saves me.
Do not handle it roughly;
The shudder would bring me down.

Our destruction is unthinkable,
More unthinkable what we endure,
More unthinkable still that a sniper
Should ever sever the quivering thread.

translated by W. H. Auden

МОТОГОНКИ ПО ВЕРТИКАЛЬНОЙ СТЕНЕ

Н. Андросовой

Завораживая, манежа,
свищет женщина по манежу!
Краги —
           красные, как клешни.
Губы крашеные — грешны.
Мчит торпедой горизонтальною,
хризантему заткнув за талию!

Ангел атомный, амазонка!
Щеки вдавлены, как воронка.
Мотоцикл над головой
электрическою пилой.

Надоело жить вертикально.
Ах, дикарочка, дочь Икара…
Обыватели и весталки
вертикальны, как «ваньки-встаньки».

В этой, взвившейся над зонтами,
меж оваций, афиш, обид,
сущность женщины
                   горизонтальная
мне мерещится и летит!

Ах, как кружит ее орбита!
Ах, как слезы к белкам прибиты!
И тиранит ее Чингисхан —
замдиректора Сингичанц…

Сингичанц: «Ну, а с ней не мука?
Тоже трюк — по стене, как муха…
А вчера камеру проколола… Интриги…
Пойду напишу
              по инстанции…
И царапается, как конокрадка».

•

WALL OF DEATH

to N. Androsova

Casting her spell and daring death,
A woman zooms round the wall of death!
With leather leggings
                                   as red as crabs' claws,
And wicked red lips that give one pause,
She hurtles — horizontal torpedo —
A chrysanthemum stuck in her belt.

Atomic angel, Amazon,
With cratered cheeks in-drawn,
Your motorcycle passes overhead,
Its noise, a power saw's.

Living vertically is such a bore,
Darling barbarian, daughter of Icarus...
It's the plight
Only of vestal virgin and suburbanite
To live vertical and upright.

In this creature who soars
Over awnings, ovations, posters, and jeers
I now can see
                        the horizontal essence of woman
Float before me!

Ah, how her orbit whirls her round the wall,
Her tears nailed to each eyeball;
And her trainer, Singichants,
Bullies her like Genghis Khan...

Says Singichants: "Let me tell you I
Have my hands full with that one, plastered up there like a fly!
And yesterday she had a flat...the little schemer...!
                                   'I'll write to the boss,' says she;
And claws at my face like a mad gypsy."
•

Я к ней вламываюсь в антракте.
«Научи, — говорю, — горизонту...»

А она молчит, амазонка.
А она головой качает.
А ее еще трек качает.
А глаза полны такой —
                                горизонтальною
                                              тоской!

During intermission I make my way
To her... "Instruct me in the horizontal!" I say.

But she stands there like lead,
The Amazon, and shakes her head;
Still shaking, dizzy from the wall,
Her eyes blurred with
                    such longing
                              for the horizontal!

translated by William Jay Smith

ОХОТА НА ЗАЙЦА

Другу Юре

Травят зайца. Несутся суки.
Травля! Травля! Сквозь лай и гам.
И оранжевые кожухи
апельсинами по снегам.

Травим зайца. Опохмелившись,
я, завгар, оппонент милиции,
лица в валенках, в хроме лица,
брат Букашкина с пацаном, —
газанем!

Газик, чудо индустриализации,
наворачивает цепя.
Трали-вали! Мы травим зайца.
Только, может, травим себя?

Полыхают снега нарядные,
сапоги на мне и тужурка,
что же пляшет прицел мой, Юрка?
Юрка, в этом что-то неладное,
если в ужасе по снегам
скачет крови живой стакан!

Страсть к убийству, как страсть к зачатию,
ослепленная и зловещая,
она нынче вопит: зайчатины!
Завтра взвоет о человечине...

Он лежал посреди страны,
он лежал, трепыхаясь слева,
словно серое сердце леса,
тишины.

Он лежал, синеву боков
он вздымал, он дышал пока еще,

HUNTING A HARE

to my friend Yuri

Hunting a hare. Our dogs are raising a racket;
Racing, barking, eager to kill, they go,
And each of us in a jellow jacket
Like oranges against the snow.

One for the road. Then, off to hound a hare,
My cabdriver friend who hates a cop, I,
Buggins' brother and his boy, away we tear.
Our jalopy,

That technological marvel, goes bounding,
Scuttling along on its snow chains. Tallyho!
After a hare we go.
Or is it ourselves we're hounding?

I'm all dressed up for the chase
In boots and jacket: the snow is ablaze.
But why, Yuri, why,
Do my gun sights dance? Something is wrong, I know,
When a glassful of living blood has to fly
In terror across the snow.

The urge to kill, like the urge to beget,
Is blind and sinister. Its craving is set
Today on the flesh of a hare: tomorrow it can
Howl the same way for the flesh of a man.

Out in the open the hare
Lay quivering there
Like the gray heart of an immense
Forest or the heart of silence:

Lay there, still breathing,
Its blue flanks heaving,

11

как мучительный глаз,
                    моргающий,
на печальной щеке снегов.

Но внезапно, взметнувшись свечкой,
он возник,
и над лесом, над черной речкой
резанул
человечий
крик!

Звук был пронзительным и чистым, как
                              ультразвук
или как крик ребенка.
Я знал, что зайцы стонут. Но чтобы так?!
Это была нота жизни. Так кричат роженицы.

Так кричат перелески голые
и немые досель кусты,
так нам смерть прорезает голос
неизведанной чистоты.

Той природе, молчально-чудной,
роща, озеро ли, бревно —
им позволено слушать, чувствовать,
только голоса не дано.

Так кричат в последний и в первый.
Это жизнь, удаляясь, пела,
вылетая, как из силка,
в небосклоны и облака.

Это длилось мгновение,
мы окаменели,
как в остановившемся кинокадре.
Сапог бегущего завгара так и не коснулся земли.

•

Its tormented eye a woe,
Blinking there on the cheek of the snow.

Then, suddenly, it got up,
Stood upright: suddenly,
Over the forest, over the dark river,
The air was shivered
By a human cry,

Pure, ultrasonic, wild,
Like the cry of a child.
I knew that hares moan, but not like this:
This was the note of life, the wail
Of a woman in travail,

The cry of leafless copses
And bushes hitherto dumb,
The unearthly cry of a life
Which death was about to succumb.

Nature is all wonder, all silence:
Forest and lake and field and hill
Are permitted to listen and feel,
But denied utterance.

Alpha and Omega, the first and the last
Word of Life as it ebbs away fast,
As, escaping the snare, it flies
Up to the skies.

For a second only, but while
It lasted we were turned to stone
Like actors in a movie still.
The boot of the running cabdriver hung in midair,

Четыре черные дробинки, не долетев,

                                         вонзились

в воздух.

Он взглянул на нас. И — или это нам показа-
лось — над горизонтальными мышцами
бегуна, над запекшимися шерстинками шеи

                                        блеснуло лицо.

Глаза были раскосы и широко расставлены,
как на фресках Феофана.

Он взглянул изумленно и разгневанно.

Он парил.

                Как бы слился с криком.

Он повис...

С искаженным и светлым ликом,
как у ангелов и певиц.

Длинноногий лесной архангел...

Плыл туман золотой к лесам.

«Охмуряет», — стрелявший схаркнул.

И беззвучно плакал пацан.

Возвращались в ночную пору.

Ветер рожу драл, как наждак.

Как багровые светофоры,
наши лица неслись во мрак.

And four black pellets halted, it seemed,
Just short of their target:
Above the horizontal muscles,
The blood-clotted fur of the neck,
A face flashed out.

With slanting eyes set wide apart, a face
As in frescoes of Theophanes,
Staring at us in astonishment and anger,
It hovered there, made one with its cry,
Suspended in space,
The contorted transfigured face
Of an angel or a singer.

Like a long-legged archangel a golden mist
Swam through the forest.
"Shit!" spat the cabdriver. "The little faking freak!":
A tear rolled down on the boy's cheek.

Late at night we returned,
The wind scouring our faces: they burned
Like traffic lights as, without remark,
We hurtled through the dark.

                                    translated by W. H. Auden

ЛОБНАЯ БАЛЛАДА

Их величеством поразвлечься
прет народ от Коломн и Клязьм.
«Их любовница —
        контрразведчица
        англо-шведско-немецко-греческая...»
Казнь!

Царь страшон: точно кляча, тощий,
почерневший, как антрацит.
По лицу проносятся очи,
как буксующий мотоцикл.

И когда голова с топорика
подкатилась к носкам ботфорт,
он берет ее
                над толпою,
точно репу с красной ботвой!

Пальцы в щеки впились, как клещи,
переносицею хрустя,
кровь из горла на брюки хлещет.
Он целует ее в уста.

Только Красная площадь ахнет,
тихим стоном оглушена:
«А-а-анхен!..»
Отвечает ему она:

«Мальчик мой государь великий
не судить мне твоей вины
но зачем твои руки липкие
солоны?

баба я
вот и вся провинность
государства мои в устах
я дрожу брусничной кровиночкой
на державных твоих усах
•

THE SKULL BALLAD

The peasants flock from miles around
To gape at the terrible Tsar
And jeer and spit at his spying bitch,
That dirty foreigner.

The Tsar is skinny as a nag
And black as anthracite;
His eyes slide over his coal-black face
Like a skidding motorbike.

Her head rolls from the blow of his ax
To the toe of his hunter's boot;
He dangles it high above the crowd
Like a red-topped turnip root.

He grips her cheeks in an iron vise,
He cracks the bridge of her nose;
The blood spurts from her golden throat
On her executioner's clothes.

He kisses her full upon the mouth,
While a groan sweeps through the crowd,
And suddenly silence stuns the square
As the death's-head speaks aloud:

"beloved one O worshipful Tsar
I will not judge thy guilt
but why do thy hands stick to my skin
and taste of my own heart's salt

let me confess my womanhood
my crime deserves the whip
I tremble where that crimson fleck
hangs on thy bristling lip
•

в дни строительства и пожара
до малюсенькой ли любви?

ты целуешь меня Держава
твои губы в моей крови

перегаром борщом горохом
пахнет щедрый твой поцелуй

как ты любишь меня Эпоха
обожаю тебя
царуй!..»

Царь застыл — смурной, малахольный,
царь взглянул с такой меланхолией,
что присел заграничный гость,
будто вбитый по шляпку гвоздь.

love is so small who cares for love
in times like these men build
and set a world on fire — you kiss
me State in blood in blood

what if you reek of borscht and peas
such passion has a flavor
Progress you drive me mad for you
I want you to rule forever"

Stock-still the greatest of the tsars
Stood black as blackest bread;
A witness from abroad jerked back
Like a spike rammed to its head.

translated by Stanley Kunitz

БЬЮТ ЖЕНЩИНУ

Бьют женщину. Блестит белок.
В машине темень и жара.
И бьются ноги в потолок,
как белые прожектора!

Бьют женщину. Так бьют рабынь.
Она в заплаканной красе
срывает ручку как рубильник
выбрасываясь

на шоссе!

И взвизгивали тормоза.
К ней подбегали тормоша.
И волочили и лупили
Лицом по лугу и крапиве...

Подонок, как он бил подробно,
стиляга, Чайльд-Гарольд, битюг!
Вонзался в дышащие ребра
ботинок узкий, как утюг.

О, упоенье оккупанта,
изыски деревенщины...
У поворота на Купавну
бьют женщину.

Бьют женщину. Веками бьют,
бьют юность, бьет торжественно
набата свадебного гуд,
бьют женщину.

А от жаровен на щеках
горящие затрещины?
Мещанство, быт — да еще как! —
бьют женщину.

Но чист ее высокий свет,
отважный и божественный.

SOMEONE IS BEATING A WOMAN

Someone is beating a woman.
In the car that is dark and hot
Only the whites of her eyes shine.
Her legs thrash against the roof
Like berserk searchlight beams.

Someone is beating a woman.
This is the way slaves are beaten.
Frantic, she wrenches open the door
and plunges out—onto the road.

Brakes scream.
Someone runs up to her,
Strikes her and drags her, face down,
In the grass lashing with nettles.

Scum, how meticulously he beats her,
Stilyága, bastard, big hero,
His smart flatiron-pointed shoe
Stabbing into her ribs.

Such are the pleasures of enemy soldiers
And the brute refinements of peasants.
Trampling underfoot the moonlit grass,
Someone is beating a woman.

Someone is beating a woman.
Century on century, no end to this.
It's the young that are beaten. Somberly
Our wedding bells start up the alarm.
Someone is beating a woman.

What about the flaming weals
In the braziers of their cheeks?
That's life, you say. Are you telling me?
Someone is beating a woman.

But her light is unfaltering
World-without-ending.

Религий — нет,
знамений — нет.
Есть
Женщина!..

...Она как озеро лежала
стояли очи как вода
и не ему принадлежала
как просека или звезда

и звезды по небу стучали
как дождь о черное стекло
и скатываясь
остужали
ее горячее чело.

There are no religions,
                    no revelations,
There are women.

Lying there pale as water
Her eyes tear-closed and still,
She doesn't belong to him
Any more than a meadow deep in a wood.

And the stars? Rattling in the sky
Like raindrops against black glass,
Plunging down,
                    they cool
Her grief-fevered forehead.

translated by Jean Garrigue

КАССИРША

Немых обсчитали.
Немые вопили.
Медяшек медали
Влипали в опилки.

И гневным протестом,
Что все это сказки,
Кассирша, как тесто,
Вздымалась из кассы.

И сразу по залам,
Сыркам, патиссонам,
Пахнуло слезами,
Как будто озоном.

О, слез этих запах
В мычащей ораве.
Два были без шапок.
Их руки орали.

А третий с беконом
Подобием мата
Ревел, как Бетховен,
Земно и лохмато!

В стекло барабаня,
Ладони ломая,
Орала судьба моя
Глухонемая!

Кассирша, осклабясь,
Косилась на солнце
И ленинский абрис
Искала
       в полсотне.

•

THE CASHIER

The dumb herd scowled:
"You've shortchanged us," they howled.
Pennies like medals stuck in the crust
Of sawdust.

The cashier flew into a rage—
"Nonsense! Be off with you! Go!"—
And rose like dough
From her glass cage.

Over counters where they sell
Cheesecakes and melons was blown
A sudden smell
Of tears and ozone.

Loud was the smell of tears
Among that lowing crowd:
The hands of one dumb pair
Howled in the air.

Clutching bacon, somebody swore,
Or so I imagined: at least, he
Gave a Beethovenish roar,
Earthy and shaggy.

Drumming of knuckle and palm
On the glass plate;
So bellowed the psalm
Of my dumb fate.

With a knowing leer
The cashier
Peered at a bill she held up to the light
To see if Lenin's profile looked all right.

•

Но не было Ленина.

Она была
          фальшью…
Была бакалея.
В ней люди и фарши.

But Lenin wasn't there anymore:
The bill was counterfeit.
It was a grocery store
Where people and farces meet.

translated by W. H. Auden

ОСЕНЬ В СИГУЛДЕ

Свисаю с вагонной площадки,
прощайте,

прощай, мое лето,
пора мне,
на даче стучат топорами,
мой дом забивают дощатый,
прощайте,

леса мои сбросили кроны,
пусты они и грустны,
как ящик с аккордеона,
а музыку — унесли.

мы — люди,
мы тоже порожни,
уходим мы,
            так уж положено,
из стен,
            матерей
                    и из женщин,
и этот порядок извечен,

прощай, моя мама,
у окон
ты станешь прозрачно, как кокон,
наверно, умаялась за день,
присядем,
друзья и враги, бывайте,
гуд бай,
из меня сейчас
со свистом вы выбегаете,
и я ухожу из вас,

о родина, попрощаемся,
буду звезда, ветла,
не плачу, не попрошайка,
спасибо, жизнь, что была,

•

AUTUMN IN SIGULDA

Hanging out of the train, I
Bid you all good-bye.

Good-bye, Summer:
My time is up.
Axes knock at the dacha
As they board it up:
Good-bye.

The woods have shed their leaves,
Empty and sad today
As an accordion case that grieves
When its music is taken away.

People (meaning us)
Are also empty,
As we leave behind
(We have no choice)
Walls, mothers, womankind:
So it has always been and will be.

Good-bye, Mother,
Standing at the window
Transparent as a cocoon: soon
You will know how tired you are.
Let us sit here a bit.
Friends and foes, adieu,
Good-bye.
The whistle has blown: it is time
For you to run out of me and I
Out of you.

Motherland, good-bye now.
I shall not whimper nor make a scene,
But be a star, a willow:
Thank you, Life, for having been.
•

на стрельбищах
в 10 баллов
я пробовал выбить 100,
спасибо, что ошибался,
но трижды спасибо, что

в прозрачные мои лопатки
вошла гениальность, как
в резиновую перчатку
красный мужской кулак,

«Андрей Вознесенский» — будет,
побыть бы не словом, не бульдиком,
еще на щеке твоей душной —
«Андрюшкой»,

спасибо, что в рощах осенних
ты встретилась, что-то спросила
и пса волокла за ошейник,
а он упирался,
спасибо,

я ожил, спасибо за осень,
что ты мне меня объяснила,
хозяйка будила нас в восемь,
а в праздники сипло басила
пластинка блатного пошиба,
спасибо,

но вот ты уходишь, уходишь,
                    как поезд отходит, уходишь...
из пор моих полых уходишь,
мы врозь друг из друга уходим,
чем нам этот дом неугоден?

ты рядом и где-то далеко,
почти что у Владивостока,

•

In the shooting gallery
Where the top score is ten,
I tried to reach a century:
Thank you for letting me make the mistake,
But a triple thank-you that into

My transparent shoulders
Genius drove
Like a red male fist that enters
A rubber glove.

Voznesensky may one day be graven
In cold stone but, meanwhile, may
I find haven
On your warm cheek as *Andrei*.

In the woods the leaves were already falling
When you ran into me, asked me something.
Your dog was with you: you tugged at his leash and called him,

He tugged the other way:
Thank you for that day.
I came alive: thank you for that September,
For explaining me to myself. The housekeeper, I remember,
Woke us at eight, and on weekends her phonograph sang
Some old underworld song
In a hoarse bass:
I give thanks for the time, the place.

But you are leaving, going
As the train is going, leaving,
Going in another direction: we are ceasing to belong
To each other or this house. What is wrong?

Near to me, I say:
Yet Siberias away!
•

я знаю, что мы повторимся
в друзьях и подругах, в травинках,
нас этот заменит и тот —
«природа боится пустот»,

спасибо за сдутые кроны,
на смену придут миллионы,
за ваши законы — спасибо,

но женщина мчится по склонам,
как огненный лист за вагоном...

Спасите!

I know we shall live again as
Friends or girlfriends or blades of grass,
Instead of us this one or that one will come:
Nature abhors a vacuum.

The leaves are swept away without trace
But millions more will grow in their place:
Thank you, Nature, for the laws you gave me.

But a woman runs down the track
Like a red autumn leaf at the train's back.

Save me!

translated by W. H. Auden

ЗАМЕРЛИ

Заведи мне ладони за плечи,
обойми,
только губы дыхнут об мои,
только море за спинами плещет.

Наши спины — как лунные раковины,
что замкнулись за нами сейчас.
Мы заслушаемся, прислонясь.
Мы — как формула жизни двоякая.

На ветру мировых клоунад
заслоняем своими плечами
возникающее меж нами —
как ладонями пламя хранят.

Если правда, душа в каждой клеточке,
свои форточки отвори.
В моих порах
                стрижами заплещутся
души пойманные твои!

Все становится тайное явным.
Неужели под свистопад
разомкнемся немым изваяньем —
как раковины не гудят?

А пока нажимай, заваруха,
на скорлупы упругие спин!
Это нас прижимает друг к другу.

Спим.

DEAD STILL

Now, with your palms on the blades of my shoulders,
Let us embrace:
Let there be only your lips' breath on my face,
Only, behind our backs, the plunge of rollers.

Our backs, which like two shells in moonlight shine,
Are shut behind us now;
We lie here huddled, listening brow to brow,
Like life's twin formula or double sign.

In folly's worldwide wind
Our shoulders shield from the weather
The calm we now beget together,
Like a flame held between hand and hand.

Does each cell have a soul within it?
If so, fling open all your little doors,
And all your souls shall flutter like the linnet
In the cages of my pores.

Nothing is hidden that shall not be known.
Yet by no storm of scorn shall we
Be pried from this embrace, and left alone
Like muted shells forgetful of the sea.

Meanwhile, O load of stress and bother,
Lie on the shells of our backs in a great heap:
It will but press us closer, one to the other.

We are asleep.

translated by Richard Wilbur

ПЕРВЫЙ ЛЕД

Мерзнет девочка в автомате,
прячет в зябкое пальтецо
все в слезах и губной помаде
перемазанное лицо.

Дышит в худенькие ладошки.
Пальцы — льдышки. В ушах — сережки.

Ей обратно одной, одной
вдоль по улочке ледяной.

Первый лед. Это в первый раз.
Первый лед телефонных фраз.

Мерзлый след на щеках блестит —
первый лед от людских обид.

FIRST FROST

A girl is freezing in a telephone booth,
huddled in her flimsy coat,
her face stained by tears
and smeared with lipstick.

She breathes on her thin little fingers.
Fingers like ice. Glass beads in her ears.

She has to beat her way back alone
down the icy street.

First frost. A beginning of losses.
The first frost of telephone phrases.

It is the start of winter glittering on her cheek,
the first frost of having been hurt.

translated by Stanley Kunitz

СТРИПТИЗ

В ревю
   танцовщица раздевается дуря...
Реву?..
Или режут мне глаза прожектора?

Шарф срывает,
    шаль срывает,
       мишуру,
как сдирают с апельсина кожуру.

А в глазах тоска такая, как у птиц.
Этот танец называется «стриптиз».

Страшен танец. В баре лысины и свист,
как пиявки,
    глазки пьяниц налились.
Этот рыжий, как обляпанный желтком,
пневматическим исходит молотком!
Тот, как клоп, —
      апоплексичен и страшон.
Апокалипсисом воет саксофон!

Проклинаю твой, Вселенная, масштаб,
марсианское сиянье на мостах,
проклинаю,
   обожая и дивясь.
Проливная пляшет женщина под джаз!..

«Вы Америка?» — спрошу, как идиот.
Она сядет, сигаретку разомнет.

«Мальчик, — скажет, — ах, какой у вас акцент!
Закажите-ка мартини и абсент».

STRIPTEASE

Playing her crazy part,
                     the dancer begins to take all
Her clothes off.... Do I bawl
Or is it the lights that make my eyes smart?

She rips off a scarf, a shawl, her tinsel and fringe,
As one would slowly peel an orange.

Her eyes like a bird's are haunted with miseries
As she does her striptease.

It's terrifying. In the bar, wolf calls, bald pates.
Like leeches with blood
The drunkards' eyes inflate.

That redhead, like someone bespattered with egg yolk,
Is transformed into a pneumatic drill!
The other, a bedbug,
                  is horrible and apoplectic;
And the saxophone howls on, apocalyptic.

Universe, I curse your lack of edges,
And the Martian lights on your sweeping bridges;
I curse you,
             adoring and marveling, as
This downpour of woman responds to jazz.

"Are you America?" I'll ask like an idiot;
She'll sit down, tap her cigarette.

"Are you kidding, kiddo?" she'll answer me.
"Better make mine a double martini!"

translated by William Jay Smith

АНТИМИРЫ

Живет у нас сосед Букашкин,
в кальсонах цвета промокашки.
Но, как воздушные шары,
над ним горят

         Антимиры!

И в них магический, как демон,
вселенной правит, возлежит
Антибукашкин, академик,
и щупает Лоллобриджид.

Но грезятся Антибукашкину
виденья цвета промокашки.

Да здравствуют Антимиры!
Фантасты — посреди муры.
Без глупых не было бы умных,
оазисов — без Каракумов.

Нет женщин —

         есть антимужчины,
в лесах ревут антимашины.
Есть соль земли. Есть сор земли.
Но сохнет сокол без змеи.

Люблю я критиков моих.
На шее одного из них,
благоуханна и гола,
сияет антиголова!..

...Я сплю с окошками открытыми,
а где-то свищет звездопад,
и небоскребы

         сталактитами
на брюхе глобуса висят.

•

ANTIWORLDS

The clerk Bukáshkin is our neighbor.
His face is gray as blotting paper.

But like balloons of blue or red,
Bright Antiworlds
               float over his head!
On them reposes, prestidigitous,
Ruling the cosmos, a demon-magician,
Anti-Bukáshkin the Academician,
Lapped in the arms of Lollobrigidas.

But Anti-Bukáshkin's dreams are the color
Of blotting paper, and couldn't be duller.

Long live Antiworlds! They rebut
With dreams the rat race and the rut.
For some to be clever, some must be boring.
No deserts? No oases, then.

There are no women—
               just anti-men.
In the forests, antimachines are roaring.
There's the dirt of the earth, as well as the salt.
If the earth broke down, the sun would halt.

Ah, my critics; how I love them.
Upon the neck of the keenest of them,
Fragrant and bald as fresh-baked bread,
There shines a perfect antihead...

...I sleep with windows open wide;
Somewhere a falling star invites,
And skyscrapers
               like stalactites
Hang from the planet's underside.

•

И подо мной
           вниз головой,
вонзившись вилкой в шар земной,
беспечный, милый мотылек,
живешь ты,
           мой антимирок!

Зачем среди ночной поры
встречаются антимиры?

Зачем они вдвоем сидят
и в телевизоры глядят?

Им не понять и пары фраз.
Их первый раз — последний раз!

Сидят, забывши про бонтон,
ведь будут мучиться потом!

И уши красные горят,
как будто бабочки сидят...

...Знакомый лектор мне вчера
сказал: «Антимиры? Мура!»

Я сплю, ворочаюсь спросонок.
Наверно, прав научный хмырь...
Мой кот, как радиоприемник,
зеленым глазом ловит мир.

There, upside down,
                              below me far,
Stuck like a fork into the earth,
Or perching like a carefree moth,
My little Antiworld,
                              there you are!

In the middle of the night, why is it
That Antiworlds are moved to visit?

Why do they sit together, gawking
At the television, and never talking?

Between them, not one word has passed.
Their first strange meeting is their last.

Neither can manage the least *bon ton*.
Oh, how they'll blush for it, later on!

Their ears are burning like a pair
Of crimson butterflies, hovering there...

...A distinguished lecturer lately told me,
"Antiworlds are a total loss."

Still, my apartment-cell won't hold me.
I thrash in my sleep, I turn and toss.

And, radiolike, my cat lies curled
With his green eye tuned in to the world.

                    translated by Richard Wilbur

ПАРАБОЛИЧЕСКАЯ БАЛЛАДА

Судьба, как ракета, летит по параболе
обычно — во мраке и реже — по радуге.

Жил огненно-рыжий художник Гоген,
богема, а в прошлом — торговый агент.
Чтоб в Лувр королевский попасть

                         из Монмартра,
он
   дал
       кругаля через Яву с Суматрой!

Унесся, забыв сумасшествие денег,
кудахтанье жен и дерьмо академий.
Он преодолел

              тяготенье земное.

Жрецы гоготали за кружкой пивною:
«Прямая — короче, парабола — круче,
не лучше ль скопировать райские кущи?»

А он уносился ракетой ревущей
сквозь ветер, срывающий фалды и уши.
И в Лувр он попал не сквозь главный порог —
параболой

        гневно
            пробив потолок!

Идут к своим правдам, по-разному храбро,
червяк — через щель, человек — по параболе.

Жила-была девочка, рядом в квартале.
Мы с нею учились, зачеты сдавали.
Куда ж я уехал!

           И нерт меня нес
меж грузных тбилисских двусмысленных звезд!

•

PARABOLIC BALLAD

Along a parabola life like a rocket flies,
Mainly in darkness, now and then on a rainbow.
Redheaded bohemian Gauguin the painter
Started out life as a prosperous stockbrocker.
In order to get to the Louvre from Montmartre
He made a detour all through Java, Sumatra,
Tahiti, the Isles of Marquesas.

       With levity
He took off in flight from the madness of money,
The cackle of women, the frowst of academies,
Overpowered the force of terrestrial gravity.

The high priests drank their porter and kept up their jabbering:
"Straight lines are shorter. less steep than parabolas.
It's more proper to copy the heavenly mansions."

He rose like a howling rocket, insulting them
With a gale that tore off the tails of their frock coats.

So he didn't steal into the Louvre by the front door
But on a parabola smashed through the ceiling.

In finding their truths lives vary in daring:
Worms come through holes and bold men on parabolas.

There once was a girl who lived in my neighborhood.
We went to one school, took exams simultaneously.
But I took off with a bang,
       I went whizzing
Through the prosperous double-faced stars of Tiflis.
•

Прости мне дурацкую эту параболу.
Простывшие плечики в черном парадном...
О, как ты звенела во мраке Вселенной
упруго и прямо — как прутик антенны!
А я все лечу,

        приземляясь по ним —
земным и озябшим твоим позывным.
Как трудно дается нам эта парабола!..

Сметая каноны, прогнозы, параграфы,
несутся искусство,

          любовь
             и история —
по параболической траектории!

В Сибирь уезжает он нынешней ночью.
А может быть, все же прямая — короче?

Forgive me for this idiotic parabola.
Cold shoulders in a pitch-dark vestibule...
Rigid, erect as a radio antenna rod
Sending its call sign out through the freezing
Dark of the universe, how you rang out to me,
An undoubtable signal, an earthly standby
From whom I might get my flight bearings to land by.
The parabola doesn't come to us easily.

Laughing at law with its warnings and paragraphs
Art, love, and history race along recklessly
Over a parabolic trajectory.

He is leaving tonight for Siberia.
                                    Perhaps
A straight line after all is the shorter one actually.

                           translated by W. H. Auden

ПОЖАР В АРХИТЕКТУРНОМ ИНСТИТУТЕ

Пожар в Архитектурном!
По залам, чертежам,
амнистией по тюрьмам —
пожар! Пожар!

По сонному фасаду
бесстыже, озорно
гориллой
        краснозадою
взвивается окно!

А мы уже дипломники,
нам защищать пора.
Трещат в шкафу под пломбами
мои выговора!

Ватман — как подраненный,
красный листопад.
Горят мои подрамники,
города горят.

Бутылью керосиновой
взвилось пять лет и зим...
Кариночка Красильникова,
ой! Горим!

Прощай, архитектура!
Пылайте широко,
коровники в амурах,
райклубы в рококо!

О юность, феникс, дурочка,
весь в пламени диплом!
Ты машешь красной юбочкой
и дразнишь язычком.

Прощай, пора окраин!
Жизнь — смена пепелищ.

FIRE IN THE ARCHITECTURAL INSTITUTE

Fire in the Architectural Institute!
through all the rooms and over the blueprints
like an amnesty through the jails...
Fire! Fire!

High on the sleepy façade
shamelessly, mischievously
like a red-assed baboon
a window skitters.

We'd already written our theses,
the time had come for us to defend them.
They're crackling away in a sealed cupboard:
all those bad reports on me!

The drafting paper is wounded,
it's a red fall of leaves;
my drawing boards are burning,
whole cities are burning.

Five summers and five winters shoot up in flames
like a jar of kerosene.
Karen, my pet,
Oi! we're on fire!

Farewell architecture:
it's down to a cinder
for all those cowsheds decorated with cupids
and those rec halls in rococo!

O youth, phoenix, ninny,
your dissertation is hot stuff,
flirting its little red skirt now,
flaunting its little red tongue.

Farewell life in the sticks!
Life is a series of burned-out sites.

Мы все перегораем.
Живешь — горишь.

А завтра, в палец чиркнувши,
вонзится злей пчелы
иголочка от циркуля
из горсточки золы...

...Все выгорело начисто.
Милиции полно.
Все — кончено!
              Все — начато!
Айда в кино!

Nobody escapes the bonfire:
if you live — you burn.

But tomorrow, out of these ashes,
more poisonous than a bee
your compass point will dart
to sting you in the finger.

Everything's gone up in smoke,
and there's no end of people sighing.
It's the end?
        It's only the beginning.
Let's go to the movies!

translated by Stanley Kunitz

БАЛЛАДА ТОЧКИ

«Баллада? О точке?! О смертной пилюле?!..»
Балда!
Вы забыли о пушкинской пуле!

Что ветры свистали, как в дыры кларнетов,
в пробитые головы лучших поэтов.

Стрелою пронзив самодурство и свинство,
к потомкам неслась траектория свиста!
И не было точки. А было — начало.

Мы в землю уходим, как в двери вокзала.
И точка тоннеля, как дуло, черна…
В бессмертье она?
Иль в безвестность она?..

Нет смерти. Нет точки. Есть путь пулевой —
вторая проекция той же прямой.

В природе по смете отсутствует точка.
Мы будем бессмертны. И это — точно!

BALLAD OF THE FULL STOP

"A ballad? A ballad of the full stop? The knockout drop?"
You dope!
What about the bullet that punctuated Pushkin!

O the winds whistled as through the stops of clarinets
Through the perforated heads of our best poets,

Zinged on their course past oppression and piggishness
On a whistling trajectory hurtling down to posterity!
There was no full stop. It was all a beginning.

We go down into earth as through the gates of a railroad station,
And the O of the tunnel is as black as a muzzle...
What's the place we are heading for?
Immortality? Oblivion?

No death. No final dot. There's the path of the bullet—
A further propulsion of the same projectile.

Our sentence in nature has no period.
We shall be deathless.
                    And that's my point!

translated by Stanley Kunitz

НЬЮ-ЙОРКСКАЯ ПТИЦА

На окно ко мне садится
в лунных вензелях
алюминиевая птица —
вместо тела

       фюзеляж

и над ее шеей гайковой
как пламени язык
над гигантской зажигалкой
полыхает

       женский

          лик!

(В простынь капиталистическую
завернувшись, спит мой друг.)

кто ты? бред кибернетический?
полуробот? полудух?
помесь королевы блюза
и летающего блюдца?

может ты душа Америки
уставшей от забав?
кто ты юная химера
с сигареткою в зубах?

но взирают не мигая
не отерши крем ночной
очи как на Мичигане
у одной

у нее такие газовые
под глазами синячки
птица что ты предсказываешь?
птица не солги!

    •

NEW YORK BIRD

On my windowsill,
monogrammed with moonlight,
               perches
an aluminum bird;
in place of a body,
               a fuselage.

And on its corkscrew neck
like the tongue of flame
on a giant cigarette lighter
blazes
        a woman's
                  face!

(Wound in his capitalistic sheet,
my traveling companion is asleep.)

Who are you? A cybernetic hallucination, who's
half robot, half creature of air?
A cross between a queen of the blues
and a flying saucer?

Perhaps you're the soul of America,
weary of playing, underneath?
Who are you, young Chimera,
that cigarette clenched between your teeth?

Unblinking, they stare
and steadily gleam—
the eyes like those of that girl somewhere
out in Chicago, face wreathed in cold cream,

circles under her eyes
as if by gas flames blurred—
What do you prophesy?
Don't lie to me, bird!

•

что ты знаешь, сообщаешь?
что-то странное извне
как в сосуде сообщающемся
подымается во мне

век атомный стонет в спальне...

(Я ору. И, матерясь,
мой напарник, как ошпаренный,
садится на матрас.)

Will you communicate, will you report
what you know? Something strange from without
rises up in me
as in a branching retort —

the atomic age groans in this hotel room...

(I shout. And my companion, crying:
"You son of a bitch!" sits bolt upright in bed,
as if he'd been scalded.)

translated by William Jay Smith

ИТАЛЬЯНСКИЙ ГАРАЖ

Б. Ахмадулиной

Пол — мозаика
как карась.
Спит в палаццо
        ночной гараж.

Мотоциклы как сарацины
или спящие саранчихи.

Не Паоло и не Джульетты —
дышат потные «шевролеты».

Как механики, фрески Джотто
отражаются в их капотах.

Реют призраки войн и краж.
Что вам снится,
        ночной гараж?

Алебарды?
или тираны?
или бабы
из ресторана?..

Лишь один мотоцикл притих —
самый алый из молодых.

Что он бодрствует? Завтра — святки.
Завтра он разобьется всмятку!

Апельсины, аплодисменты...
Расшибающиеся —
                бессмертны!
Мы родились — не выживать,
а спидометры выжимать!..

Алый, конченый, жарь! Жарь!
Только гонщицу очень жаль...

ITALIAN GARAGE

to Bella Akhmadulina

The floor's a mosaic —
A trout's back stippled with light.

The garage in the palazzo sleeps.
                                    It is night.

In rows the motorcycles rest
Like Saracens or slumbering locusts.

No Paolos here, no Juliets —
Only Chevrolets that pant and sweat.

Figures in the Giotto frescoes are
Like mechanics mirrored in each car.

Ghosts of feuds and battles range at large;
What do you summon in your dreams, garage?

Is it halberds
                    or tyrants that haunt
You? Or women
                    picked up in restaurants?

One motorcycle seems to brood —
The reddest of the little brood.

Why is it still awake? Is it because
Tomorrow is Christmas and tomorrow it will crash?

Oranges, applause...
                        Those who smash
Themselves to pieces never die.

Give her the gun, doomed one, bloodred!
And for the girl who rides you it's too bad.

We were not born to survive, alas,
But to step on the gas.

translated by William Jay Smith

БАЛЛАДА-ДИССЕРТАЦИЯ

Нос растет в течение всей жизни.
(Из научных источников)

Вчера мой доктор произнес:
«Талант в вас, может, и возможен,
но Ваш паяльник обморожен,
не суйтесь из дому в мороз».

О нос!..

Неотвратимы, как часы,
у нас, у вас, у капуцинов
по всем
            законам
                    Медицины
торжественно растут носы!

Они растут среди ночи
у всех сограждан знаменитых,
у сторожей,
                у замминистров,
сопя бессонно, как сычи,
они прохладны и косы,
их бьют боксеры,
                    щемят двери,
но в скважины, подобно дрели,
соседок ввинчены носы!

(Их роль с мистической тревогой
интуитивно чуял Гоголь.)

Мой друг Букашкин пьяны были,
им снился сон:
                подобно шпилю,
сбивая люстры и тазы,
пронзая потолки разбуженные,

THE NOSE

The nose grows during the whole of one's life.
(from scientific sources)

Yesterday my doctor told me:
"Clever you may be, however
Your snout is frozen."
So don't go out in the cold,
Nose!

On me, on you, on Capuchin monks,
According to well-known medical laws,
Relentless as clocks, without pause
Nose-trunks triumphantly grow.

During the night they grow
On every citizen, high or low,
On janitors, ministers, rich and poor,
Hooting endlessly like owls,
Chilly and out of kilter,
Brutally bashed by a boxer
Or foully crushed by a door,
And those of our feminine neighbors
Are foxily screwed like drills
Into many a keyhole.

Gogol, that mystical uneasy soul,
Intuitively sensed their role.

My good friend Buggins got drunk: in his dream
It seemed that, like a church spire
Breaking through washbowls and chandeliers,
Piercing and waking startled ceilings,
Impaling each floor like
Receipts on a spike,

над ним
   рос
     нос,
       как чеки в булочной,
нанизывая этажи!

«К чему б?» — гадал он поутру.
Сказал я: «К Страшному суду.
К ревизии кредитных дел!»

30-го Букашкин сел.

О, вечный двигатель носов!
Носы длиннее — жизнь короче.
На бледных лицах среди ночи,
как коршун или же насос,
нас всех высасывает нос,

и говорят, у эскимосов
есть поцелуй посредством носа...

Но это нам не привилось.

Higher and higher
              rose
          his nose.

"What could that mean?" he wondered next morning.
"A warning," I said, "of Doomsday: it looks
As if they were going to check your books."
On the 30th poor Buggins was haled off to jail.

Why, O Prime Mover of Noses, why
Do our noses grow longer, our lives shorter,
Why during the night should these fleshly lumps,
Like vampires or suction pumps,
Drain us dry?

They report that Eskimos
Kiss with their nose.

Among us this has not caught on.

translated by W. H. Auden

ГОЛОВА ЛИ ОТ ВЕТРА КРУЖИТСЯ?

Голова ли от ветра кружится?
Или память клубком раскручивается?
Будто крутится радиолой
марш охрипший и одиозный.

Ты не пой, пластинка, про Сталина.
Это песенка не простая,
непроста усов седина,
то — прозрачна, а то — мутна...

Те усы свисали над трубкой
выдающегося конструктора,
разбирались в шайбочках, в винтиках,
человека только не видели!

Кто в них верил? И кто в них сгинул,
как иголка в седой копне?
Их разглаживали при Гимне.
Их мочили в красном вине.

И торжественно над страною,
точно птица хищной красы,
плыли
          с красною
                              бахромою
государственные усы!

Ты не пой, пластинка, про Сталина.
Быть нам винтиком не пристало.
Было. Больше не угорим
вислым дымом его седин.

DOES A HIGH WIND MAKE ME REEL?

Does a high wind make me reel
Or does memory unwind like a spool?
I hear on a record player
A vile marching air.

Of Stalin do not sing;
That is no simple song,
But mixed like his gray mustaches,
Cloudy at times, then clear.

They looped about the pipe
Of the Great Engineer,
Nuts and bolts surveying,
Blind to human beings.

How many were impounded,
Needles in that gray stack,
Stroked when the anthem sounded,
Dipped in wine bloodred?

Majestic over the land,
The wings of a bird of prey,
They hovered,
              tinged with red,
Great mustaches of state.

Of Stalin do not sing;
We are more than nuts and bolts;
And no more shall we choke
On his blue-bearded smoke.

translated by William Jay Smith

ВЫЙДУ ЛИ К ПАРКУ

Выйду ли к парку, в море ль плыву —
туфелек пара стоит на полу.

Левая к правой набок припала,
их не поправят — времени мало.

В мире не топлено, в мире ни зги,
вы еще теплые, только с ноги,

в вас от ступни потемнела изнанка,
вытерлось золото фирменных знаков...

Красные голуби просо клюют.
Кровь кружит голову — спать не дают!

Выйду ли к пляжу — туфелек пара,
будто купальщица в море пропала.

Где ты, купальщица? Вымыты пляжи.
Как тебе плавается? С кем тебе пляшется?..

...В мире металла, на черной планете,
сентиментальные туфельки эти,

как перед танком присели голубки —
нежные туфельки в форме скорлупки!

HER SHOES

When I walk in the park or swim in the sea,
A pair of her shoes waits there on the floor.

The left one leaning on the right,
Not enough time to set them straight.

The world is pitch-black, cold and desolate,
But they are still warm, right off her feet.

The soles of her feet left the insides dark,
The gold of the trademark has rubbed off.

A pair of red doves pecking seed,
They make me dizzy, rob me of sleep.

I see the shoes when I go to the beach
Like those of a bather drowned in the sea.

Where are you, bather? The beaches are clean.
Where are you dancing? With whom do you swim?

In a world of metal, on a planet of black,
Those silly shoes look to me like

Doves perched in the path of a tank, frail
And dainty, as delicate as eggshell.

translated by William Jay Smith

ТЫ СЕГОДНЯ, 16-ГО, СПРАВЛЯЕШЬ ДЕНЬ РОЖДЕНИЯ

Ты сегодня, 16-го, справляешь день рождения в ресторане «Берлин». Зеркало там на потолке.

Из зеркала вниз головой, как сосульки, свисали гости. В центре потолка нежный, как вымя, висел розовый торт с воткнутыми свечами.

Вокруг него, как лампочки, ввернутые в элегантные черные розетки костюмов, сияли лысины и прически. Лиц не было видно. У одного лысина была маленькая, как дырка на пятке носка. Ее можно было закрасить чернилами.

У другого она была прозрачна, как спелое яблоко, и сквозь нее, как зернышки, просвечивали три мысли (две черные и одна светлая — недозрелая).

Проборы щеголей горели, как щели в копилках.

Затылок брюнетки с прикнопленным прозрачным нейлоновым бантом полз, словно муха по потолку.

Лиц не было видно. Зато перед каждым, как таблички перед экспонатами, лежали бумажки, где кто сидит.

И только одна тарелка была белая, как пустая розетка.

«Скажите, а почему слева от хозяйки пустое место?»

«Генерала, может, ждут?» «А может, помер кто?»

Никто не знал, что там сижу я. Я невидим. Изящные денди, подходящие тебя поздравить, спотыкаются об меня, царапают вилками.

Ты сидишь рядом, но ты восторженно чужая, как подарок в целлофане.

Модного поэта просят: «Ах, рваните чего-то этакого! Поближе к жизни, не от мира сего... чтобы модерново...»

Поэт подымается (вернее, опускается, как спускают трап с вертолета). Голос его странен, как бы антимирен ему.

AT HOTEL BERLIN

You are celebrating your birthday today — the 16th — in the banquet room of the Berlin. The ceiling there has a mirror.

The guests hang head downward from the ceiling. A pink wedding cake with candles stuck in it hangs down, like an udder, from the center of the ceiling.

Round about it, like electric bulbs screwed into the black sockets of their suits and dresses, bald pates and hairdos glow. One can't see their faces. One of them has a small bald patch, no bigger than a hole in the heel of a stocking — you could block it out with black ink.

Another bald head is as translucent as a ripe apple and through the skin you can see — like pips — three thoughts: two of them black, and the third light in color: it has not yet matured.

The partings of well-groomed hair shine like the slits in piggy banks.

The neck of a brunette with a transparent nylon band pinned to it glides over the ceiling like a fly.

One can't see their faces. But they have cards in front of them giving their names, like labels on exhibits in a museum.

Only one plate is white and empty.

"Tell me," someone asks. "Why is the place next to our hostess vacant?"

"Perhaps they're waiting for a general? Or perhaps somebody's died?"

Nobody realizes that I am sitting there. I am invisible. All those elegant fellows coming up to wish you many happy returns bump into me and scratch me with their forks.

You sitting there next to me, but you are splendidly remote, like a gift wrapped in cellophane.

People beg a fashionable poet: "Do let's have something — you know what: something close to life, something out of this world...as long as it's modern...."

The poet gets up (or rather, drops down, in the way a rope ladder is lowered from a helicopter). His voice is strange and, so to speak, antiworldly, as though he were only intoning somebody else's words.

Читая, он запрокидывает лицо. И на его белом лице, как на тарелке, горел нос, точно болгарский перец.

Все кричат: «Браво! Этот лучше всех. Ну, и тостик!» Слово берет следующий поэт. Он пьян вдребезину. Он свисает с потолка вниз головой и просыхает, как полотенце. Только несколько слов можно разобрать из его бормотанья.

Все замолкают.

Слово берет тамада Ъ.

Он раскачивается вниз головой, как длинный маятник. «Тост за новорожденную». Голос его, как из репродуктора, разносится с потолка ресторана. «За ее новое рождение, и я, как крестный... Да, а как зовут новорожденную?» (Никто не знает.)

Как это все напоминает что-то! И под этим подвешенным миром внизу расположился второй, наоборотный, со своим поэтом, со своим тамадой Ъ. Они едва не касаются затылками друг друга, симметричные, как песочные часы. Но что это? Где я? В каком идиотском измерении? Что это за потолочно-зеркальная реальность? Что за наоборотная страна?!

Задумавшись, я машинально глотаю бутерброд с кетовой икрой.

Но почему висящий напротив, как окорок, периферийный классик с ужасом смотрит на мой желудок? Боже, ведь я-то невидим, а бутерброд реален! Он передвигается по мне, как красный джемпер в лифте.

Классик что-то шепчет соседу.

Слух моментально пронизывает головы, как бусы на нитке.

Красные змеи языков ввинчиваются в уши соседей. Все глядят на бутерброд.

«А нас килькой кормят!» — вопит классик.

Надо спрятаться! Ведь если они обнаружат меня, кто же выручит тебя: кто же разобьет зеркало?!

Я выпрыгиваю из-за стола и ложусь на красную дорожку пола. Рядом со мной, за стулом, стоит пара

As he reads, he throws back his head and his nose shines on the white plate of his face like a Bulgarian red pepper.

People shout: "Bravo! He's the best of the lot! Here's to him."

He is followed by another poet, who is dead drunk. He hangs down from the ceiling like a towel drying on a clothes line. It is only possible to make out a few muttered words.

Everybody is silent.

The next to speak is X, the Toastmaster.

He swings head downward as though he were a pendulum. "I give you the health of our guest of honor." His voice booms from the ceiling like a loudspeaker. "Here's many happy returns to her and, as her godfather, I . . . what's her name now?" (Nobody knows.)

It is all vaguely familiar. Under this world suspended on the ceiling there is a second world, an upside-down one, which also has its poet and its toastmaster. The napes of their necks almost touch — they are counterpoised like the two halves of an hourglass. But what is all this and where are we? In what preposterous dimension? What is this reality reflected in the ceiling? What is this upside-down country?

Lost in these thoughts, I absentmindedly started eating a red-caviar sandwich. Why is that provincial celebrity, who hangs opposite me like a smoked ham, looking at my stomach with such horror? God, how stupid! I'd clean forgotten that I am invisible, but that sandwiches aren't — this was something that H. G. Wells warned us about. It moves down me like a red sweater in an elevator.

He whispers in his neighbor's ear and immediately heads are threaded together by rumor as beads on a string.

Red snakes of tongues dart into neighboring ears. Everybody looks at my caviar sandwich.

"And all *we* get is sardines!" the celebrity hisses.

I must hide! If they catch me, who will save you, who will smash the mirror?

I jump up from the table and lie flat on the floor, which has a red carpet. Next to me, behind a chair, I see a pair of shoes.

туфелек. Они, видимо, жмут кому-то. Левая припала к правой. (Как все напоминает что-то!) Тебя просят спеть...

Начинаются танцы. Первая пара с хрустом проносится по мне. Подошвы! Подошвы! Почему все ботинки с подковами? Рядом кто-то с хрустом давит по туфелькам. Чьи-то каблучки, подобно швейной машинке, прошивают мне кожу на лице. Только бы не в глаза!..

They must have been slipped off because they hurt. The left one has fallen against the right one (how familiar it all is!). People ask you to sing something. . . .

Now they've begun to dance. The soles of their shoes! The first couple passes over me with a crunch. Why do they all have studs on their soles? Somebody tramples on the little shoes next to me. A pair of heels goes rat-a-tat-tat over the skin of my face as though it were being stitched by a sewing machine. As long as they don't get my eyes!

translated by Max Hayward

ПЛАЧ ПО ДВУМ НЕРОЖДЕННЫМ ПОЭМАМ

Аминь.

Убил я поэму. Убил, не родивши. К Харонам!
Хороним.
Хороним поэмы. Вход всем посторонним.
Хороним.

На черной Вселенной любовниками
                          отравленными
лежат две поэмы,
           как белый бинокль театральный.
Две жизни прижались судьбой половинной —
две самых поэмы моих
                  соловьиных!
Вы, люди,
      вы, звери,
            пруды, где они зарождались
                  в Останкине, —

в с т а н ь т е!

Вы, липы ночные,
           как лапы в ветвях хиромантии, —
встаньте,
дороги, убитые горем,
            довольно валяться в асфальте,
как волосы дыбом над городом,
вы встаньте.

Раскройтесь, гробы,
           как складные ножи гиганта,
вы встаньте, —
        Сервантес, Борис Леонидович,
                Данте,
вы б их полюбили, теперь они тоже останки,
встаньте.

И Вы, Член Президиума Верховного Совета
           товарищ Гамзатов,

LAMENT FOR TWO UNBORN POEMS

Amen.

I have killed a poem. Killed it, unborn. To hell with it!
We bury.
We bury poems. Come see.
We bury.

On the black Universe like poisoned lovers
the poems lie,
         or like an ivory pair of opera glasses,
two half-lives locked together—
my two most lyric
           poems!

You people,
     you dumb creatures,
         ponds, where they were conceived
                 in Ostankino,
rise!
You, nocturnal linden trees,
like the calligraphy of a hand outstretched for the palmist,
rise,
roads killed by grief,
         erupt from the asphalt,
rise above the metropolis
like hair standing on end.

Open, you coffins,
like the jackknife of a giant,
rise, you—
     Cervantes, Pasternak, Bramante,
you who would have loved them, though they are dust now,
rise.

And you, Comrade Gamzatov, Presidium member
                 of the Supreme Soviet,

встаньте,
погибло искусство, незаменимо это,
                              и это не менее важно,
                                        чем речь
                         на торжественной дате,
встаньте.
Их гибель — судилище. Мы — арестанты.
Встаньте.

О, как ты хотела, чтоб сын твой шел чисто
                                        и прямо,
встань, мама.

Вы встаньте в Сибири,
                 в Париже, в глухих
                              городишках,
встаньте,
мы столько убили
            в себе,
                    не родивши,
встаньте,
Ландау, погибший в косом лаборанте,
встаньте,
Коперник, погибший в Ландау галантном,
встаньте,
вы, девка в джаз-банде,
                 вы помните школьные банты?
Встаньте,

геройские мальчики вышли в герои, но в анти,
встаньте

(я не о кастратах — о самоубийцах,
кто саморастратил
                 святые крупицы),
встаньте.
                 •

rise —
the irreversible condition
is that art has died, passed beyond reach,
more important than a speech
by an official rhetorician —
rise.
Their death is our judgment. It is we who are tried.
Rise.

Oh, you who wanted your son's road straight and true,
rise, mother.

Rise, you in Siberia,
in Paris, in provincial towns,
we have killed so much
within,
without giving birth,
rise;
Landau, you who died in a cross-eyed labworker,
rise,
Copernicus, you who died in a gallant Landau,
rise;
you, slut in a jazz band, what remains
of the schoolgirl ribbons in your hair?
you daring boys turned into heroes, meaning antiheroes,
rise,

(I do not refer to the castrates or suicides,
those who squandered
their holy grains),

rise.
•

Погибли поэмы. Друзья мои в радостной
                                        панике —
«Вечная память!»
Министр, вы мечтали, чтоб юнгой
                              в Атлантике плавать,
вечная память,
громовый Ливанов, ну, где ваш несыгранный Гамлет?
Вечная память,
где принц ваш, бабуся? А девственность
                    можно хоть в рамку обрамить
вечная память,
зеленые замыслы, встаньте как пламень,
вечная память,
мечта и надежда, ты вышла на паперть?
Вечная память!..

Аминь.

Минута молчанья. Минута — как годы.
Себя промолчали — все ждали погоды.
Сегодня не скажешь, а завтра уже
                              не поправить.
Вечная память.

И памяти нашей, ушедшей как мамонт,
вечная память.

Аминь.

Тому же, кто вынес огонь сквозь
                        потраву, —
        Вечная слава!
        Вечная слава!

Poems have died. My good friends cannot wait to cry
"Eternal Memory!"
Minister of State, you dreamed of sailing the Atlantic as a cabin boy?
Eternal memory...
Thunderous Livanov, what of your unplayed Hamlet?
Eternal memory...
Granny, where is your prince? You can take your virginity
    and frame it.
Eternal memory...
Green thought, rise like a flame.
Eternal memory...
Poor dream and hope, have you joined the beggars on the
    church steps?
Eternal memory!...

Amen.

A minute of silence. A minute — like years.
We lost ourselves through silence — we waited for fair weather.
If you hold your tongue today, nothing will be right tomorrow.

Eternal memory.

And to our memory, which shall have vanished like the mammoth,
eternal memory.

Amen.

      To him who bore the fire
              in a time of persecution,
    Eternal glory!
    Eternal glory!

translated by Stanley Kunitz

ЗОВ ОЗЕРА

Памяти жертв фашизма

Певзнер 1903, Лебедев 1916, Бирман 1938,
Бирман 1941, Дробот 1907...

Наши кеды как приморозило.
Тишина.
Гетто в озере. Гетто в озере.
Три гектара живого дна.

Гражданин в пиджачке гороховом
зазывает на славный клев,
только кровь
            на крючке его крохотном,
кровь!

«Не могу, — говорит Володька, —
а по рылу — могу,
это вроде как
            не укладывается в мозгу!

Я живою водой умоюсь,
может, чью-то жизнь расплещу.
Может, Машеньку или Мойшу
я размазываю по лицу.

Ты не трожь воды плоскодонкой,
уважаемый инвалид,
ты пощупай ее ладонью —
болит!

Может, так же не чьи-то давние,
а ладони моей жены,
плечи, волосы, ожидание
будут кем-то растворены?

●

THE CALL OF THE LAKE

to the memory of the victims of fascism

Pevsner 1903, Lebedev 1916, Birman 1938,
Birman 1941, Drobot 1907...

As if our sneakers froze to the ground...
Stillness.
Ghetto in the lake. Ghetto in the lake.
Three bottom acres teeming with life.

A fellow in a pea-green jacket
hails us with news the fishing's good;
but look at the blood
                on his tiny hook,
blood!

"No! No!" — says Volodka —
"I want to smack him on the jaw;
it's really more
                than I can bear.

"It would be desecrating life
to wash myself in this place,
like smearing Mary or Moishe
over my face.

"Your boat is muddying the lake.
Don't, buddy.
Just touch the water with your palm,
feel how it burns!

"Hands that liquefy below
could belong to my bride —
not some girl who lived long ago —
her breasts, her hair, her need.

•

А базарами колоссальными
барабанит жабрами в жесть
то, что было теплом, глазами,
на колени любило сесть…

— Не могу, — говорит Володька, —
лишь зажмурюсь —

                    в чугунных ночах,
точно рыбы на сковородках,
пляшут женщины и кричат!»

Третью ночь, как Костров пьет.
И ночами зовет с обрыва.
И к нему
является
рыба
чудо-юдо озерных вод!

        «Рыба,
            летучая рыба,
                с гневным лицом мадонны,
                    с плавниками, белыми,
                        как свистят паровозы,
                                            рыба,
Рива тебя звали,
        золотая Рива,
                Ривка, либо как-нибудь еще,
с обрывком
        колючки проволоки или рыболовным
                                            крючком
            в верхней губе, рыба,
рыба боли и печали,
        прости меня,
                прокляни,
                    но что-нибудь ответь…»
Ничего не отвечает рыба.

    •

"And the body of her warmth
that loved to sit on my knees
could be slapping in a pail
amid the market crowds..."

"No! No!"—says Volodka—
"on these iron nights,
            as soon as I close my eyes,
women sputter and dance
like fish in a frying pan!"

He's been on a three-day binge.
And at night he calls from the cliff.
And to him
A Jewfish
appears,
The Genius of the Lake!

"Fish,
        flying fish,
                with wrathful madonna's face,
                        with fins as white
                                as locomotive whistles,
                                        fish,

"Your name was Riva,
            golden Riva,
                    Rivka—any name you wish—
with a sliver
        of barbed wire or a fishhook
            caught in your upper lip—fish,
fish of pain and sorrow—
            forgive me, curse me, but speak to me..."

Silence.
•

Тихо.
Озеро приграничное.
Три сосны.

Изумленнейшее хранилище
жизни, облака, вышины.

Лебедев 1916, Бирман 1941, Румер 1902, Бойко оба 1933.

No word.
The lake is close to the border.
Three pines.

The stunned reservoir
of life, of a cloud, of height.

Lebedev 1916, Birman 1941, Rumer 1902, Boiko (twice) 1933.

translated by Stanley Kunitz

II

Ностальгия
по настоящему

II

Nostalgia for the Present

НОСТАЛЬГИЯ ПО НАСТОЯЩЕМУ

Я не знаю, как остальные,
но я чувствую жесточайшую
не по прошлому ностальгию —
ностальгию по настоящему.

Будто послушник хочет к господу,
ну а доступ лишь к настоятелю —
так и я умоляю доступа
без посредников к настоящему.

Будто сделал я что-то чуждое,
или даже не я — другие.
Упаду на поляну — чувствую
по живой земле ностальгию.

Нас с тобой никто не расколет,
но когда тебя обнимаю —
обнимаю с такой тоскою,
будто кто тебя отнимает.

Когда слышу тирады подленькие
оступившегося товарища,
я ищу не подобья — подлинника,
по нему грущу, настоящему.

Одиночества не искупит
в сад распахнутая столярка.
Я тоскую не по искусству,
задыхаюсь по-настоящему.

И когда мне хохочет в рожу
идиотствующая мафия,
говорю: «Идиоты — в прошлом.
В настоящем — рост понимания.»

Хлещет черная вода из крана,
хлещет ржавая, настоявшаяся,

NOSTALGIA FOR THE PRESENT

I don't know about the rest of you,
but I feel the cruelest
nostalgia—not for the past—
but nostalgia for the present.

A novice desires to approach the Lord
but is permitted to do so only by her Superior.
I beg to be joined, without intermediary,
to the present.

It's as if I had done something wrong,
Not I even—but others.
I fall down in a field and feel
nostalgia for the living earth.

No one can ever tear you away,
and yet when I embrace you again
I feel overcome by terrible pain
as if you were being stolen from me.

When I hear the nasty tirades
of a friend who has taken a false step,
I don't look for what he seems to be,
I grieve for what he really is.

A window opening on a garden
will not redeem loneliness.
I long not for art—I choke
on my craving for reality.

And when the Mafia laughs in my face
idiotically, I say:
"Idiots are all in the past. The present
calls for fuller understanding."

Black water spurts from the faucet,
Brackish water, stale water,

хлещет красная вода из крана,
я дождусь — пойдет настоящая.

Что прошло, то прошло. К лучшему.
Но прикусываю как тайну
ностальгию по настоящему,
что настанет. Да не застану.

rusty water flows from the faucet—I'll wait
for the real water to come.

Whatever is past is past. So much the better.
But I bite at it as at a mystery,
nostalgia for the impending
present.
  And I'll never catch hold of it.

translated by Vera Dunham and H. W. Tjalsma

ЧАСТНОЕ КЛАДБИЩЕ

Памяти Р. Лоуэлла

Ты проходил переделкинскою калиткой,
голову набок, щекою прижавшись к плечу —
как прижимал недоступную зрению скрипку.
Скрипка пропала. Слушать хочу!

В домик Петра ты вступал близоруко.
Там на двух метрах зарубка, как от топора.
Встал ты примериться под зарубку —
встал в пустоту, что осталась от роста Петра.

Ах, как звенит пустота вместо бывшего тела!
Новая тень под зарубкой стоит.
Клены на кладбище облетели.
И недоступная скрипка кричит.

В чаще затеряно частное кладбище.
Мать и отец твои. Где же здесь ты?..
Будто из книги вынули вкладыши,
и невозможно страничку найти.

Как тебе, Роберт, в новой пустыне?
Частное кладбище носим в себе.
Пестик тоски в мировой пустоте,
мчащийся мимо, как тебе имя?
Прежнее имя как платье лежит на плите.

Вот ты и вырвался из лабиринта.
Что тебе, тень, под зарубкой в избе?
Я принесу пастернаковскую рябину.
Но и она не поможет тебе.

FAMILY GRAVEYARD

to the memory of Robert Lowell

At Peredelkino you passed through the gate,
Your head to one side, your cheek on your shoulder tight
As on a violin held somehow out of sight;
I listen now, but it is there no more.

In Moscow, nearsighted, you entered Peter's hut,
Examining a notch some six feet from the floor
Hacked as by an ax; you stood below that notch
And measured yourself against Great Peter's height.

Once filled by a body, how the void resounds!
Beneath the notch a new ghost fills the air;
The maples in the graveyard now are bare;
And through the dark the violin thinly sounds.

The family graves lie deep within the wood:
Your parents both are there, but where in the dark are you?
The bookmarks in the book have been removed,
One cannot find the page as one leafs through.

How is it, Robert, there in your wild land?
Within us we all bear our family graves;
How can we name the heart of sorrow's flower
As it races past us through dark cosmic waves?
Here on the stone the name that you once had rests like discarded
    clothes.

So through the labyrinth you've made your way?
And yet beneath that notch I still hear you,
And bring these berries from Pasternak's rowan tree
For all the good that rowanberries do.

translated by William Jay Smith and Fred Starr

САГА

Ты меня на рассвете разбудишь,
проводить необутая выйдешь.
Ты меня никогда не забудешь.
Ты меня никогда не увидишь.

Заслонивши тебя от простуды,
я подумаю: «Боже всевышний!
Я тебя никогда не забуду.
Я тебя никогда не увижу».

Эту воду в мурашках запруды,
это Адмиралтейство и Биржу
я уже никогда не забуду
и уже никогда не увижу.

Не мигают, слезятся от ветра
безнадежные карие вишни.
Возвращаться — плохая примета.
Я тебя никогда не увижу.

Даже если на землю вернемся
мы вторично, согласно Гафизу,
мы, конечно, с тобой разминемся.
Я тебя никогда не увижу.

И окажется так минимальным
наше непониманье с тобою
перед будущим непониманьем
двух живых с пустотой неживою.

И качнется бессмысленной высью
пара фраз, залетевших отсюда:
«Я тебя никогда не забуду.
Я тебя никогда не увижу».

SAGA

You will awaken me at dawn
And barefoot lead me to the door;
You'll not forget me when I'm gone,
You will not see me anymore.

Lord, I think, in shielding you
From the cold wind of the open door:
I'll not forget you when I'm gone,
I shall not see you anymore.

The Admiralty, the Stock Exchange
I'll not forget when I am gone.
I'll not see Leningrad again,
Its water shivering at dawn.

From withered cherries as they turn,
Brown in the wind, let cold tears pour:
It's bad luck always to return,
I shall not see you anymore.

And if what Hafiz says is true
And we return to earth once more,
We'll miss each other if it's true;
I shall not see you anymore.

Our quarrels then will fade away
To nothing when we both are gone,
And when one day our two lives clash
Against that void to which they're drawn.

Two silly phrases rise to sway
On heights of madness from earth's floor:
I'll not forget you when I'm gone,
I shall not see you anymore.

translated by William Jay Smith and
Vera Dunham

ВАСИЛЬКИ ШАГАЛА

Лик ваш серебряный, как алебарда.
Жесты легки.
В вашей гостинице аляповатой
в банке спрессованы васильки.

Милый, вот что вы действительно любите!
С Витебска ими раним и любим.
Дикорастущие сорные тюбики
с дьявольски
                    выдавленным
                                голубым!

Сирый цветок из породы репейников,
но его синий не знает соперников.
Марка Шагала, загадка Шагала —
рупь у Савеловского вокзала!

Это росло у Бориса и Глеба,
в хохоте нэпа и чебурек.
Во поле хлеба — чуточку неба.
Небом единым жив человек.

В небе коровы парят и ундины.
Зонтик раскройте, идя на проспект.
Родины разны, но небо едино.
Небом единым жив человек.

Как занесло васильковое семя
на Елисейские, на поля?
Как заплетали венок Вы на темя
Гранд Опера, Гранд Опера!

В век ширпотреба нет его, неба.
Доля художников хуже калек.
Давать им сребреники нелепо —
небом единым жив человек.

Ваши холсты из фашистского бреда
от изуверов свершали побег.

CHAGALL'S CORNFLOWERS

Your face is all of silver like a halberd,
your gestures light.
In your vulgar hotel room
you keep pressed cornflowers.

Dear friend, so this is what you truly love!
Since Vitebsk, cornflowers have wounded
and loved you — those wildflower tubes
of squeezed-out
                    devilish
                            sky-blue.

An orphaned flower of the burdock family,
its blue has no rival.
The mark of Chagall, the enigma of Chagall —
a tattered ruble note at a remote Moscow station.

It grew around St. Boris and St. Gleb,
around guffawing speculators with their greasy fingers.
In a field of grain, add a patch of sky.
Man lives by sky alone.

Cows and water nymphs soar in the sky.
Open your umbrella as you go out on the street.
Countries are many, the sky is one.
Man lives by sky alone.

How did a cornflower seed chance to fall
on the Champs-Elysées, on those fields?
What a glorious garland you wove
for the Paris Opéra.

In the age of consumer goods there is no sky.
The lot of the artist is worse than a cripple's.
Giving him pieces of silver is silly —
man lives by sky alone.

Your canvases made their escape
from the fascist nightmare, from murder,

Свернуто в трубку запретное небо,
но только небом жив человек.

Не протрубили трубы господни
над катастрофою мировой —
в трубочку свернутые полотна
воют архангельскою трубой!

Кто целовал твое поле, Россия,
пока не выступят васильки?
Твои сорняки всемирно красивы,
хоть экспортируй их, сорняки.

С поезда выйдешь — как окликают!
По полю дрожь.
Поле пришпорено васильками,
как ни уходишь — все не уйдешь...

Выйдешь ли вечером — будто захварываешь,
во поле углические зрачки.
Ах, Марк Захарович, Марк Захарович,
все васильки, все васильки...

Не Иегова, не Иисусе,
ах, Марк Захарович, нарисуйте
непобедимо синий завет —
Небом Единым Жив Человек.

the forbidden sky rolled up in a tube,
but man lives by sky alone.

While God failed to trumpet
over the horror,
your canvases rolled up in a tube
still howl like Gabriel's horn.

Who kissed your fields, Russia,
until cornflowers bloomed?
Your weeds become glorious in other countries,
you ought to export them.

How they hail you, when you leave the train.
The fields tremble.
The fields are studded with cornflowers.
You can't get away from them.

When you go out in the evening—you seem ill.
Eyes of the unjustly condemned stare from the field.
Ah, Marc Zakharovich, Marc Zakharovich,
is it all the fault of those cornflowers?

Let not Jehovah or Jesus
but you, Marc Zakharovich, paint a testament
of invincible blue—
Man Lives by Sky Alone.

translated by Vera Dunham and H. W. Tjalsma

ПРОВИНЦИАЛЬНАЯ ХРОНИКА

Мы с другом шли. За вывескою «Хлеб»
ущелье дуло, как депо судеб.

Нас обступал сиропный городок.
Местный вампир у донорского пункта
на бампере клиентов ждал попутных.

Мой друг хромал. И пузыри земли,
я уточнил бы — пузыри асфальта —
нам попадаясь, клянчили на банку.

«Ты помнишь Анечку-официантку?»

Я помнил. Удивленная лазурь
ее меж подавальщиц отличала.
Носила косу. Говорят, свою.
Когда б не глаз цыганские фиалки
ее бы мог писать Венецианов.
Спешила к сыну с сумками, полна
такою темно-золотою силой,
что женщины при приближеньи Аньки
мужей хватали, как при крике: «Танки!»

Но иногда на зов «Официантка!»
она душою оцепеневала,
и встрепенувшись, шла: «Спешу! Спешу!»

Я помнил Анечку-официантку,
что не меня, а друга целовала
и в деревянном домике жила.
Спешила вечно к сыну. Сын однажды
ее встречал. На нас комплексовал.
К ней, как вьюнок белесый, присосался,
Потом из кухни в зеркало следил
и делал вид, что учит Песни Данте.

•

PROVINCIAL SCENE

While wind swept down the gorge as from the depot of the fates
I walked with my friend the quiet little streets
below a bakery sign in a sweet southern town.
Beside a blood bank a local vampire
leaned on the bumper of his car, awaiting clients.
My friend limped along, and bubbles from the earth
(or rather, bubbles rising between chinks
in the asphalt) came toward us like bums cadging drinks. . . .

"You remember Annie, the little waitress, don't you?"

I did, of course. It was the astonished blue
of her eyes that distinguished her from her fellow hash-slingers.
She wore a braid, thought to be her own.
Had it not been for the gypsy violet of
her eyes, she might have modeled for Venetsianov.
She was always hurrying to her son with shopping bags of food.
Filled with such dark, golden strength
that any woman who saw her would grab her husband and disappear
as if someone had cried, "Look out, the tanks are here!"

Often when customers shouted, "Miss!"
her soul would freeze as if she mistook this
for some other signal, and then, waking up, would reply, "I'm
    coming, coming."

I remembered her clearly,
little Annie, the waitress —
she had slept with my friend, but not with me —
lived in a shack,
always hurrying to her son. Once the son
stood waiting, felt uneasy with us,
and clung to her like a pale vine; then he
kept watching us in the mirror
while pretending to study his Dante.
•

«Ты помнишь Анечку-официантку?
Ее убил из-за валюты сын.
Одна коса от Анечки осталась.»

Так вот куда ты, милая, спешила...

«Он бил ее в постели молотком,
вьюночек, малолетний сутенер, —
у друга на ветру блеснули зубы. —
Ее ассенизаторы нашли,
ее нога отсасывать мешала.
Был труп утоплен в яме выгребной,
как грешница в аду. Старик, Шекспир...»

Она летела над ночной землей.
Она кричала: «Мальчик потерялся!»
Заглядывала форточкой в дома —
«Невинен он, — кричала, — я сама
ударилась! Сметана в холодильнике.
Проголодался? Мальчика не вижу!»
И безнадежно отжимала жижу.

И с круглым люком мерзкая доска
скользила нимбом, как доска иконы.
Нет низкого для Божьей чистоты!

«Ее пришел весь город хоронить.
Гадали — кто? Его подозревали.
Ему сказали: «Поцелуй хоть мать».
Он отказался. Тут и раскололи.
Он не назвал сообщников, дебил».
Сказал я другу: «Это ты убил».

Ты утонула в наших головах
меж новостей и скучных анекдотов.
Не существует рая или ада.

"You remember Annie, the little waitress? She's dead,
killed by her son for her money;
all that was left was her false braid."

So that is where you were hurrying, Annie.

"He beat her with a hammer while she slept,
the little clinging vine, the teenage pimp."
My friend's teeth glittered in the wind.
"She was found by the sanitation crew
when her leg blocked their pump.
Her corpse was stuffed down the outhouse hole—
like in Shakespeare, bud, like a sinner in hell."

Over the night earth I saw her fly,
and "I've lost my boy!" I heard her cry
as she gazed in at the windows.
"He is not guilty!" I heard her scream.
"I hit myself with the hammer!
In the icebox there is sour cream.
Aren't you hungry, honey? I can't see my boy..."
and she tried to wipe away the excrement....

But the vile board surrounded her all the while
like the hatch of a conning tower or the nimbus of an icon:
In God's eyes nothing is vile.

"The whole town came to her funeral.
They guessed who'd done it. Suspecting him,
they said: 'Kiss your mother';
he refused.
And it was then that they found him out.
But he would not say who his accomplices had been."
"You were the killer!" I said to my friend.

Yes, Annie, you drowned in our minds
between news reports and dirty jokes...
heaven and hell do not exist—

Ты стала мыслью. Кто же ты теперь
в той новой, ирреальной иерархии —
клочок Ничто? тычиночка тоски?
приливы беспокойства пред туманом?
Куда спешишь, гонимая причиной,
необъяснимой нам? зовешь куда?

Прости, что без нужды тебя тревожу.
В том океане, где отсчета нет,
ты вряд ли помнишь 30-40 лет,
субстанцию людей провинциальных
и на кольце свои инициалы?
Но вдруг ты смутно помнишь зовы эти
и на мгновенье оцепеневаешь,
расслышав фразу на одной планете:

«Ты помнишь Анечку-официантку?»

Гуляет ветр судеб, судебный ветер.

you drift somewhere in between. Who are you now
in your new hierarchy?

A little scrap of nothing, are you? Stamen dusted with grief,
the rush of anxiety that comes before fog descends. . . .
Where are you hurrying now, driven by what we do not know;
where in the world do you want us to go?

Sorry to disturb you for no reason.
Now in that ocean where one can't begin to count,
you have no doubt forgotten your thirty or forty years,
the fabric of provincial people, the initials in your ring.
But maybe you dimly remember their calls,
and for one second your soul may freeze,
catching a phrase that from a planet will descend.

"You remember Annie, the little waitress, don't you?"

The wind of judgment blows, the fateful wind.

translated by William Jay Smith

ПОХОРОНЫ ГОГОЛЯ НИКОЛАЯ ВАСИЛЬИЧА

1. Завещаю тела моего не погребать до тех пор, пока не покажутся явные признаки разложения. Упоминаю об этом потому, что уже во время самой болезни находили на меня минуты жизненного опомения, сердце и пульс переставали биться...

Н. В. Гоголь. (Завещание)

I

Вы живого несли по стране!
Гоголь был в летаргическом сне.
Гоголь думал в гробу на спине:

Разве я некрофил? Это вы!
Любят похороны витии,
поминают, когда мертвы,
забывая, пока живые.

Вы вокруг меня встали в кольцо,
наблюдая, с какой кручиной
погружается нос мой в лицо,
точно лезвие в нож перочинный.

II

«Поднимите мне веки, соотечественники мои,
в летаргическом веке
пробудитесь от галиматьи.
Поднимите мне веки!
Разбуди меня, люд молодой,
мои книги читавший под партой,
потрудитесь понять, что со мной.
Нет, отходят попарно!

Грешный дух бронирован в плоть,
безучастную, как каменья.
Помоги мне подняться, Господь,
чтоб упасть пред тобой на колени».

THE INTERMENT OF NIKOLAI VASILICH GOGOL

I direct that my body not be buried until such time as it shows signs
of decomposition. I mention this because during my illness there
have already been moments of deathly numbness when my heart
and pulse stopped beating.

N. V. Gogol, *Last Will and Testament*

I

You carried him alive through the country,
Gogol in a deep sleep.
Gogol lay in his coffin thinking:

"I'm not necrophiliac; you are.
Russia loves funerals. Forgetting the living,
it prays for you
when you're dead.

"You've gathered in a circle
around me. With such agony
my nose like the blade of a penknife
sinks deeply into my face.

II

"Raise my eyelids, my compatriots,
in our lethargic age
wake up from gibberish.
Raise my eyelids!
Young people who read my books
under your school desks, wake me up.
Try to understand what I'm about.
No, they are going away, two by two!
My sinful spirit is clad in flesh,
indifferent as stone.
Help me arise, Lord, so I may
fall on my knees before Thee.

«Из-под фрака украли исподнее.
Дует в щель. Но в нее не просунуться.
Что там муки Господние
перед тем, как в могиле проснуться!»
Крик подземный глубин не потряс.
Двое выпили на могиле.
Любят похороны, дивясь,
детвора и чиновничий класс,
как вы любите слушать рассказ,
как Гоголя хоронили.

Вскройте гроб и застыньте в снегу.
Гоголь, скорчась, лежит на боку.
Вросший ноготь подкладку прорвал сапогу.

"They've stolen my linen from under my frock coat.
There's a draft through a crack. But there's no way to get through it.
Even Christ suffered less
before waking up in the grave!"
The subterranean cry did not shake the depths.
Two men had a drink on the grave.
We enjoy funerals just as
you enjoy hearing how Gogol was buried.

Unseal his coffin freezing in the snow.
Gogol, writhing, lies on his side.
His twisted toenail has torn the lining in his boot.

translated by Vera Dunham and H. W. Tjalsma

АВТОМАТ

Москвою кто-то бродит,
накрутит номер мой.
Послушает и бросит —
отбой…

Чего вам? Рифм кило?
Автографа в альбом?
Алло!..
Отбой…

Кого-то повело
в естественный отбор!
Алло!..
Отбой…

А может, ангел в кабеле,
пришедший за душой?
Мы некоммуникабельны.
Отбой…

А может, это совесть,
потерянная мной?
И позабыла голос?
Отбой…

Стоишь в метро конечной
с открытой головой,
и в диске, как в колечке,
замерзнул пальчик твой.

А за окошком мелочью
стучит толпа отчаянная,
как очередь в примерочную
колечек обручальных.

Ты дунешь в трубку дальнюю,
и мой воротничок
от твоего дыхания
забьется как флажок…

•

PHONE BOOTH

Someone is loose in Moscow who won't stop
Ringing my phone.
Whoever-it-is listens, then hangs up.
Dial tone.

What do you want? A bushel of rhymes or so?
An autograph? A bone?
Hello?
Dial tone.

Someone's lucky number, for all I know,
Is the same, worse luck, as my own.
Hello!
Dial tone.

Or perhaps it's an angel calling collect
To invite me to God's throne.
Damn, I've been disconnected.
Dial tone.

Or is it my old conscience, my power of choice
To which I've grown
A stranger, and which no longer knows my voice?
Dial tone.

Are you standing there in some subway station, stiff
And hatless in the cold,
With your finger stuck in the dial as if
In a ring of gold?

And is there, outside the booth, a desperate throng
Tapping its coins on the glass, chafing its hands,
Like a line of people who have been waiting long
To be measured for wedding bands?

I hear you breathe and blow into some remote
Mouthpiece, and as you exhale
The lapels of my coat
Flutter like pennants in a gale.

•

Порвалась связь планеты.
Аукать устаю.
Вопросы без ответов.
Ответы в пустоту.

Свело. Свело. Свело.
С тобой. С тобой. С тобой.
Алло. Алло. Алло.
Отбой. Отбой. Отбой.

The planet's communications are broken.
I'm tired of saying *hello*.
My questions might as well be unspoken.
Into the void my answers go.

Thrown together, together
With you, with you unknown.
Hello. Hello. Hello there.
Dial tone. Dial tone. Dial tone.

translated by Richard Wilbur

СТРЕЛА В СТЕНЕ

Тамбовский волк тебе товарищ
и друг,
когда ты со стены срываешь
подаренный пенджабский лук!

Как в ГУМе отмеряют ситец,
с плеча откинется рука,
стрела задышит, не насытясь,
как продолжение соска.

С какою женственностью лютой
в стене засажена стрела —
в чужие стены и уюты.
Как в этом женщина была!

Стрела — в стене каркасной стройки,
во всем, что в силе и в цене.
Вы думали — век электроники?
Стрела в стене!

Горите, судьбы и державы!
Стрела в стене.
Тебе от слез не удержаться
наедине, наедине,

над украшательскими нишами,
как шах семье,
ультимативно нищая
стрела в стене!

Шахуй, оторва белокурая!
И я скажу:
«У, олимпийка!» И подумаю:
«Как сжались ямочки в тазу».

«Агрессорка, — добавлю, — скифка...»
Ты скажешь: «Фиг-то»...
•

AN ARROW IN THE WALL

You'd look right with a wolf from Tambov
For sidekick and friend,
As you tear my Punjabi bow
Down from the wall, and bend it.

Your hand pulls back from the shoulder
As if measuring cloth by the yard;
The arrow pants, and is eager,
Like a nipple extended and hard.

And now, with what feminine fury,
Into the wall it goes —
All the walls of the snug and secure.
There's a woman in that, God knows!

In towers of skeletal steel, — an arrow!
In pomposities one and all.
Who says it's the electronic era?
There's an arrow in the wall!

Burn, privilege and power!
There's an arrow in the wall.
Soon, in a drained and lonely hour,
Your tears will fall.

But dark now, doubly dark,
Over rich embrasures which crawl
With elaborate moldings, your stark
Arrow is in the wall!

All right, you cheeky blonde,
Checkmate me, and I'll say
"Oh, you Olympian!," thinking fondly
Of how your belly dimples play.

"You Scythian," I shall add, "you shrew..."
And you'll say, "To hell with you...."
●

Отдай, тетивка сыромятная,
наитишайшую из стрел
так тихо и невероятно,
как тайный ангел отлетел.

На людях мы едва знакомы,
но это тянется года.
И под моим высотным домом
проходит темная вода.

Глубинная струя влеченья.
Печали светлая струя.
Высокая стена прощенья.
И боли четкая стрела.

Release, O rawhide bowstring,
The stillest arrow, a dart
So incredibly hushed, one might suppose
An angel was departing.

In public, we're barely friends,
But for years it's been going on:
Beneath my high-rise window
Dark waters run.

A deep stream of love.
A bright rapids of sorrow.
A high wall of forgiveness.
And pain's clean, piercing arrow.

translated by Richard Wilbur

СТАРАЯ ПЕСНЯ

Г. Джагарову

«По деревне янычары детей
отбирают...»
Болгарская народная песня

Пой, Георгий, прошлое болит.
На иконах — конская моча.
В янычары отняли мальца.
Он вернется — родину спалит.

Мы с тобой, Георгий, держим стол.
А в глазах — столетия горят.
Братия насилуют сестер.
И никто не знает, кто чей брат.

И никто не знает, кто чей сын,
материнский вырезав живот.
Под какой из вражеских личин
раненая родина зовет?

Если ты, положим, янычар,
не свои ль сжигаешь алтари,
где чужие — можешь различать,
но не понимаешь, где свои.

Безобразя рощи и ручьи,
человеком сделавши на миг,
кто меня, Георгий, отлучил
от древесных родичей моих?

Вырванные груди волоча,
остолбеневая от любви,
мама, отшатнись от палача.

Мама! У него глаза — твои.

OLD SONG

to G. Dzhagarov

*The janissaries carry off our children from village
after village.*

Bulgarian folk song

The past hurts, George, but sing and be merry,
with horses' urine our icons burn.
Each stolen baby becomes a janissary
who will scourge his homeland on his return.

You and I, George, let us drink together,
in our eyes the wild fires of centuries glow.
Each sister is raped by her own brother,
and nobody knows whose brother is who.

With the mother's uterus cut out,
whose son is whose no need to ask.
Our wounded motherland cries out
beneath God knows what enemy mask.

Let us say that we are Turkish soldiers;
aren't we burning our own altars then?
We can understand who our enemies are,
but fail to recognize our own men.

Now ruining forest, field, and stream,
who cut me off, George, tell me please,
the moment I became a human being
from my oldest ancestors, the trees?

Your slashed breast dragging the earth, Mother,
transfixed with love more than surprise,
reel back now from your murderer, Mother!

Mother, look—he has your eyes!

translated by William Jay Smith and Vera Dunham

СМЕРТЬ ШУКШИНА

Хоронила Москва Шукшина,
хоронила художника, то есть
хоронила страна мужика
и активную совесть.

Он лежал под цветами на треть,
недоступный отныне.
Он свою удивленную смерть
предсказал всенародно в картине.

В каждом городе он лежал
на отвесных российских простынках.
Называлось не кинозал —
просто каждый пришел и простился.

Он сегодняшним дням — как двойник.
Когда зябко курил он чинарик,
так же зябла, подняв воротник,
вся страна в поездах и на нарах.

Он хозяйственно понимал
край как дом — где березы и хвойники.
Занавесить бы черным Байкал
словно зеркало в доме покойника.

ON THE DEATH OF SHUKSHIN

Moscow was burying Shukshin,
burying an artist;
the nation was burying a man,
burying its conscience.

Inaccessible henceforth,
he lay with flowers half covering him,
having publicly foretold his death
by acting it out in a popular film.

Vertically on the screen as on a sheet
he lay in every city: people came by
in what were no longer theaters
simply to stop and say good-bye.

He was a double for his time:
When he shivered, puffing on a cigarette butt,
in trains and on wooden bunks the country
turned up its collar, and shivered with him.

He was master of the house
in a country of fir trees and birches.
Let Lake Baikal be covered with black
as a mirror is draped in mourning.

translated by William Jay Smith and Vera Dunham

ИРОНИЧЕСКАЯ ЭЛЕГИЯ, РОДИВШАЯСЯ В ВЕСЬМА СКОРБНЫЕ МИНУТЫ, КОГДА НЕ ПИШЕТСЯ

Я — в кризисе. Душа нема.
«Ни дня без строчки», — друг мой точит.
А у меня —
ни дней, ни строчек.

Поля мои лежат в глуши.
Погашены мои заводы.
И безработица души
зияет страшною зевотой.

И мой критический истец
в статье напишет, что, окрысясь,
в безкризиснейшей из систем
один переживаю кризис.

Мой друг, мой северный,
                     мой неподкупный друг,
хорош костюм, да не по росту,
внутри все ясно и вокруг —
но не поется.

Я деградирую в любви.
Дружу с оторвою трактирною.
Не деградируете вы —
я деградирую.

Был крепок стих, как рафинад.
Свистал хоккейным бомбардиром.
Я разучился рифмовать.
Не получается.

Чужая птица издали
простонет перелетным горем.
Умеют хором журавли.
Но лебедь не умеет хором.

•

AN IRONICAL ELEGY BORN IN THOSE MOST DISTRESSING MOMENTS WHEN ONE CANNOT WRITE

I'm in a crisis. My spirit is mute.
"A line a day," my friend insists.
But I have neither
Days nor lines.

My fields lie fallow;
My factories are dark.
My soul, unemployed,
Gapes, yawning wide.

My critic, my accuser,
Will say with a snarl
That in this most immune-to-crisis system
I alone experience a crisis.

My incorruptible fellow countryman,
The suit is perfect, but it doesn't fit.
Everything's clear inside and out—
But poetry doesn't come...

I go to pieces in love,
Take to squiring a cheap whore.
You don't go to pieces—
I go.

My verse was solid—like crystal;
A hockey puck, it zinged to its goal.
But I can't rhyme anymore;
I've lost the knack.

A migratory bird
Will mourn in flight.
Cranes sing in unison;
A swan will not.
•

О чем, мой серый, на ветру
ты плачешь белому Владимиру?
Я этих нот не подберу.
Я деградирую.

Семь поэтических томов
в стране выходит ежесуточно.
А я друзей и городов
бегу, как бешеная сука,

в похолодавшие леса
и онемевшие рассветы,
где деградирует весна
на тайном переломе к лету...

Но верю я, моя родня —
две тысячи семьсот семнадцать
поэтов нашей федерации —
стихи напишут за меня.

Они не знают деградации.

Gray bird, what do you lament
in the wind before white Vladimir?
I cannot catch those notes;
I go to pieces.

Seven books of poetry
Are published daily;
But I flee friends and towns,
A mad dog,

Into forests gone to frost,
Into dawns turned numb,
Where spring goes to pieces,
Breaking secretly into summer.

And yet I trust my colleagues—
The twenty-five hundred and fifteen
Poets of our federation;
They will write poems even if I can't;

They never go to pieces.

translated by William Jay Smith and
Nicholas Fersen

МОРОЗНЫЙ ИППОДРОМ

В. Аксенову

Табуном рванулись трибуны к стартам.
В центре — лошади,
                          вкопанные в наст.
Ты думаешь,
              мы на них ставим?
Они, кобылы, поставили на нас.

На меня поставила вороная иноходь.
Яблоки по крупу — ё-мое...
Умеет крупно конюшню вынюхать.
Беру все финиши, а выигрыш — ее.

Королю кажется, что он правит.
Людям кажется, что им — они.
Природа и рощи на нас поставили.
А мы — гони!

Колдуют лошади, они шепочут.
К столбу Ханурик примерз цепочкой.
Все-таки 43°...
Птица замерзла в воздухе, как елочная
                                    игрушка.
Мрак, надвигаясь с востока, замерз посредине
                          неба, как шторка
у испорченного фотоаппарата.
А у нас в Переделкине, в Доме творчества,
              были открыты 16 форточек.
Около каждой стоял круглый плотный комок
                    комнатного воздуха.
Он состоял из сонного дыхания, перегара,
                          тяжелых идей.
Некоторые закнопливают фортки марлей,
чтобы идеи не вылетали из комнат,
как мухи.
У тех воздух свисал тугой и плотный,
              как творог в тряпочке...

•

WINTER AT THE TRACK

to Vasili Aksyonov

The stands go stampeding to the starting post
Down to where the horses paw the ground.
And, Vasya, you think we're betting on them?
They're betting on us — it's the other way round.

That black mare has put all her money on me —
Just look at her dappled rump;
A hot tip tells her whom to pick;
And I always win, but the take is hers.

So the rulers think it is they who rule,
While the people think they rule the rulers.
The woods and the hills have gambled on us;
So what can we do but race like hell?

The horses whisper, chafing at the bit.
Barfly pisses on the post, linked to it
By a frozen yellow chain:
                              it is forty below.
A Christmas tree ornament, a bird freezes up there.
Night, moving in from the east, is caught congealed midair,
The shutter of a broken camera.
But at Peredelkino, in the writers' club,
Sixteen windows are open a crack.
In front of each hangs a chunk of frozen air —
Congealed hot air.
Some writers cover the windows with gauze
So their portentous ideas won't escape like flies.
And the air balloons, sagging, thick and slimy,
As with curds in a cloth.

•

127

Взирают лошади в городах:
как рощи в яблоках о четырех стволах...
Свистят Ханурику.

                    Но кто свистит?
Свисток считает, что он свистит.
Сержант считает, что он свистит.
Закон считает, что он свистит.

Планета кружится в свистке горошиной,
но в чьей свистульке? Кто свищет? Глядь —
упал Ханурик. Хохочут лошади —
кобыла Дунька, Судьба, конь Блед.

Хохочут лошади.
Их стоны жутки:
«Давай, очкарик! Нажми! Андрей!»
Их головы покачиваются,

                        как на парашютиках,
на паре, выброшенном из ноздрей.

Понятно, мгновенно замерзшем.
Все-таки 45°...
У ворот ипподрома лежал Ханурик.
Он лежал навзничь. Слева — еще пять.
Над его круглым ртом,
короткая, как вертикальный штопор,
открытый из перочинного ножа, стояла
замерзшая Душа.
Она была похожа на поставленную торчком
винтообразную сосульку.
Видно, испарялась по спирали,
да так и замерзла.
И как, бывает, в сосульку вмерзает листик или веточка,
внутри ее вмерзло доказательство добрых

                                        дел,
взятое с собой. Это был обрывок заявления
на соседа за невыключенный радиоприемник.
Над соседними тоже стояли Души, как пустые

                                        бутылки.
Между тел бродил Ангел.

Horses gaze about them, penned up in cities
Like groves of dappled four-trunked trees.
Now they're whistling at Barfly,
But who is whistling?
The whistle thinks the whistle's whistling.
The policeman thinks that he is whistling.
The law thinks that it is whistling.

The planet twirls, a pea in a whistle,
But in whose whistle? Who's whistling — wait!
Look, Barfly's down. And the others laugh —
Russian Filly, Pale Horse, Fate.

The horses laugh,
Making terrible sounds:
"Come on, Egghead, let's go! Get a move on!"
While their heads sway on tiny parachutes
Of steam exhaled from their nostrils
And frozen at once.

It is forty-five below:
Barfly lies at the starting post —
On his back: to the left, five others.
Above his open mouth, blunt as a corkscrew
Sticking up from a penknife, his frozen soul,
A screw-shaped icicle protruding into the air;
It has spiraled and condensed.
And as a leaf or twig freezes in an icicle,
Frozen within is its final Certificate of Good Deeds;
(In reality, the denunciation of a neighbor for not turning off
   his radio).

Souls like empty bottles are poised above the other horses,
While among their bodies wanders an angel.

Он был одет в сатиновый халат
                              подметальщика.
Он собирал Души, как порожние бутылки.
                              Внимательно
проводил пальцем — нет ли зазубрин.
Бракованные скорбно откидывал через плечо.
Когда он отходил, на снегу оставались
                    отпечатки следов с подковками...

...А лошадь Ангел — в дыму морозном
ноги растворились,
                    как в азотной кислоте,
шейку шаловливо отогнула, как полозья,
сама, как саночки, скользит на животе!..

In a street cleaner's smock, it strolls along,
Collecting the souls, the empty bottles,
Drawing its finger carefully over each to see if it is broken,
Sadly tossing the rejects over its shoulder,
Leaving behind the print of horseshoes in the snow...

And the Angel Horse, in the frozen haze,
Legs dissolving as in nitric acid,
Playfully arches its neck like the curved runner of a sleigh,
And then, on its belly, slides away.

translated by William Jay Smith and Max Hayward

НЕ ЗАБУДЬ

Человек надел трусы,
майку синей полосы,
джинсы белые, как снег,
надевает человек.
Человек надел пиджак,
на пиджак нагрудный знак
под названьем «ГТО».
Сверху он надел пальто.
На него, стряхнувши пыль,
он надел автомобиль.
Сверху он надел гараж
(тесноватый — но как раз!),
сверху он надел наш двор,
как ремень надел забор,
сверху он надел жену,
и вдобавок — не одну,
сверху наш микрорайон,
область надевает он.
Опоясался как рыцарь
государственной границей.
И, качая головой,
надевает шар земной.
Черный космос натянул,
крепко звезды застегнул,
Млечный Путь — через плечо,
сверху — кое-что еще...

Человек глядит вокруг.
Вдруг —
у созвездия Весы
вспомнил, что забыл часы.
(Где-то тикают они
позабытые, одни?..)

Человек снимает страны,
и моря, и океаны,

DO NOT FORGET

Somewhere a man puts on his shorts,
his blue-striped T-shirt,
his blue jeans;
a man puts on
his jacket on which there is a button
reading COUNTRY FIRST,
and over the jacket, his topcoat.

Over the topcoat,
after dusting it off, he puts on his automobile,
and over that he puts on his garage
(just big enough for his car),
over that his apartment courtyard,
and then he belts himself with the courtyard wall.
Then he puts on his wife
and after her the next one
and then the next one;
and over that he puts on his subdivision
and over that his county
and like a knight he then buckles on
the borders of his country;
and with his head swaying,
puts on the whole globe.

Then he dons the black cosmos
and buttons himself up with the stars.
He slings the Milky Way over one shoulder,
and after that some secret beyond.

He looks around:
Suddenly
in the vicinity of the constellation Libra
he recalls that he has forgotten his watch.
Somewhere it must be ticking
(all by itself).
The man takes off the countries,
the sea,
the oceans,

и машину, и пальто.
Он без Времени — ничто.

Он стоит в одних трусах,
держит часики в руках.
На балконе он стоит
и прохожим говорит:
«По утрам, надев трусы,
НЕ ЗАБУДЬТЕ ПРО ЧАСЫ!»

the automobile, and the topcoat.
He is nothing without Time.

Naked he stands on his balcony
and shouts to the passersby:
"For God's sake, do not forget your watch!"

translated by William Jay Smith and Vera Dunham

ХОР НИМФ

Я 41-я на Плисецкую,
26-я на пледы чешские,
30-я на Таганку,
35-я на Ваганьково,
кто на Мадонну — запись на Морвокзале,
а Вы с ребенком, тут не стояли!
Кто был девятая. станет десятой,
Борисова станет Мусатовой,
я 16-я к глазному,
75-я на Глазунова,
110-я на аборты
(придет очередь — подработаю),
26-я на фестивали,
а Вы с ребенком, тут не стояли!
47-я на автодетали
(меня родили — и записали),
я уже 1000-я на автомобили
(меня записали — потом родили),
что дают? кому давать?
а еще мать!
Я 45-я за «35-ми»,
а Вы с ребенком, чего тут пялитесь?
Кто на Мадонну — отметка в 10-ть.
А Вы с ребенком — и не надейтесь!
Не вы, а я — 1-я на среду,
а Вы — первая куда следует...

A CHORUS OF NYMPHS

I'm 41st in line for Plisetskaya,
26th for plaid blankets from Czechoslovakia,
30th for a ticket to the Taganka,
35th for a place in Vagankovo Cemetery,
whoever wants to see the Madonna — sign up
at Seaport Hall — hey, you with the kid,
you weren't in line before!
Whoever was ninth goes back to tenth,
Rimskaya becomes Korsakova,
I'm 16th at the optician's,
and 75th for Glazunov,
110th for an abortion
(not pregnant now, but ready when my turn comes).
You with the kid, you weren't here before,
47th for spare car parts
(they signed me up at birth).
No. 1000 for a new car
(signed up before birth).
What are they giving out? Who should be bribed?
And you're a mother besides!
I'm 45th behind everybody with a 35,
and, you with the kid, what are you staring at?
Those who want to see the Madonna, check in at ten o'clock.
But, you with the kid, you won't make it.
Because I'm first for Wednesday,
and you're first to go to hell.

translated by Vera Dunham and H. W. Tjalsma

НТР

Моя бабушка — староверка,
но она —
научно-техническая революционерка.
Кормит гормонами кабана.

Научно-технические коровы
следят за Харламовым и Петровым,
и, прикрываясь ночным покровом,
сексуал-революционерка Сударкина,
в сердце,
            как в трусики-безразмерки,
умещающая пол-Краснодара,
подрывает основы
семьи,
            частной собственности

                        и государства.

Научно-технические обмены
отменны.
Посылаем Терпсихору —
получаем «Пепси-колу».

И все-таки это есть Революция —
в умах, в быту и в народах целых.
К двенадцати стрелки часов крадутся —
но мы носим лазерные, без стрелок!

Я — попутчик
            научно-технической революции.
При всем уважении к коромыслам
хочу, чтобы в самой дыре завалющей
был водопровод
            и движенье мысли.

•

TECHNOLOGY

My grandmother is an Old Believer,
a technological revolutionary;
she fattens her pig on hormones.

Her technological cows
watch a hockey game on TV.
And under cover of night,
taking half her provincial city
to heart,
      into her elastic panties,
there is a sexual revolutionary
who undermines the basis
of the family,
      private property,
         and the state.

Official technological exchanges
are a good idea:
We send them our best ballerinas
and get Pepsi-Cola in return.

And yet this is a Revolution—
in the minds and lives of peoples.
Toward midnight the hands of clocks get stolen,
but we wear digital watches
      that have no hands.

I'm a fellow traveler
      of this technological revolution.
With all due respect to samovars,
in the very middle of this provincial hole,
I long for plumbing and freedom
      of thought.

•

Революция в опасности!
                    Нужны меры.
Она саботажникам не по нутру.
Научно-технические контрреволюционеры
не едят синтетическую икру.

But this Revolution is in danger!
S.O.S.
Technological counterrevolutionaries,
refuse to eat synthetic caviar!

*translated by William Jay Smith and
Vera Dunham*

ИСПОВЕДЬ

Ну что тебе надо еще от меня?
Чугунна ограда. Улыбка темна.
Я музыка горя, ты музыка лада,
ты яблоко ада, да не про меня!

На всех континентах твои имена
прославил. Такие отгрохал лампады!
Ты музыка счастья, я нота разлада.
Ну что тебе надо еще от меня?

Смеялась: «Ты ангел?» — я лгал, как змея.
Сказала: «Будь смел» — не вылазил из спален.
Сказала: «Будь первым» — я стал гениален,
ну что тебе надо еще от меня?

Исчерпана плата до смертного дня.
Последний горит под твоим снегопадом.
Был музыкой чуда, стал музыкой яда,
ну что тебе надо еще от меня?

Но и под лопатой спою, не виня:
«Пусть я удобренье для Божьего сада,
ты — музыка чуда, но больше не надо!
Ты случай досады. Играй без меня».

И вздрогнули складни, как створки окна.
И вышла усталая и без наряда.
Сказала: «Люблю тебя. Больше нет сладу.
Ну что тебе надо еще от меня?»

THE ETERNAL QUESTION

What more on this earth do you want from me?
Iron is the railing protecting your smile.
I am all discord, you are all harmony,
But the apple you offer's not from heaven but hell.

I have carried your name far across the sea,
And the purest of candles have lighted for you.
Your music brings joy, while mine brings decay:
What more on this earth do you want from me?

"You're pure?" you said, and, a serpent, I lied.
"Be brave, be a man!" So I slept with each whore.
"Be first!" you cried, and a genius I was:
What more on this earth do you want? What more?

I paid with my life till I couldn't pay more,
I died, and lay burning beneath your snowfall;
My words were of wonder, and you poisoned them all:
What more on this earth do you want? What more?

When they shoveled the last of the earth on my grave,
I still spoke no ill, and had only one claim:
That to freshen God's garden my bones might serve,
And if Error you are, then play your own game.

The mirrors behind you opened into a door,
And glittering, naked you stood before me.
"I love you," you said. "What more then of me—
What more on this earth do you want? What more?"

translated by William Jay Smith

ИЮНЬ-68

Лебеди, лебеди, лебеди...
К северу. К северу. К северу!..
Кеннеди... Кеннеди... Кеннеди...
Срезали...

Может, в чужой политике
не понимаю что-то?
Но понимаю залитые
кровью беспомощной щеки!

Баловень телепублики
в траурных лимузинах...
Пулями, пулями, пулями
бешеные полемизируют!..

Помню, качал рассеянно
целой еще головою,
смахивал на Есенина
падающей копною.

Как у того, играла,
льнула луна на брови...
Думали — для рекламы,
а обернулась — кровью.

Незащищенность вызова
лидеров и артистов,
прямо из телевизоров
падающих на выстрел!

Ах, как тоскуют корни,
отнятые от сада,
яблоней на балконе
на этаже тридцатом!..

•

JUNE '68

Wild swans, wild swans, wild swans,
Northward, northward bound
Kennedy... Kennedy... the heart
Breaks at the sound.

Of foreign politics
Not much may be understood;
But I do understand
A white cheek bathed with blood.

The idol of TV screens
In his funereal auto rides...
With bullets, bullets, bullets
Madmen proselytize.

When absently he shook
That head while yet intact
I thought of Yesenin
With his tumbling forelock:

As on that poet's brow
A sickle moon would brood—
For public effect, they thought,
But it proved to be for blood.

How defenseless the challenger,
Politician or poet,
When he topples to gunshot
Right through the TV set!

Oh, the roots of apple trees
Torn from orchard soil
Mourn high on her balcony
There on the thirtieth floor!
•

Яблони, яблони, яблони —
к дьяволу!..

Яблони небоскребов —
разве что для надгробьев.

Apple trees, apple trees...
Curse those bloody trees!

Let skyscraper-apples grieve,
Good but to guard a grave.

translated by William Jay Smith
and Nicholas Fersen

ЗАБАСТОВКА СТРИПТИЗА

Стриптиз бастует! Стриптиз бастует!
Над мостовыми канкан лютует.

Грядут бастующие — в тулупах, в джинсах.
«Черта в ступе!
            Не обнажимся!»

Эксплуататоров теснят, отбрехиваясь.
Что там блеснуло?
            Держи штрейкбрехершу!

Под паранджою чинарь запаливают,
а та на рожу чулок напяливает.

Ку-ку, трудящиеся эстрады!
Вот ветеранка в облезлом страусе,
едва за тридцать — в тираж пора:
«Ура, сестрички,
            качнем права!

Соцстрахование, процент с оваций
и пенсий ранних — как в авиации...»

«А производственные простуды?»
Стриптиз бастует.
«А факты творческого зажима?
Не обнажимся!»

Полчеловечества вопит рыдания:
«Не обнажимся.
Мы — солидарные!»

Полы зашивши
(«Не обнажимся!»)
В пальто к супругу
жена ложится.

•

STRIPTEASE ON STRIKE

The strippers are out on strike,
a fierce cancan drums on the sidewalks —
the strikers are marching in fur coats and blue jeans:
"To hell with it!
          We won't strip no more!"

They shove their exploiters, kick and claw them.
"Look at that bright bare ass! —
          Stop the scabbing bitch!"
There's one in a yashmak — sneaking a smoke behind it,
and that one's pulled a stocking over her face.

"Hey there, workers of the stage!
See that old-timer with her mangy ostrich feathers?
Just pushing thirty and it's time to retire,
come on, girls, stick up for your rights:
social security, a commission on encores
and early pensions, like in the air force.

"And what about colds caught in line of duty?"
The strippers are out on strike.
"And they're always trampling
on our sensibilities!
We won't strip no more!"

Half of mankind cries out with them:
"Why should we bare ourselves?
Let's show our solidarity!"

A woman gets in her husband's bed
all sewn up tight in a heavy coat:
"We won't strip no more."
•

Лежит, стервоза,
и издевается:
«Мол, кошки тоже
не раздеваются...»

А оперируемая санитару:
«Сквозь платье режьте — я солидарна!»
«Мы не позируем», —
вопят модели.

«Пойдем позырим,
на Венеру надели
синенький халатик в горошек,
с коротенькими рукавами!..»
Мир юркнул в раковину.
Бабочки, сложив крылышки, бешено
                            заматывались в куколки.
Церковный догматик заклеивал тряпочками
нагие чресла Сикстинской капеллы,
                        штопором он пытался
вытащить пуп из микеланджеловского
Адама.
Первому человеку пуп не положен!

Весна бастует. Бастуют завязи.
Спустился четкий железный
                            занавес.
Бастует там истина.
                    Нагая издавна,
она не издана, а если издана,
то в ста обложках под фразой фиговой —
попробуй выковырь!
•

She just lies there, the bitch,
and pokes fun at the man:
"Cats don't take their coats off either!"

A woman under the knife
says to the surgeon:
"Cut through my dress! Solidarity forever!"

"We're sick of posing,"
the models yell,
"Let's go look at Venus de Milo—
they've got her up
in short-sleeved navy polka dots."

The world's ducking into its shell,
butterflies fold their wings
and struggle back, frantic,
into their cocoons.

A zealot's covering up the
naked loins in the Sistine Chapel,
and, with a corkscrew, he's trying
to take the navel out of Michelangelo's Adam:
the First Man wasn't supposed to have one.
Same mentality as the old biddies of Sarato.

Coverers-up of the world unite!
Spring is on strike, so are the buds—
There is the Iron Curtain.

Truth is on strike. Always naked,
it can't be printed, and if it is,
there's a fig leaf on it.
How to get at it?

•

Земля покрыта асфальтом города.
Мир хочет голого,
                   голого,
                           голого.
У мира дьявольский аппетит.
Стриптиз бастует. Он победит!

The earth's under asphalt,
it longs to be naked.
The world has a hell of an appetite.
The world will win.
The stripteasers will win!

translated by Max Hayward

НЬЮ-ЙОРКСКИЕ ЗНАЧКИ

Блещут бляхи, бляхи, бляхи,
возглашая матом благим:
«Люди — предки обезьян»,
«Губернатор — лесбиян»,
«Непечатное — в печать!»,
«Запретите запрещать!»

«Бог живет на улице Пастера, 18. Вход со двора».

Обожаю Гринич Вилидж
в саркастических значках.
Это кто мохнатый вылез,
как мошна в ночных очках?

Это Ален, Ален, Ален!
Над смертельным карнавалом,
Ален, выскочи в исподнем!
Бог — ирония сегодня.
Как библейский афоризм
гениальное «Вались!»

Хулиганы? Хулиганы.
Лучше сунуть пальцы в рот,
чем закиснуть куликами
буржуазовых болот!

Бляхи по местам филейным,
коллективным Вифлеемом
в мыле давят трепака —
«мини» около пупка.

Это Селма, Селма, Селма
агитирующей шельмой
подмигнула и — во двор:
«Мэйк лав, нот уор!»*
•

* «Твори любовь, а не войну!» (англ.)

154

AMERICAN BUTTONS

Buttons flash, buttons, buttons, buttons
shouting at the tops of their lungs
"Men are the ancestors of apes"
"Ronald Reagan is a lesbian"
"Fuck censorship"
"If it moves, fondle it"

GOD LIVES AT 18 PASTEUR ST.
REAR ENTRANCE PLEASE

I love Greenwich Village
with its sarcastic buttons.
Who's the shaggy one who showed up
cock & balls in dark glasses?
It's Allen, Allen, Allen!
Leap over Death's carnival,
Allen, in your underwear!
Irony is God today.
"Power to the People" is a holy slogan.

Better to stick your fingers in your mouth and whistle
than to be silent *booboisie*.

Button-stars of Bethlehem
on everybody's bottom,
miniskirts on bellybuttons.

A wild girl agitator
winks from a dark corner
"Make love not war!"
•

Бог и ирония сегодня.
Блещут бляхи над зевотой.
Тем страшнее, чем смешней,
и для пули — как мишень!

«Бог переехал на проспект Мира, 43. 2 звонка».

И над хиппи, над потопом
ироническим циклопом
блещет Время, как значком,
округлившимся зрачком!

Ах, Время,
сумею ли я прочитать, что написано
                          в твоих очах,
мчащихся на меня,
                    увеличиваясь, как фары?
Успею ли оценить твою хохму?..
Ах, осень в осиновых кружочках...
Ах, восемь
подброшенных тарелочек жонглера,
            мгновенно замерших в воздухе,
будто жирафа убежала,
                    а пятна от нее
                                остались...

Удаляется жирафа
в бляхах, будто мухомор,
на спине у ней шарахнуто:
«Мэйк лав, нот уор!»

Irony is God today.
Buttons flash over yawns.
The funnier they are, the more terrifying
And like bull's-eyes for bullets.

GOD HAS MOVED TO 43 AVENUE OF PEACE.
RING TWICE.

And above the Hippies, — above the Flood
like an ironic Cyclops
Time flashes its button eye!

TIME,
Can I read what's written in your eyes,
rushing at me —
          growing bigger and bigger, like headlights?
Can I see through your antics?

O autumn with round leaves
O eight plates
tossed up by a juggler
                    frozen for an instant in air,
as if a giraffe had run away,
                          and left its spots
                                          behind!

The giraffe retreats
with a sacred mushroom-button on its bottom:
"Make Love Not War"

translated by Lawrence Ferlinghetti

МОЛЧАЛЬНЫЙ ЗВОН

Их, наверно, тыщи — хрустящих лакомок!
Клесты лущат семечки в хрусте крон.
Надо всей Америкой
                             хрустальный благовест.
Так необычаен молчальный звон.

Он не ради славы, молчальный благовест,
просто лущат пищу — отсюда он.
Никакого чуда, а душа расплакалась —
молчальный звон!..

Этот звон молчальный таков по слуху,
будто сто отшельничающих клестов
ворошат волшебные погремухи
или затевают сорок сороков.

Птичьи коммуны, не бойтесь швабры!
Групповых ансамблей широк почин.
Надо всей Америкой — групповые свадьбы.
Есть и не поклонники групповщин.

Групповые драки, групповые койки.
Тих единоличник во фраке гробовом.
У его супруги на всех пальцах —
                                кольца,
видно, пребывает
                       в браке групповом...

А по-над дорогой хруст серебра.
Здесь сама работа звенит за себя.
Кормят, молодчаги, детей и жен,
ну а получается
                 молчальный звон!

В этом клестианстве — антипод свинарни.
Чистят короедов — молчком, молчком!

SILENT TINGLING

Must be thousands of sweet gourmets rustling through
leaf crowded branches, thrushes cracking seedling shells
all over America like crystalline carillon bells,
a really strange silent tingling.

Silent carillons, not to celebrate Main Street
but rustling up some food their only scene—
No miracle but millions of hungry souls
silently tingling.

This tingling silence heralds
an orgy of hermit thrushes eating,
like thousands of song-men's clapsticks clacking
or faraway Moscow's million bells
—some dream collective—generational vogue.

Thrush communes don't be afraid of the big Broom,
your flock continues an ancient tradition,
now all over America—collective marriage;
though some detractors put down your in-group, not big enough!

A silent Individualist in top hat & tails drest
coffinlike denounces your collective struggles in bed—
but his own wife wears rings on every finger,
as if she wound up in a group marriage.

This gentle gang's only enemy's insects,
cleaning up bark parasites—silently, silently—
Anybody can crush bones and oink louder
but can't beat this silent tingling.

Fast New York Sydney chicks—
thanks Brisbane birds & Chicago thrushes

Пусть вас даже кто-то
                              превосходит в звонарности,
но он не умеет
                      молчальный звон!

Юркие ньюйоркочки и чикагочки,
за ваш звон молчальный спасибо,
                                                клесты.
Звенят листы дубовые,
                              будто чеканятся
византийски вырезанные кресты.

В этот звон волшебный уйду от ужаса,
посреди беседы замру, смущен.
Будто на Владимирщине —
                                прислушайся! —
молчальный звон...

for your own silent tingling—your cities' trees'
leaves tremble like golden curlicues on Byzantine crosses.

Maybe someday our descendants
'll ask about this poet—What'd he sing about?
I didn't ring Halleluiah bells, I didn't clang leg-irons,
I was silently tingling.

translated by Allen Ginsberg

ПОРНОГРАФИЯ ДУХА

Отплясывает при народе
с поклонником голым подруга.
Ликуй, порнография плоти!
Но есть порнография духа.

Докладчик порой на лектории,
в искусстве силен как стряпуха,
раскроет на аудитории
свою порнографию духа.

В Пикассо ему все не ясно,
Стравинский — безнравственность слуха.
Такого бы постеснялась
любая парижская шлюха.

Подпольные миллионеры,
когда твоей родине худо,
являют в брильянтах и нерпах
свою порнографию духа.

Конечно, спать вместе не стоило б...
Но в скважине голый глаз
значительно непристойнее
того, что он видит у вас...

Клеймите стриптизы экранные,
венерам закутайте брюхо.
Но все-таки дух — это главное.
Долой порнографию духа!

PORNOGRAPHY OF THE MIND

Naked the woman dances in public
with her naked partner.
Hail to pornography of the flesh,
but beware pornography of the mind.

The lecturing official knows as much
about art as a short-order cook;
he reveals to his audience
the pornography of the mind.

To him Picasso makes no sense,
Stravinsky offends his ear;
any whore off the street
knows better.

When things go badly for the people,
you secret millionaires
parade in your sables and diamonds,
pornographers of the mind.

Naked lovemaking may be shameful indeed,
but more shameful
the naked eye
at the crack in the wall.

Denounce striptease on the screen,
Wrap up the bellies of Venuses;
But what matters is the mind—
Down with pornography of the mind.

translated by William Jay Smith and Vera Dunham

СКРЫМТЫМНЫМ

«Скрымтымным» — это пляшут омичи?
скрип темниц? или крик о помощи?
или у Судьбы есть псевдоним,
темная ухмылочка — скрымтымным?

Скрымтымным — то, что между нами.
То, что было раньше, вскрыв, темним.
«Ты-мы-ыы…» — с закрытыми глазами
в счастье стонет женщина: скрымтымным.

Скрымтымным — языков праматерь.
Глупо верить разуму, глупо спорить с ним.
Планы прогнозируем по сопромату,
но часто не учитываем скрымтымным.

«Как вы поживаете?» — «Скрымтымным…»
«Скрымтымным!» — «Слушаюсь. Выполним».

Скрымтымным — это не силлабика.
Лермонтов поэтому непереводим.
Лучшая Марина зарыта в Елабуге.
Где ее могила? — скрымтымным…

А пока пляшите, пьяны в дым:
«Шагадам, магадам, скрымтымным!»
Но не забывайте — рухнул Рим,
не поняв приветствия: «Скрымтымным».

DARKMOTHERSCREAM

Darkmotherscream is a Siberian dance,
cry from prison or a yell for help,
or, perhaps, God has another word for it—
ominous little grin—darkmotherscream.

Darkmotherscream is the ecstasy of the sexual gut;
We let the past sink into darkmotherscream also.
You, we—oooh with her eyes closed
woman moans in ecstasy—darkmother, darkmotherscream.

Darkmotherscream is the original mother of languages.
It is silly to trust mind, silly to argue against it.
Prognosticating by computers
We leave out darkmotherscream.

"How's it going?" Darkmotherscream.
"Motherscream! Motherscream!"
          "OK, we'll do it, we'll do it."

The teachers can't handle darkmotherscream.
That is why Lermontov is untranslatable.
When the storm sang in Yelabuga,
What did it say to her? Darkmotherscream.

Meanwhile go on dancing, drunker and drunker.
"Shagadam magadam—darkmotherscream."
Don't forget—Rome fell
not having grasped the phrase: darkmotherscream.

translated by Robert Bly

III

*прибавьте тиражи ...
журавлям*

III

"Release the Cranes"

КНИЖНЫЙ БУМ

Попробуйте купить Ахматову.
Вам букинисты объяснят,
что черный том ее агатовый
куда дороже, чем агат.

И многие не потому ли —
как к отпущению грехов —
стоят в почетном карауле
за томиком ее стихов?

«Прибавьте тиражи журналам», —
мы молимся книгобогам,
прибавьте тиражи желаньям
и журавлям!

Все реже в небесах бензинных
услышишь журавлиный зов.
Все монолитней в магазинах
сплошной Массивий Муравлев.

Страна желает первородства.
И, может, в этом добрый знак —
Ахматова не продается,
не продается Пастернак.

BOOK BOOM

Just try to buy Akhmatova—
sold out. The booksellers say
her black, agate-colored tome
is worth more than agate today.

Those who once attacked her—
as if to atone for their curse—
stand, a reverent honor guard,
for a single volume of her verse.

"Print more copies of magazines,"
we beg of the great book gods.
"Give us more copies of our dreams,
release the cranes, vanished birds."

It's rare in our polluted skies
to hear the crane's lonely cries,
while every bookstore's lined with stacks
of monolithic published hacks.

The country demands its birthright,
and maybe that's as well:
Akhmatova will not sell out,
nor Pasternak, although he sell.

translated by William Jay Smith and
Vera Dunham

ПОЧЕМУ ДВА ВЕЛИКИХ ПОЭТА

Почему два великих поэта,
проповедники вечной любви,
не мигают, как два пистолета?
Рифмы дружат, а люди — увы...

Почему два великих народа
холодеют на грани войны,
под непрочным шатром кислорода?
Люди дружат, а страны — увы...

Две страны, две ладони тяжелые,
предназначенные любви,
охватившие в ужасе голову
черт те что натворившей Земли!

THE GREAT CONFRONTATION

Why must two great poet-teachers,
from whom eternal love should flow,
stare unblinking like two pistols?
Rhymes can be friends, but people, no.

Why must two great nations then
freeze on the edge of war also?
Under their fragile oxygen tent
people stay friends, but nations, no.

Two countries like two heavy hands,
guiltily tying nonlove's knot,
grasp in terror now Earth's head,
Earth that has wrought God knows what.

translated by William Jay Smith and
Vera Dunham

АВТОЛИТОГРАФИЯ

На обратной стороне Земли,
как предполагают, в год Змеи,
в частной типографийке в Лонг-Айленде
у хозяйки домика и рифа
я печатал автолитографии
за станком, с семи и до семи.
После нанесенья изошрифта
два немногословные Сизифа —
Вечности джинсовые связисты —
уносили трехпудовый камень.
Амен.

Прилетал я каждую субботу.
В итальянском литографском камне
я врезал шрифтом наоборотным
«Аз» и «Твердь», как принято веками,
верность контролируя в зерцало.
«Тьма-тьма-тьма» — врезал я по овалу,
«тьматьматьма» — пока не проступало:
«мать-мать-мать». Жизнь обретала речь.
После оттиска оригинала
(чтобы уникальность уберечь)
два Сизифа, следуя тарифу,
разбивали литографский камень.
Амен.

Что же отпечаталось в сознанье?
Память пальцев и тоска другая,
будто внял я неба содроганье
или горних ангелов полет,
будто перестал быть чужестранен.
Мне открылось, как страна живет —
мать кормила, руль не выпуская,
тайная Америки святая,
и не всякий песнь ее поймет.
Черные грузили лед и пламень.
У обеих океанских вод
США к утру сушили плавки,

AUTOLITHOGRAPHY

On the reverse side of the earth—
as ordained in the year of the serpent—
at a small private press on Long Island,
in a little domain of the mistress of a reef,
I printed lithographs of my life
on a block from dawn till dusk.
When the print (in reverse) had been cut,
two laconic Sisyphi,
Eternity's signalmen, clad in jeans,
carried off the three-stone stone:
Amen.

I came each Saturday, and on
Italian lithographic stone
I cut in reverse script
"O" and "M", as in ancient times,
holding the letters firmly in the mirror.
"OM—OM—REHT—OM"—I cut along the oval—
"REHT—OM—REHTOM"—until "MOTHER—MOTHER"
at last showed through; and life began to speak.
After the original impression
(so its uniqueness might be retained)
the two Sisyphi, collecting their due,
shattered the lithographic stone:
Amen.

What imprint on the mind remained?
A memory of fingers, and some deeper longing,
as though I had seen heaven shudder
or a flight of angels high above,
as though I had ceased to be an alien
and had found, at the helm, a country's life revealed:
suckling her babe, hand firmly on the wheel,
the secret madonna of America,
whose song not everyone can grasp.
Blacks were loading fire and ice
on the shores of both oceans.
My people hung up my intellectual pelt
to dry, while, toward morning, the U.S.A.

а Иешуа бензозаправки
на дороге разводил руками.

И конкистадор иного свойства,
Петр Великий иль тоскливый Каин,
в километре над Петрозаводском
выбирал столицу или гавань...
Истина прощалась с метафизикой.
Я люблю Америку созданья,
где снимают в Хьюстоне Сизифы
с сердца человеческого камень.
Амен.

Не понять Америку с визитом
праздным рифмоплетам назиданья,
лишь поймет сообщник созиданья,
с кем преломят бутерброд с вязигой
вечности усталые Сизифы,
когда в руки въелся общий камень.
Амен.

Ни одно- и ни многоэтажным
я туристом не был. Я работал.
Боб Раушенберг, отец поп-арта,
на плечах с живой лисой захаживал,
утопая в алом зоопарке.
Я работал. Солнце заходило.
Я мешал оранжевый в белила.
Автолитографии теплели.
Как же совершилось преступленье?
Камень уничтожен, к сожаленью.
Утром, нумеруя отпечаток,
я заметил в нем — как крыл зачаток —
оттиск смеха, профиль мотыльковый,
лоб и нос, похожие на мамин.
Может, воздух так сложился в складки?
Или мысль блуждающая чья-то?

laid out its swimming trunks;
and the Jesus of the filling stations
threw up his arms on the highway;
and a conquistador of another persuasion,
Peter the Great or the melancholy Cain,
chose to place both capital and harbor
miles above Petrozavodsk:
Truth bids farewell to metaphysics.
I love the America of creation,
where, in Houston, Sisyphi remove
from the human heart a stone:
Amen.

Those idle, self-righteous, versifying visitors
cannot understand America;
only that creative partner can
with whom you've shared your bit of gristle.
Weary are the eternal Sisyphi
when their hands are eaten by the common stone:
Amen.

I am neither a one-story nor a many-floored
tourist, but one who worked.
Bob Rauschenberg, the father of pop art,
a live fox on his shoulder, dropped in,
wallowing in a vermilion zoo.
I worked: the sun was setting.
I mixed some orange in with the white;
the autolithographs warmed up.
How, then, was the crime committed?
The stone, alas, has been destroyed.
In the morning, numbering the prints,
I saw wings sprouting from the stone,
the print of a laugh, the flutter of a profile,
a forehead and a nose, resembling Mother's.
Perhaps the air had folded in this way
or was it someone's errant thought?

Или дикий ангел бестолковый
зазевался — и попал под камень?..
Амен.

Что же отпечаталось в хозяйке?
Тень укора, бегство из Испании,
тайная улыбка испытаний,
водяная, как узор Госзнака.
Что же отпечаталось во мне?
Честолюбье стать вторым Гонзаго?
Что же отпечаталось извне?

Что же отпечатается в памяти
матери моей на Юго-Западе?
Что же отпечатает прибой?
Ритм веков и порванный «Плейбой»?
Что заговорит в Раушенберге?
«Вещь для хора и ракушек пенья»?
Что же в океане отпечаталось?
Я не знаю. Это знает атлас.
Что-то сохраняется на дне —
связь времен, первопечать какая-то...
Все, что помню — как вы угадаете, —
только типографийку в Лонг-Айленде,
риф, и исчезающий за ним
ангел повторяет профиль мамин.
И с души отваливает камень.

Аминь.

Or did some playful, mixed-up angel
totter and fall into that stone?
Amen.

And what print was left by the mistress of the house?
A shade of her reproach, her flight from Spain,
the hidden smile of hardship,
invisible as the paper's watermark.
What then was the imprint that I made?
Ambition to become a second Gonzago?
What then was the imprint from without?
And in her quarter of Moscow
what will mark my mother's memory?
What will the breakers then imprint—
the rhythm of ages, a torn *Playboy*?
What will the dove-blue Sisyphi remember
of all this when they come of age?
What will resound in Rauschenberg?
"A Composition for Seashell with Chorus"?
What then was printed on the ocean?
I know not; only the atlas knows.
Whatever is preserved on the sea floor—
the bonds of time, an elemental grief—
all I remember, you may surmise—
is that small press on Long Island,
a reef, behind whose radiance lies
an angel outlining my mother's profile;
and from my soul there falls a stone:
All's done—Amen.

translated by William Jay Smith and Vera Dunham

МАТЬ

Охрани, Провидение, своим махом шагреневым,
                  пощади ее хижину —
мою мать — Вознесенскую Антонину Сергеевну,
                  урожденную Пастушихину.

Воробьишко серебряно пусть в окно постучится:
«Добрый день, Антонина Сергеевна,
                  урожденная Пастушихина!»

Дал отец ей фамилию, чтоб укутать от Времени.
Ее беды помиловали, да не все, к сожалению.

За житейские стыни, две войны и пустые деревни
родила она сына и дочку, Наталью Андреевну.

И, зайдя за калитку, в небесах над речушкою
подарила им нитку — уток нитку жемчужную.

Ее серые взоры, круглый лоб без морщинки,
коммунальные ссоры утишали своей
                  беззащитностью.

Любит Блока и Сирина, режет рюмкой пельмени.
Есть другие россии. Но мне эта милее.

Что наивно просила, насмотревшись по телеку:
«Чтоб тебя не убили, сын, не езди в Америку...»

Назовите по имени веру женскую,
                  независимую пустынницу —
Антонину Сергеевну Вознесенскую,
                  урожденную Пастушихину.

MOTHER

Protect, O Providence, with the broad sweep of your wing,
        in her small dwelling,
my mother—Antonina Sergeevna Voznesenskaya—
        née Pastushikhina.

May a tiny sparrow give a silver knock at her window:
"Good day, Antonina Sergeevna Voznesenskaya, née Pastushikhina."

Her father gave her a name to cushion her against time.
Misfortunes have spared her, but, alas, not every time.

Having endured a harsh life, barren trees, two wars,
she bore a daughter, Natalia Andreevna, and a son.

Pointing to a flight of wild ducks above her river,
she gives her children strings of pearls that last forever.

She loves Blok and Sirin, with a glass cuts dumpling dough.
There may be other Russias; this one's the best I know.

"Don't go to America, son. You won't go, will you?"
she asks, frightened by TV. "Don't go, they'll kill you."

May woman's enduring faith everywhere bear the blessing
of one Antonina Sergeevna Voznesenskaya, née Pastushikhina.

                    translated by William Jay Smith and Vera Dunham

МАТЬ

Я отменил материнские похороны.
Не воскресить тебя в эту эпоху.

Мама, прости эти сборы повторные.
Снегом осело, что было лицом.
Я тебя отнял у крематория
и положу тебя рядом с отцом.

Падают страшные комья весенние
Новодевичьего монастыря.
Спят Вознесенский и Вознесенская —
жизнью пронизанная земля.

То, что к тебе прикасалось, отныне
стало святыней.
В сквере скамейки, Ордынка за ними
стали святыней.
Стал над березой екатерининской
свет материнский.

Что ты прошла на земле, Антонина?
По уши в ландыши влюблена,
интеллигентка в косынке Рабкрина
и ермоловская спина!

В скрежет зубовный индустрий и примусов,
в мире, замешенном на крови,
ты была чистой любовью, без примеси,
лоб-одуванчик, полный любви.

Ты — незамеченная Россия,
ты охраняла очаг и порог,
беды и волосы молодые,
как в кулачок, зажимая в пучок.

Как ты там сможешь, как же ты сможешь
там без родни?
Носик смешливо больше не сморщишь
и никогда не поправишь мне воротник.

.

ELEGY FOR MY MOTHER

I canceled your funeral, Mother;
you can't be resurrected in this day and age.

Mama, forgive these repeated gatherings.
I know your face has long since turned to snow;
I have taken you from the crematorium
and will place you now beside Father.

This spring we let earth fall
into your grave at the Novodevichi Monastery:
Voznesensky and Voznesenskaya rest there now
and the earth is given new life.

Whatever you touched has become holy:
the benches in the square, and Ordynka Street
behind them, are holy;
over Catherine's birch tree
shines your maternal light.

What did earth offer you, Antonina?
Mad for lilies of the valley,
you were an intellectual in a worker's kerchief
with the backbone of a tragedienne.

Industries and furnaces belched forth
their calls for blood throughout the world,
but you were pure, unpolluted love,
a dandelion head, packed with love.

Unsung Russia you were,
guarding hearth and home;
a young wife, you combed out troubles, drew them,
with your hair, back into a bun tight as a fist.

How will you manage there without us
children always at your heels?
You'll never again be able to wrinkle up your nose
as you joke and straighten my collar.

•

Будешь ночами будить анонимно.
Сам распахнется ахматовский томик.
Что тебя мучает, Антонина,
Тоня?

В дождь ты стучишься. Ты не простудишься.
Я ощущаю присутствие в доме.
В темных стихиях ты наша заступница,
Тоня...

Рюмка стоит твоя после поминок
с корочкой хлебца на сорок дней.
Она испарилась наполовину.
Или ты вправду притронулась к ней?

Не попадает рифма на рифму,
но это последняя связь с тобой!
Оборвалось. Я стою у обрыва,
малая часть твоей жизни земной.

«Благодарю тебя, что родила меня
и познакомила этим с собой,
с тайным присутствием идеала,
что приблизительно звали — любовь.

Благодарю, что мы жили бок о бок
в ужасе дня или радости дня,
робкой любовью приткнувшийся лобик —
лет через тысячу вспомни меня».

Я этих слов не сказал унизительно.
Кто прочитает это, скорей
матери ландышей принесите.
Поздно — моей, принесите — своей.

Now you'll be a stranger when you waken me at night;
the little Akhmatova volume will fly open on its own:
What is it that torments you, Antonina,
Tonya?

You knock at my door in the rain and do not catch cold,
but I sense your presence in the house;
and you will intercede for us with the dark elements,
Tonya.

After the funeral your wineglass stood
with a crust of bread for forty days.
It had half evaporated;
or had you touched it?

Rhyme no longer resounds with rhyme,
but this is my last link to you.
You were torn from me. I stand here
on the edge now, your last bit of earthly life.

I thank you for having given me life,
and for touching that life with yours,
with the secret presence of that ideal
which is loosely called love.

I thank you for allowing us to live side by side
in the joy and horror of every day,
little forehead bent over me with tender love,
remember me in a thousand years.

I have not spoken these words with condescension:
Whoever reads them, please do not wait.
Rush with lilies of the valley to your mother,
for mine I cannot — it is too late.

translated by William Jay Smith and F. D. Reeve

ВОДИТЕЛЬ

Я впрыгнул в грузовик, идущий к побережию.
Шофер длинноволос, совсем еще дитя.
На лобовом стекле — изображенье Цезаря.
Садясь, я произнес: «Приветствую тебя!»

Что знаешь ты, пацан, о Цезаре по сути?
Что значит талисман? Что молодость слепа?
Темнело. По пути мы брали голосующих.
И каждый говорил: «Приветствую тебя».

«Приветствую тебя», — леса голосовали.
И сотни новых рук хватались за борта.
И памятники к нам тянулись с пьедестала.
«Убитые тобой приветствуют тебя».

А Цезарь пролетал, глаза от ветра сузив.
Что ты творишь, пацан, срывая скоростя?
Их всех не уместить в твой пятитонный кузов.
Убитые тобой преследуют тебя.

Отец твой из земли привстал благоговейно.
Сидело за рулем убитое дитя.
И хор перерастал в иные поколенья:
«Убитые собой приветствуют тебя».

THE DRIVER

I jumped in a truck headed for the shore.
The driver was long-haired, still just a kid.
On the windshield there was a picture of "Caesar."
As I got in, I declared: "Hail to thee!"

What do you really know about Caesar, kid?
What does your mascot mean? How blind are the young?
It was getting dark. We kept picking up hand-raisers.
And each one repeated: "Hail to thee!"

"Hail to thee!" The autumn trees voted.
And hundreds of new hands clutched at the rail.
And statues leaned down to us from their pedestals:
"The ones that you killed cry hail to thee!"

And Caesar flew on, squinting into the wind.
What're you doing slowing down, kid?
You can't get them all in your five-ton box.
The ones that you killed keep following you.

Your father respectfully rose from the soil.
The child, now dead, sat hunched at the wheel.
And the chorus developed into new generations:
"The ones that killed themselves cry hail to thee!"

translated by F. D. Reeve

ПЕВЕЦ

Эта слава и цветы —
дань талантищу.
Любят голос твой. Но ты —
всем до лампочки.

Пара падает в траву,
сломав лавочку,
под мелодию твою...
Ты им — до лампочки.

Друг на исповедь пришел,
пополам почти.
Ну, а что с твоей душой —
ему до лампочки.

Муза в местной простыне
ждет лавандово
твой автограф на спине.
Ты ей до лампочки.

Телефонят пол-Руси,
клубы, лабухи —
хоть бы кто-нибудь спросил:
«Как ты, лапочка?»

Лишь врагу в тоске ножа,
в страстной срочности
голова твоя нужна,
а не творчество.

Но искусство есть комедь,
смысл Ламанческий.
Прежде, чем перегореть,
ярче лампочка.

THE SINGER

All this fame and flowers — they're
    the dues to a huge talent.
People love your voice. But yourself —
    you're in up to the light bulb.

A pair of lovers falls on the grass,
    having broken their little bench
listening to your melody —
    But you're in up to the light bulb.

One day a friend came to confess,
    to share fifty-fifty, almost.
But what you might have wanted to get off your chest —
    you're in up to the light bulb.

Smelling of lavender and wrapped in a sheet,
    a local muse is waiting for you
to autograph her back. Think she cares?
    You're in up to the light bulb.

Half of Russia's always calling,
    the nightclubs and the combos —
If only someone cared to ask,
    "How you doing, buddy?"

Knife ready, anxiously waiting,
    passionately sure of the date,
only your enemy wants your head —
    and not your creative work.

But art is, indeed, a bitter comedy,
    its sense that of the Man from La Mancha's.
Before burning out forever
    it flares up — the light bulb.

translated by F. D. Reeve

ПАМЯТИ ВЛАДИМИРА ВЫСОЦКОГО

Ты жил, играл и пел с усмешкою,
любовь российская и рана.
Ты в черной рамке не уместишься.
Тесны тебе людские рамки.

EPITAPH FOR VYSOTSKY

You lived, you played, you sang with a bitter grin;
Russia's love you were and heartbreak for us all.
A black frame now can never hold you in;
and a human frame for you is far too small.

translated by William Jay Smith

ЯБЛОКОПАД

Я посетил художника после кончины
вместе с попутной местной чертовкой.
Комнаты были пустынны, как рамы,
                              что без картины.
Но из одной доносился Чайковский.

Припоминая пустые залы,
с гостьей высокой в афроприческе,
шел я, как с черным воздушным шаром.
Из-под дверей приближался Чайковский.

Женщина в кресле сидела за дверью.
40 портретов ее окружали.
Мысль, что предшествовала творенью,
сделала знак, чтобы мы не мешали.

Как напряженна работа натурщицы!
Мольберты трудились над ней на треногах.
Я узнавал в их все новых конструкциях
характер мятущийся и одинокий —

то гвоздь, то три глаза, то штык трофейный,
как он любил ее в это время!
Не находила удовлетворенья
мысль, что предшествовала творенью.

Над батареею отопленья
крутился Чайковский, трактуемый Геной
Рождественским. Шар умолял его в небо
выпустить. В небе гроза набрякла.
Туча пахла, как мешок с яблоками.

Это уже ощущалось всеми:
будто проветривали помещенье —
мысль, что предшествовала творенью,
страсть, что предшествовала творенью,
тоска, предшествующая творенью,
шатала строения и деревья!

•

APPLEFALL

I visited an artist after his demise
with a local witch at her devilish work.
The rooms were like frames emptied of their pictures
but from one of them poured the strains of Tchaikovsky.

Remembering empty concert halls,
I followed my tall dark friend with her Afro
hairdo like a black balloon
while Tchaikovsky grew louder under the doors.

A woman in an armchair sat behind a door,
forty portraits of herself surrounding her.
The idea that preceded creation, she
signaled to us not to interfere.

How intense is a living model's work!
Above, the easels labored on their tripods:
In every new construction I could see
a lonely character crumple up before me.

Recorded with a spike, three eyes, or captured bayonet,
ah, how she fascinated him in all those guises,
but the idea that preceded his creation
took no pleasure in any of them now.

Above a battery of heating pipes
Tchaikovsky swirled, interpreted by Gena
Rozhdestvensky. The balloon begged him to be
released to the sky. In the sky a storm was brewing;
the storm cloud smelled like a bag of apples.

Everyone could see what was happening;
now everything was tossed into the air:
the idea that preceded creation,
the passion that preceded creation,
the depression coming before creation
rocked the buildings and the trees.

•

Мысль в виде женщины в кресле сидела.
Была улыбка — не было тела.
Мысль о собаке лизала колени.
Мыслью о море стояла аллея.
Мысль о стремянке, волнуя, белела —
в ней перекладина, что отсутствовала,
мыслью о ребре присутствовала.

Съезжалось общество потребления.
Мысль о яблоке катилась с тарелки.
Мысль о тебе стояла на тумбочке.
«Как он любил ее!» — я подумал.
«Да», — ответила из передней
недоуменная тьма творенья.

Вот предыстория их отношений.
Вышла студенткой. Лет было мало.
Гения возраст — в том, что он гений.
Верила, стало быть, понимала.
Как он ревнует ее, отошедши!
Попробуйте душ принять в его ванной —
душ принимает его очертанья.
Роман их длится не для посторонних.

Переворачивался двусторонний
Чайковский. В мелодии были стоны
антоновских яблонь. Как мысль о создателе,
осень стояла. Дом конопатили.
Шар об известку терся щекою.
Мысль обо мне заводила Чайковского,
по старой памяти, над парниками.
Он ставил его в шестьдесят четвертом.
Гости в это не проникали.
«Все оправдалось, мэтр полуголый,
что вы сулили мне в стенах шершавых
гневным затмением лысого шара,
локтями черными треугольников».

●

Idea in the form of woman sat in the armchair.
There was a smile — but there was no body.
The idea of a dog licked at her knees.
The avenue stood like an idea of the sea.
Wavering, the idea of a ladder faded;
from it the rung that was missing
emerged as the idea of a rib.

A consumer society came together here:
the idea of an apple rolled off a plate;
the idea of you stood on the night table.
"How he loved her!" I thought.
"Indeed," the puzzled darkness of creation
answered me from out in the hall.

The background of this relationship:
Married in her student days. Very young,
the age of genius — and he was a genius.
She believed in him, believed, and understood.
How jealous he is of her now that he's gone!
Try taking a shower in his bathroom —
the water takes on the outline of his physique:
their affair does not continue for outsiders.

Tchaikovsky got turned over
on his backside: his melody evoked the groaning
of Antonov apple trees. Like the idea of the creator,
outside there was fall. In the house caulked tight,
the balloon rubbed against the whitewashed wall.
The idea of myself kept rewinding the Tchaikovsky,
calling forth past times over the cold frames.
He staged that show in sixty-four;
people beat down the door to get in.
"Everything has come true, half-naked master,
what you promised me then on those rough walls —
in the angry eclipse of the bald balloon
and the black elbowing of the triangles."
•

Море сомнительное манило.
Сохла сомнительная малина.
Только одно не имело сомненья —
мысль о бессмысленности творенья.
Цвела на террасе мысль о терновнике.
Благодарю вас, мэтр модерновый!
Что же есть я? Оговорка мысли?
Грифель, который тряпкою смыли?
Я не просил, чтоб меня творили!
Но заглушал мою говорильню
смысл совершаемого творенья —
ссылка на Бога была б трафаретной —
Материя. Сад. Чайковский, наверное.

Яблоки падали. Плакали лабухи.
Яблок было — греби лопатой!
Я на коленях брал эти яблоки
яблокопада, яблокопада.
Я сбросил рубаху. По голым лопаткам
дубасили, как кулаки прохладные.
Я хохотал под яблокопадом.
Не было яблонь — яблоки падали.
Связал рукавами рубаху казнимую.
Набил плодами ее, как корзину.
Была тяжела, шевелилась, пахла.
Я ахнул —
сидела женщина в мужской рубахе.

Тебя я создал из падших яблок,
из праха — великую, беспризорную!
Под правым белком, косящим набок,
прилипла родинка темным зернышком.
Был я соавтором сотворенья.
Из снежных яблок там во дворе мы
бабу слепляем. Так на коленях
любимых лепим. Хозяйке дома
тебя представил я гостьей якобы.
Ты всем гостям раздавала яблоки.
И изъяснялась по-черноземному.

•

The sea beckoned dubiously;
the dubious raspberry shriveled up.
About one thing only there was no doubt:
the senselessness of all creation.
The idea of the prickly pear blossomed on the terrace.
I thank you, modernist master!
What am I then? The stipulation of an idea?
A slate wiped clean with a rag?
I did not ask to be created!
But the sense of perfectible creation
did not stop my endless chatter
and any reference to God would smack of the commonplace.
Matter. Garden. The effect of Tchaikovsky, no doubt.

Apples were falling; instruments wept.
Apples there were — to be shoveled up.
On my knees I gathered the apples
of this applefall, this applefall.
I tore off my shirt. On my bare shoulder blades
apples beat down like cold fists.
I roared with laughter under the applefall.
There were no apple trees — but apples were falling.
I tied up the sleeves of my tortured shirt
and filled it with fruit like a basket.
It was heavy; it moved; it gave off an aroma.
I cried out —
and there sat a woman in a man's shirt.

I created you from fallen apples,
from dust — great homeless one!
Under your right eyeball, turned to one side,
a mole had settled like a dark seed.
I was the coauthor of creation.
Out of snow apples there in the yard
we could forge an old woman. So on our knees
we model those we love. To our hostess
I introduced you as one of her guests.
You gave apples to all those present
and expressed yourself in your earthy way.
•

Стояла яблонная спасительница,
моя стеснительная сенсация.
Среди диванов глаза просили:
«Сенца́ бы!»
Откуда знать тебе, улыбавшейся,
в рубашке, словно в коротком платьице,
что, забывшись, влюбишься, сбросишь

                                        рубашку
и как шары по земле раскатишься!..

Над автобусной остановкой
туча пахла, как мешок с антоновкой.
Шар улетал. В мире было ветрено.
Прощай, нечаянное творенье!

Вы ночевали ли в даче создателя,
на одиночестве колких дерюжищ?
И проносилось в вашем сознании:
«Благодарю за то, что даруешь».

Благодарю тебя, автор творенья,
что я случился частью твоею,
моря и суши, сада в Тарусе,
благодарю за то, что даруешь,
что я не прожил мышкой-норушкой,
что не двурушничал с тобой, время,
даже когда ты мне даришь кукиш,
и за удары остервенелые,
даже за то, что дошел до ручки,
даже за это стихотворенье,
даже за то, что завтра задуешь, —
благодарю тебя, что даруешь
краткими яблоками коленей!
За гениальность твоих натурщиц,
за безымянность твоей идеи...
И повторяли уже в сновиденье:
«Боготворю за то, нто даруешь».

•

There stood my apple-made woman savior,
my delicate sensation.
Among the sofas all eyes begged:
"Do something!"
How were you to know, you who smiled
in your miniskirt shirt
that you would relax, fall in love, tear off the shirt
and float off over the world like a balloon?

Above the bus stop
the storm cloud smelled like a bag of Antonovs;
the balloon flew off. A wind swept through the world:
farewell, accidental creation!

Did you spend that night in your creator's dacha,
in the solitude of his prickly sacking?—
while running through your consciousness
were the words: "Thank you for what you have given."

I thank you, author of creation,
that I happen to be part of you.
I thank you for the sea and the land, for the garden in Tarusa,
thank you for what you have given,
for my not having lived in some rat hole,
for my not having tried to cheat on time;
even when you have given me the finger,
I thank you for the frenzied blows I strike,
I thank you for taking up my pen
and for this poem also,
and even for what you extinguish tomorrow.
I thank you for the gift
of apple-dimpled knees,
for the genius of your models,
for the anonymity of your idea....
And as we say in our dreams:
I worship you for what you give.
•

В мир открывались ворота ночные.
Вы уезжали. Собаки выли.
Не посещайте художника после кончины,
а навещайте, пока вы живы.

The night gates opened on the world.
You drove off. Dogs howled.
Do not visit an artist after his demise
but call upon him while still alive.

translated by William Jay Smith and F. D. Reeve

ДИАЛОГ

— Итак,
в прошедшем поэт, в настоящем просящий суда,
свидетель себя и мира в 60-е года?
— Да!
— Клянетесь ответствовать правду в ответ?
— Да.
— Живя на огромной, счастливейшей из планет,
песчиночке из моего решета...
— Да.
— ...вы производили свой эксперимент?
— Да.
— Любили вы петь и считали, что музыка — ваша
звезда?
— Да.
— Имели вы слух или голос и знали хотя бы предмет?
— Нет.
— Вы знали ли женщину с узкою трубочкой рта?
И дом с фонарем отражался в пруду, как бубновый
валет?
— Нет.
— Все виски просила без соды и льда?
— Нет, нет, нет!
— Вы жизнь ей вручили. Где женщина та?
— Нет.
— Вы все испытали — монаршая милость, политика,
деньги, нужда,
все только бы песни увидели свет,
дешевую славу с такою доплатою вслед!
— Да.
— И все ж, мой отличник, познания ваши на «2»?
— Да.
— Хотели пустыни — а шли в города,
смирили ль гордыню, став модой газет?
— Нет.

— Вы были ль у цели, когда стадионы ревели вам
«Дай»!
— Нет.

DIALOGUE

—So,
in the past a poet, now a plaintiff, witness to yourself and the
world of the sixties?
—Yes!
—Do you swear to tell the truth, the whole truth?
—Yes.
—Living on this huge and happiest-of-all-planets, a grain of
sand in my sieve...
—Yes.
—You did your experiment?
—Yes.
—You liked to sing and considered music your thing?
—Yes.
—Had you an ear, or a voice, and did you know your
subject?
—No.
—Did you know a woman with a little tube of a mouth?
And a house with a light reflected in a pond like the jack of
diamonds?
—No.
—Always asked for whiskey neat?
—No, no, no!
—You brought her to life. Where's that woman?
—No.
—You've known everything—monarchal favor, politics,
money, want—all so your songs would see the light, a cheap
celebrity, the rest of the payment to follow?
—Yes.
—All the same, my star pupil, you get a B for what you
know?
—Yes.
—Wanted the desert but headed for town, swallowed your
pride, became a celebrity?
—No.

—You were near the goal when the stadiums roared, "Go,
go, go!"
—No.

— В стишках все — вопросы, в них только и есть что
вреда,
производительность труда падает, читая сей бред?
— Да.
— И все же вы верите в некий просвет?
— Да.

— Ну, мальчики, может,
                            ну, девочки, может...
                        Но сникнут под ношею лет.
Друзья же подались в искусство «дада»?
— Кто да.
— Все — белиберда,
                        в вас нет смысла, поэт!
— Да, если нет.
— Вы дали ли счастье той женщине, для которой
трудились, чей образ воспет?
— Да,
то есть нет.
— Глухарь стихотворный, напяливший джинсы, поешь,
наступая на горло собственной жизни? Вернешься
домой — дома стонет беда?
— Да.
— Хотел ли свободы парижский Конвент?
Преступностью ль стала его правота?
— Да.
— На вашей земле холода, холода, такие пространства,
хоть крикни — все сходит на нет?..
— Да.
— Вы лбом прошибали из тьмы ворота, а за
воротами — опять темнота?
— Да.
— Не надо, не надо, не надо, не надо, не надо, случится
беда,
вам жаль ваше тело, ну ладно.
                        Но маму, но тайну оставшихся лет?
— Да.
— Да?

—Your little poems are all queries, nothing good in them;
productivity declines because people read such rubbish?
   —Yes.
—Yet still you believe in some ray of hope to come?
   —Yes.

—Well, boys, perhaps,
                    well, girls, perhaps...
                    But they shrink into themselves under
                    the burden of years.
Your friends became Dadaists?
   —Some, yes.
—It's all absurd.
                    You're not making sense, poet!
   —Yes, if I'm not.
—Did you make the woman happy, the one for whose sake
you worked so hard, whose image you celebrated?
   —Yes.
I mean, no.
   —You rhyming pigeon tight in your jeans, you sing by
stepping on the throat of your own life? When you go home,
does the house groan with trouble?
   —Yes.
—You wanted the freedom of the Paris Convention, but didn't
its justice become criminality?
   —Yes.
—On our earth there are such cold, cold, vast spaces that,
shout as you will, nothing comes of anything?
   —Yes.
—With your forehead you pounded down the gates from the
dark but, outside, found only more darkness?
   —Yes.
—Don't, don't, don't, don't, don't—something happens, you
get upset about your physical self, well, okay.
                    But what about Mama, the secret of the remaining
                    years?
   —Yes.
—Yes?

— Нет.
— ?..
— Нет.
— Итак, продолжаете эксперимент? Айда!

Обрыдла мне исповедь,
вы — сумасшедший, лжеидол, балда, паразит!
Идете витийствовать? зло поразить? иль простить?
Так в чем же есть истина? В «да» или в «нет»?
— С п р о с и т ь.

В ответы не втиснуты
судьбы и слезы.
В вопросе и истина.
Поэты — вопросы.

—No.

—?

—No.

—So, you're going on with the experiment? Oho!

The confession irked me;
crazy fool, false idol, knob on a stick, parasite!
You off to poetize? astound evil? or forgive?
So, where's the truth? "Yes" or "No"?
    —Ask me.

Fates and tears
aren't squeezed into answers.
In a question there's truth,
and poets are questions.

                    translated by F. D. Reeve

ЧЕМ БОЛЬШЕ ОТ СЕРДЦА ОТРЫВАЕШЬ

Мамонт пролетел над Петрозаводском,
трубя о своем сиротстве.
Чем больше от сердца отрываешь,
тем больше на сердце остается.

Раздайте себя немедля,
даруя или простивши,
единственный рубль имея,
отдайте другому тыщу!

Вовеки не загнивает
вода в дающих колодцах.
Чем больше от сердца отрываешь,
тем больше в нем остается.

Так мать — хоть своих орава —
чужое берет сиротство,
чем больше от сердца отрываешь,
тем больше в нем остается.

Люблю перестук товарный
российского разноверстья —
сколько от себя оторвали,
сколько еще остается!

Какое самозабвенье
в воздухе над покосами,
как будто сердцебиение,
особенно — над погостами.

Пекущийся о народе,
раздай бриллиант редчайший,
и станешь моложе вроде,
и сразу вдруг полегчает.

Бессмертие, милый Фауст,
простое до идиотства, —

THE MORE YOU TEAR OFF, THE MORE YOU KEEP

A mammoth flew over Petrozavodsk
trumpeting his orphan state.
The more you tear from your heart,
the more you keep.

Give all at once,
making gifts of yourself and forgiving;
having but one ruble,
give someone a thousand!

The water in living wells
does not stagnate;
the more you tear from your heart
the more of it you keep.

A mother with many children
takes in an orphan;
the more you tear from your heart
the more you keep.

I love the clatter of freight cars
through endless varied Russian miles:
however much is torn from you,
that much you'll still have to give.

What self-sacrifice there is
in the air over new-mown hay:
it's as if the hearts of the dead could beat,
especially over country graves.

You who worry so about people,
give away your earnings;
you will become younger
and your burden will lighten.

Immortality, dear Faustus,
is idiotically simple —

чем больше от сердца отрываешь,
тем больше жить остаешься.

Нищему нет пожарищ.
Беда и победа — сестры.
Чем больше от сердца отрываешь,
тем больше ему достается.

the more you tear from your heart,
the longer you will live.

But a beggar's house cannot burn;
trouble and triumph are brothers;
the more you tear from your heart,
the more that heart will hurt.

*translated by William Jay Smith and
Vera Dunham*

ПОРТРЕТ

Я так долго тебя не писал —
лоб и дом, что никак не наладишь,
запрокинутых зубок печаль —
каждый снизу зазубрен, как ландыш.

Как я долго тебе не писал!
По чащобам, свершая порубки,
я на ландыши наступал —
на твои задышавшие зубки.

PORTRAIT

It has been years since I painted you—
your house in disarray, your forehead slightly creased,
you lying back with your legs stretched and smiling
like bells of lily of the valley with white serrated edges.

It has been years since I wrote to you!
In the days when I used to chop down trees,
thinning the forest, I stepped on lilies of the valley—
on your white, moist, newly breathing, little teeth.

translated by Diana Der Hovanessian

БЕСЕДА В РИМЕ

Я спросил у Папы римского:
                              «Вы верите в тарелки?»
Улыбнувшись, как нелепости,
                              мне ответил Папа: «Нет».
И Христос небес касался,
                              легкий, как дуга троллейбуса,
чтоб стекала к нам энергия, движа мир две тыщи лет.
В папскую библиотеку петербургский дух
                                            наведывался,
и шуршал рукав папирусный.
                              Был по времени обед.
Где-то к Висле мчались лебеди.
                              Шла сикстинская побелка.
И на дне реки познанья поблескивал стилет.
Пазолини вел на лежбище
                      по Евангелью и Лесбосу.
Боже, где надежда теплится?
                              Кому вернуть билет?
Бах ослеп от математики,
                      если только верить Лейбницу.
И сибирской группы «Примус» римский пел
                                        эквивалент.
Округлив иллюминаторы,
                      в виде супницы и хлебницы
проплыла Капелла Паццы, как летающий объект.
В небесах на телеспутнике
                      СиБиЭс сражалась с ЭйБиСи.
Жили жалко. Жили мелко. Не было идеи.
Землю, как такси по вызову,
                              ждала зеленая тарелка.
Кто-то в ней спросил по рации:
                              «Вы верите в людей?»

A CONVERSATION IN ROME

I asked the Pope:
> "Do you believe in flying saucers?"
Smiling at what seemed absurd,
> the Pope replied: "No."
Christ reached to the sky,
> arched and easy, like a trolleybus,
so energy flowed down to us,
> ran the world two thousand years.
A Petersburg spirit came and went
> among the papal books,
rustling its papyrus sleeve.
> Dinnertime, the clock showed.
Swans were rushing toward the Vistula somewhere.
> The Sistine Chapel was being whitewashed.
On the bottom of the river of knowledge a stiletto sparkled.
Pasolini led to a breeding ground
> via Lesbos and the Gospel.
Lord, where's there a ray of hope?
> Who'll we return the ticket to?
Bach went blind from mathematics,
> if Leibnitz can be believed.
A Roman rock group like the Siberian "Primus"
> knocked out a beat.
With sidelights as round
> as soup plates and breadbaskets,
the Pazzi Chapel sailed past, like a huge flying object.
By communication satellite in space
> CBS fought ABC.
We've lived shamefully. Pettily. Without a sense of purpose.
A flying saucer with a green light on like an empty taxi
> was waiting for Earth.
From inside it someone asked over the CB network:
> "Do you believe in people?"

translated by F. D. Reeve

213

ДВА СТИХОТВОРЕНИЯ

I

Над темной молчаливою державой
такое одиночество парить!
Завидую тебе, орел двуглавый —
ты можешь сам с собой поговорить.

II

Виснут шнурами вечными
лампочки под потолком.
Но только поэт подвешен
на белом нерве спинном.

TWO POEMS

I

Over a dark and quiet empire
alone I fly—and envy you,
two-headed eagle who at least
have always yourself to talk to.

II

To hang bare light bulbs from a ceiling
simple cord will always serve;
it's only the poet who must hang
by his glaring white spinal nerve.

translated by William Jay Smith and
Patricia Blake

ЛИНКОЛЬНУ

Приду попробить микрофон
с актрисою билингвельно.
Пустой театр, простой плафон —
но здесь убили Линкольна.

Какие духи здесь фонят?
Какое эхо вклинено?
Не оператор виноват,
я думаю — дух Ли́нкольна.

По-русски говорят Линко́льн.
Его для уха русского
я звал бы «Мистер Колокольн»
за рост и за акустику.

Я первый русский, кто взошел
на эту сцену с лирикой.
Читать охрипший мой глагол
Уитмену и Линкольну.

Искусство — на крови собор.
И тем оно великое.
Кто приволок цветы с собой —
их отнесите Линкольну.

AT FORD'S THEATER

With an actress here this afternoon
I've come to test the microphone:
An empty stage, a simple light,
where Abraham Lincoln was shot one night.

What spirits are there lurking here?
What echo somehow pierces through?
It's not the fault of the engineer—
it's the ghost of Lincoln, I am sure.

In Russian Lincoln speaks to me—
or it's his ghost that so speaks out.
Mr. Belltower he might be
with that deep voice and that great height.

I'm the first Russian to appear
upon this famous haunted stage
for Lincoln and Whitman to recite
my poems in a quavering voice.

Art is a church that's built on blood;
in blood alone has it verity.
Let's leave these flowers for in truth
they belong to Lincoln, not to me.

translated by William Jay Smith and
Inna Bogachinskaya Perlin

ЧЕКОЛЕК

Человек меняет кожу,
боже мой! — и челюсть тоже,
он меняет кровь и сердце.
Чья-то боль в него поселится?

Человек меняет голову
на учебник Богомолова,
он меняет год рожденья,
он меняет убежденья
на кабинет в учрежденье.
Друг, махнемся — помоги!
Дам мозги за три ноги.
Что еще бы поменять?
Человек меняет мать.

Человек сменил кишки
на движки,
обновил канализацию,
гол, как до колонизации,
человек меняет вентиль,
чтоб не вытек,
человек меняет пол.
Самообслуживанье ввел.

Человек меняет голос,
велочек немяет логос,
меночек осляет Сольвейг,
елечвок левмяет ослог...
Бедный локис, бедный век!
Он меняет русла рек,
чудотворец-человек.

Наконец он сходит в ад.
Его выгнали назад:
«Здесь мы мучаем людей,
а не кучу запчастей».
Он обиделся, сопя,
И пошел искать себя.

A MAN IS CHANGING HIS SKIN

A man is changing his skin,
my God! and his jaw also,
changing his blood and his heart.
And taking on another's pain?

A man is exchanging his head
for a textbook of Bogomolov,
changing the year in which he was born;
a man is exchanging his convictions
for a fine position without restrictions.
Come on now and help me, friend.
For three legs I'll give up my brain.
What else is there to exchange?
A man is exchanging his mother.

The man has turned in his intestines
for rollers that are mechanized;
nude, as before he was colonized,
new ventilation he has devised
so that his valves no longer leak;
and now the man is changing his sex.
He has introduced self-service.

The man is changing his voice,
teh nam si ganching sih cevoi,
eht anm si asgchin solveig,
mnanm si nasgich goslvo...
Poor man entrapped, poor century!
He's changing the channel of the river,
this magic man, this wonder-worker.

The fellow finally goes to hell.
But no sooner down there, he departs.
"We don't want any of your kind here.
We torment people, not spare parts."
Offended, the man wipes away a tear.
And goes off to find himself.

translated by William Jay Smith and
F. D. Reeve

СОН

Человек проснулся трезвый —
он не врезал,
не дерябнул политуры
с гением литературы,
с настроенья неважнецкого
не набрался под Жванецкого,
бормотухи роковой
не занюхал рукавом,
вышел в путь без «посошка».
Жив пока.

Странен мир безалкогольный.
И стоят среди страны,
как холмы без колоколен,
безбутыльные столы.

Сократился рост дебилов.
Входят любящие в дом:
«Давай, милый, без бутылки
двойняшек заведем».

Трезвый шеф приходит в трест.
И водопроводчик трезв.
И высокие персоны
протрезвели от трезвона.

Не двоятся, не троятся
показатели реляций.
Вежлив, как миссионер,
трезвый милиционер.

Изменения целебны.
Вытрезвитель сорвал план.
В церквах служатся молебны
по вернувшимся мужьям.

Свадьба чокается чаем,
Сократилось число «Чаек».

A DREAM

A man woke up sober—
he hadn't gotten potted;
hadn't polished off rotgut
stinking with literary odors;
feeling himself a nogoodnik
hadn't gotten high listening to Zhvanetsky;
hadn't downed wine on an empty belly
while wiping his nose;
had left without one for the road.
And had come up alive.

The nonalcoholic world's peculiar.
All across the countryside,
like rolling hills without church steeples,
tables have no bottles on them.

The increase of Mongoloids has stopped.
Lovers coming home rush in:
"Honey, no need to pop a top,
let's just make us some little twins."

A sober boss arrives at work,
finds even that the plumber's sober.
And the highest of the higher-ups
have sobered up from all the chatter.

Production indices have stopped
lying two and three times over.
On every corner a sober cop
is as polite as a missionary.

The changes are restorative,
the sobering-station's bonuses, unearned.
Te Deums are being sung in churches
for husbands who at last returned.

Wedding toasts are made with tea;
there aren't more Chaikas around, but fewer;

И никто не хочет, трезв,
засолить всю реку Днестр.

Сколько пропили соколики!
Сколько с этих пьяных слез
сквозь универмаг в Сокольниках
миллионов пронеслось!

Набирает правда силу.
И надеждами полна
протрезвевшая Россия,
ясноглазая страна.

And, sober, no one fancies he
would ever try to salt the Dnestr.

What the good old boys spent on drink!
How many millions from those drunken tears
found their way through the diamond ring
of the Sokolniki department store!

Truth is gaining the upper hand.
Russia once again is sober
and full of hope,
a clear-eyed land.

translated by F. D. Reeve

ВЕЧЕР В «ОБЩЕСТВЕ СЛЕПЫХ»

Милые мои слепые,
слепые поводыри,
меня по своей России,
невидимой, повели.

Зеленая, голубая,
розовая на вид,
она, их остерегая,
плачет, скрипит, кричит.

Прозрейте, товарищ зрячий,
у озера в стоке вод.
Вы слышите — оно плачет?
А вы говорите — цветет.

Скажу я вам — цвет ореховый,
вы скажете — гул ореха.
Я говорю — зеркало,
вы говорите — эхо.

Вам кажется Паганини
красивейшим из красавцев,
Сильвана же Помпанини —
сиплая каракатица.

Пытаться читать стихи
в обществе слепых —
пытаться скрывать грехи
в обществе святых.

Плевать им на куртку кожаную,
на показуху рук,
они не прощают кожею
наглый и лживый звук.

И дело не в рифмах бедных —
они хорошо трещат, —

AN EVENING AT THE SOCIETY FOR THE BLIND

My dear blind people,
blind leaders of the blind,
have guided me across
their invisible Russia.

Green, light blue—
or pink it would appear—
watching over them,
weeps and creaks and cries aloud.

Look clearly, you who see,
at the water flowing into the lake.
Listen—can you hear it weep?
No—you say—I see it bloom.

Let me tell you—what you call
nut-brown is the walnut's roar.
I say—mirror;
you say—echo.

Paganini seems to you
the handsomest of handsome men
while Silvana Pompanini
is a hoarse and ugly lump.

Trying to read one's poems
at the Society for the Blind
is like trying to hide one's sins
in the company of saints.

They don't give a damn for a leather jacket
and they scorn a show of hands
and yet they bridle at
any false or insolent sound.

It's not a question of bad rhymes—
those crackle well enough along—

но пахнут, чем вы обедали,
а надо петь натощак!

И в вашем слепом обществе,
всевидящем, как Вишну,
вскричу, добредя ощупью:
вижу!

зеленое зеленое зеленое
заплакало заплакало заплакало
зеркало зеркало зеркало
эхо эхо эхо

and yet they smell what you had for supper
and so you must sing on an empty stomach!

In your blind society,
all-seeing like Vishnu,
I cry out, groping my way along:
"I see!"

green green green
weeping weeping weeping
mirror mirror mirror
echo echo echo

translated by William Jay Smith and
F. D. Reeve

СКУЛЬПТОР СВЕЧЕЙ

Скульптор свечей, я тебя больше года вылепливал.
Ты — моя лучшая в мире свеча.
Спички потряхиваю, бренча.
Как ты пылаешь великолепно
волей создателя и палача!

Было ль, чтоб мать поджигала ребенка?
Грех работенка, а не барыш.
Разве сжигал своих детищ Коненков?
Как ты горишь!

На два часа в тебе красного воска.
Где-то у коек чужих и афиш
стройно вздохнут твои краткие сестры,
как ты горишь.

Как я лепил свое чудо и чадо!
Весны кадили. Капало с крыш.
Кружится разум. Это от чада.
Это от счастья, как ты горишь!

Круглые свечи. Красные сферы.
Белый фитиль незажженных светил.
Темное время — вечная вера.
Краткое тело — черный фитиль.

«Благодарю тебя и прощаю
за кратковременность бытия,
пламя пронзающее без пощады
по позвоночнику фитиля.

Благодарю, что на миг озаримо
мною лицо твое и жилье,
если ты верно назвал свое имя,
значит, сгораю во имя Твое».

Скульптор свечей, я тебя позабуду,
скутер найму, умотаю отсюда,

THE CANDLE SCULPTOR

A candle sculptor, I spent more than a year modeling you.
You are my best candle in the world.
I shake my matchbox, rattle it.
How splendidly you blaze
by the will of your creator and executioner.

Did ever a mother burn her babe?
A sin, this product, never a gain.
Did Calder ever melt down his children?
How you burn!

Two hours of red wax I've given you:
by other posters, at other bedsides,
your skinny sisters sigh and flicker out,
but how you burn!

How I have shaped your image, my child!
Springs scattered their incense; water dripped from the eaves.
The mind reels; from all the fumes,
from all the joy at how you burn!

Round candles. Red spheres.
White wick of unillumined planets.
A dark time—eternal faith,
a short body—a black wick.

"I thank you and forgive you
for my too-brief life,
for the flame that chewed mercilessly away
on the spine of my wick.

"I thank you for letting me
light up briefly your face and your house;
and if you faithfully spoke your name,
then it is in Thy name I burn."

A candle sculptor, I'll forget you,
rent a scooter and get the hell out,

свеч наштампую голый столбняк.
Кашляет ворон ручной от простуды.
Жизнь убывает, наверное, так,
как сообщающиеся сосуды,
вровень свече убывает в бутылке коньяк.

И у свечи, нелюбимой покуда,
темный нагар на реснице набряк.

leaving all my candles to harden in one bloody pool.
The raven on the wrist coughs with a cold:
life runs out like the liquid in so many communicating vessels
or like that bottle of cognac, keeping level with its candle.

And the candle, unloved for a while,
has gathered dark snuff on its eyelash.

translated by William Jay Smith and F. D. Reeve

ШКОЛЬНИК

Твой кумир тебя взял на премьеру.
И Любимов — Ромео!
И плечо твое онемело
от присутствия слева.

Что-то будет! Когда бы час пробил,
жизнь ты б отдал с восторгом
за омытый сиянием профиль
в темноте над толстовкой.

Вдруг любимовская рапира —
повезло тебе, крестник! —
обломившись, со сцены влепилась
в ручку вашего кресла.

Стало жутко и весело стало
от такого событья!
Ты кусок неразгаданной стали
взял губами, забывшись.

«Как люблю вас, Борис Леонидович! —
думал ты, — повезло мне родиться.
Моя жизнь передачей больничною,
может, вам пригодится...»

Распрямись, мое детство согбенное.
Детство. Самозабвенье.
И пророческая рапира.
И такая Россия!..

Через год пролетал он над нами
в белом гробе на фоне небес,
будто в лодке — откинутый навзничь,
взявший весла на грудь — гребец.

•

THE SCHOOLBOY

Your idol invited you to opening night.
Lyubimov played Romeo,
and your shoulder went numb, so close
to the presence on your left.

Something will happen! If the last hour struck
you'd ecstatically give life up
for the radiant profile in the dark
above the Tolstoy blouse.

Suddenly Lyubimov's foil—
you were lucky, godson!—
snapping, plunged from the stage into
the arm of your seat.

How terrifying, how exciting
it was, happening like that!
Beside yourself, you put your lips
on the mysterious steel.

"How I love you, Boris Pasternak!"
you thought. "How lucky to be alive.
Perhaps in some medical transfer
my life may be useful to you..."

Stand up straight, hunched-over childhood.
My childhood. Selfless time.
And oracular foil.
Such a Russia it was!

A year later he flew high above us
in a white coffin through the sky,
as if in a rowboat, laid back, an oarsman
with the oars pulled to his chest.
•

Это было не погребенье.
Была воля небесная скул.
Был над родиной выдох гребельный —
он по ней слишком сильно вздохнул.

It wasn't an interment. It was
the cheekbones' will to glory.
It was the rower's letting out his breath
in the country he had breathed too deeply for.

translated by F. D. Reeve

ВОР ВОСПОМИНАНИЙ

От тех времен ключи еще лежат.

Я отпер дверь, как триста лет назад.
Я свет зажег. И озарились снизу
под потолком, протянутые в ряд —
как яйца в холодильнике стоят —
ионики ампирного карниза.

Я вор воспоминаний. Где хранят
предметы чувства в тысячи карат?
куски тоски? и хризопраз каприза?
Где ты их держишь? Тюбики помад
меня не узнавали. Вырыт клад.
Мое письмо торчало из корзины.

Был тепл утюг. Шел терпкий аромат
халата. Твой салат кончала крыса.
«Сестра, — успел подумать, — я твой брат!»
И запустил ключами по карнизу.
И скорлупа посыпалась в салат.

И сразу трясануло укоризной
в сто киловатт. Ионики трещат.
И вылупились — мне не объяснят
как — тыщи птиц, горластых, белых, сизых.
«Ты виноват! Ты виноват! Ты виноват!
грабитель гнезд!..» Толкаются, кричат.
И пачкают издания Совписа.

Я узнаю вас, страстный зоосад —
вожак тоски, слепые самки шиза,
подстриженные крылья божьей жизни
и состраданья мокрый снегопад —
как мы кормили чаек в Симеизе.

•

THE THIEF OF MEMORIES

The keys to those days are still lying around.

I unlocked the door, like three hundred years ago.
I turned on a light. And lit up from the bottom,
stretched in a row along the ceiling's edge —
as in an icebox door a rack of standing eggs —
was the Ionic molding of the Empire cornice.

I'm a thief of memories. Where do they keep
the thousand-carat objects of sentiment?
The bits of nostalgia? the chrysoprase caprice?
Where have you put them? The little tubes of lipstick
didn't recognize me. The cabinet was empty.
My letter was sticking out of the wastepaper basket.

The iron was still warm. The tart aroma
of a bathrobe passed. A rat was finishing your lettuce.
"Sister," I thought, looking at the rat, "I'm your brother."
And flung the keys at the Empire cornice.
And eggshells rained down on the lettuce.

And suddenly a hundred-kilowatt reproach
shook everything. The Ionic molding cracked.
And there hatched forth — no way I can explain it —
thousands of loudmouthed, white, blue-gray birds.
"It's all your fault! It's all your fault! It's all your fault!
You nest robber!" They shoved each other and shouted.
And they dirtied all the hot-shit publisher's books.

I know you well, you zoological garden
of passion — nostalgia's guide, blind females
of two minds, clipped wings of the divine life
and the wet snowfall of compassion —
as once we fed the gulls at Simeiz.
•

И ты войдешь с коронною репризой:
«Так твою мать! Опять в квартире ад».

«Вы к Лизе?
Ах, прошлая хозяйка анфилад?
Та съехала. В загранку, говорят.
Дом на сигнализации...» Наряд
милиции подымался снизу.

Я дверь закрыл, как триста лет назад.

And in you come with the crowning rebuff:
"Goddamn it! Again the place looks like hell!"

"You want to see Liza?
Ah, the previous tenant?
She left. Went abroad, I heard.
The building has an alarm system..." A
squad of cops was coming up the stairs.

I shut the door, like three hundred years ago.

translated by F. D. Reeve

ЧЕЛОВЕК ПОРОДЫ СЕНБЕРНАР

Выбегает утром на бульвар
человек породы сенбернар.
Он передней лапой припадал,
говорили — будучи в горах,
прыгнул за хозяином в завал
и два дня собой отогревал.
Сколько таких бродит по Руси!
Пес небесный, меня спаси.

Я его в компаниях видал.
Неуклюжий и счастливый раб,
нас сквозь снег до трапа провожал,
оставляя отпечатки лап.
Сенбернар, подбрось в аэропорт!
Сенбернар, сгоняй за коньяком!
И несется к вам во весь опор
верный пар над частым языком.

Изо всех людей или собак
сенбернары ближе к небесам.
Мы не знали, где его чердак.
Без звонка он заявлялся сам.
Может, то не лапы, а шасси?
Пес небесный, меня неси.

Пес, никто не брал тебя всерьез.
Но спасал, когда нас забывал
человек по имени Христос,
человек породы сенбернар.

Вдруг в одной из наших Галатей
он увидел бедственный сигнал
и, как в пропасть, бросился за ней.
Брось! Будь человеком, сенбернар.

Позабыл, что взят ты напрокат.
Наша жизнь — практически буран!
Женщинам не надо серенад,
был бы на подхвате сенбернар.

•

A SAINT BERNARD OF A MAN

Each morning a Saint Bernard of a man
runs out to the avenue. He's lame
in one front leg. The story goes
that up in the mountains when it snowed
he leapt after his master into a drift
and kept him warm for two whole days.
How many like him in Russia there be!
Heavenly hound, rescue me.

I used to see him in different crowds.
A clumsy but a happy slave,
he'd guide to the ladder through the snow,
leaving behind the prints of his paws.
Saint Bernard, drop me at the airport!
Saint Bernard, round up a cognac!
And full tilt at us there he'd come,
faithful breathing above a panting tongue.

Of all the people and dogs there are
the closest to Heaven are Saint Bernards.
We never knew in what garret he slept.
He always showed up without being called.
Maybe he came on wheels, not paws?
Heavenly hound, pick me up, too.

No one took you seriously, dog.
But when we were forgotten or lost
by a man everyone knows as Christ,
a Saint Bernard of a man would save us.

Suddenly from one of our Galateas
he spotted a signal of distress
and dashed to her side as if into a pit.
Lay off! Be a man, Saint Bernard.

You've forgotten you're for hire.
Our life, in fact, is one huge snowstorm.
No point to serenading women
when, below, a Saint Bernard will catch them.

•

«Я родился быть твоим рабом,
волочить из бездны на краю.
Только жизнь тебе я подарю
на снегу, от вмятин голубом».
«Будь же человеком, дуралей!
Разбудил. Замучил. Отдышал.
Ты — четвероногая метель,
мой уже последний перевал».

Для других спасает сенбернар.
Человек влюбился для себя.
Мы на возмущенный семинар
собирались, кару торопя…

Он пришел. Нашарил в кухне газ.
Снял ошейник. Музыку врубил.
И лежал, не открывая глаз,
пока сенбернара не убил.

С той поры в компаниях пропал
человек породы сенбернар.
Как метель гуляет по Руси!
Пес небесный, меня прости.

"I was born to be your slave,
to drag you from the canyon to the rim.
Here where the snow has been pressed blue
I come only to bring you back to life."
"Oh, come on; be a man, you ass!
You woke me, pestered me, breathed all over me.
You're a four-legged blizzard by yourself,
the last pass I have to travel through."

A Saint Bernard saves for others' sakes,
the man fell in love for his own.
Gathered round in indignation,
our seminar planned retribution—

He came in. Fumbled with the gas
in the kitchen. Took off his collar. Tuned in to
some music, and lay there, his eyes closed,
until he had killed the Saint Bernard.

Since then, nobody in town has seen
the Saint Bernard of a man around.
He wanders Russia like a blizzard!
Heavenly hound, grant me pardon.

translated by F. D. Reeve

КАБАНЬЯ ОХОТА

Он прет
          на тебя, великолепен.
Собак
          по пути позарезав.
Лупи!
          Ну, а ежели не влепишь —
нелепо перезаряжать!
Он черен.
              И он тебя заметил.
Он жмет
          по прямой, как глиссера.
Уже
          между вами десять метров.
Но кровь твоя четко-весела.

Очнусь — стол как операционный.
Кабанья застольная компанийка
на 8 персон.
И порционный,
одетый в хрен и черемшу,
как паинька,
на блюде ледяной, саксонской,
с морковочкой, как будто с соской,
смиренный, голенький лежу.

Кабарышни порхают меж подсвечников.
Копытца их нежны, как подснежники.
Кабабушка тянется к ножу.

В углу продавил четыре стула
центр тяжести литературы.
Лежу.

Внизу, элегически рыдая,
полны электрической тоски,
коты с окровавленными ртами,
вжимаясь в скамьи и сапоги,
визжат, как точильные круги!
•

THE BOAR HUNT

He bears down
          on you, magnificent,
having torn hounds
            to pieces on the way.
Hit him!
        But if you don't get him—
reloading's ridiculous!
He's black.
        And he has sighted you.
He presses
        straight ahead like a hydroplane.
Between you
        no more than ten yards.
But your blood is high-spirited and clear.

I come to—as on an operating table.
A boar-run private party room
for eight.
Sliced up,
dressed in horseradish and wild garlic
like a good boy,
I'm lying on a cold, Saxon platter
with a little carrot, like a teat,
peaceful, naked.

Young girl boars flutter among the candlesticks.
Their hooves are tender, like snowdrops.
An old granny boar reaches for the knife.

In the corner, the center of literary
gravity has crushed four chairs.
I lie still.

Down below, sobbing elegiacally,
filled with electric languor,
cats with bloody mouths,
squeezing onto benches and into boots,
howl like grindstones!

•

(А кот с головою стрекозы,
порхая капронными усами,
висел над столом и, гнусавя,
просил кровяной колбасы.)

Озяб фаршированный животик.
Гарнир умирающий поет.
И чаши торжественные сводят
над нами хозяева болот.

Собратья печальной литургии,
салат, чернобыльник и другие,
ваш хор
меня возвращает вновь к Природе,
оч.хор
и зерна, как кнопки на фаготе,
горят сквозь моченый помидор.

Кругом умирали культуры —
садовая, парниковая, византийская,
кукурузные кудряшки Катулла,
крашеные яйца редиски
(вкрутую),
селедка, нарезанная как клавиатура
перламутрового клавесина,
попискивала.
Но не сильно.

А в голубых листах капусты,
как с рокотовских зеркал,
в жемчужных париках и бюстах
век восемнадцатый витал.

Скрипели красотой атласной
кочанные ее плеча,
мечтали умереть от ласки
и пугачевского меча.
•

(A cat with a dragonfly head,
twitching its nylon whiskers,
hung above the table and, speaking through its nose,
begged some blood sausage.)

The little chopped-meat belly felt chilled.
The dying garnish sings.
And the swamp hosts bring
the ceremonial cups together over us.

Fellow members of the sad liturgy,
lettuce, wormwood and others,
your chorus
restores me anew to Nature,
OK
and the seeds, like the keys on a bassoon,
glow through a wet tomato.

Cultures were dying out all around —
garden, seedbed, Byzantine,
Catullus' corn-colored curls,
the dyed eggs of the radish
(hard-boiled).
A pickled herring sliced like the keyboard
of a mother-of-pearl harpsichord
squeaked a little,
but not loudly.

In the blue leaves of cabbage
as if in a hall of mirrors
in pearly wigs and busts
the eighteenth century soared past.

Her cabbaged shoulders
screeched in satin beauty,
dreamed of dying from caresses
and Pugachev's sword.

•

Прощальною позолотой
петергофская нимфа лежала,
как шпрота,
на черством ломтике пьедестала.

Вкусно порубать Расина!
И, как гастрономическая вершина,
дрожал на столе
аромат Фета, застывший в кувшинках,
как в гофрированных формочках для желе.
И умирало колдовство
в настойке градусов под сто.

Пируйте, восьмерка виночерпиев.
Стол, грубо сколоченный, как плот.
Без кворума Тайная Вечеря.
И кровь предвкушенная и плоть.

Клыки их вверх дужками закручены.
И рыла тупые над столом —
как будто в мерцающих уключинах
плывет восьмивесельный паром.

Так вот ты, паромище Харона,
и Стикса пустынные воды.
Хреново.
Хозяева, алаверды!

Я пью за страшенную свободу
отплыть, усмехнувшись, в никогда.
Мишени несбывшейся охоты,
рванем за усопшего стрелка!

Чудовище по имени Надежда,
я гнал за тобой, как следопыт.

The Peterhof nymph lay
in farewell gilding
like a sardine
on its dry slice of pedestal.

Racine is tasty all chopped up!
And, a gastronomic treat,
the aroma of Fet, congealed in water lilies,
trembled on the table
like jelly in goffered molds.
Sorcery faded away
in standing liquor some 200 proof.

Feast on, you eight winescoopers.
Crudely knocked together, the table is like a raft.
No quorum at the Last Supper.
The blood has been pretasted, and the flesh.

Their tusks are curved in little arches.
And their stupid snouts above the table—
as if between shimmering rowlocks—
move like an eight-oared ferry.

So there you are, ferryman Charon,
and the empty water of the Styx.
Horseradish.
My hosts, *alla verde*!

I drink to the most terrifying freedom
of sailing off into nowhere with a smile.
Bull's-eyes of an imaginary hunt,
we'll rip them up for the dead marksman's sake.

Monster called Hope,
I pursued you like a tracker.

Все пули уходили, не задевши.
Отходную! Следует допить.

За пустоту по имени Искусство.
Но пью за отметины дробин.
Закусывай!
Не мсти, что по звуку не добил.

А ты кто? Я тебя, дитя, не знаю.
Ты обозналась. Ты вина чужая!
Молчит она. Она не ест, не пьет.
Лишь на губах поблескивает лед.

А это кто? Ты?! Ты ж меня любила.
Я пью, чтоб в тебе хватило силы
взять ножик в чудовищных гостях.
Простят убийство —

                промах не простят.

Пью кубок свой преступный, как агрессор
и вор,
который, провоцируя окрестности,
производил естественный отбор!

Зверюги прощенье ощутили:
разлукою и хвоей задышав.
И слезы скакали по щетине,
и пили на брудершафт.

Очнулся я, видимо, в бессмертье.
Мы с ношей тащились по бугру.
Привязанный ногами к длинной жерди,
отдав кишки жестяному ведру,
качался мой хозяин на пиру.

И по дороге, где мы проходили,
кровь свертывалась в шарики из пыли.

All the bullets missed, then vanished.
Write them off! Drink her down.

To the emptiness called Art!
But I drink to the small-shot marks.
Have a bite!
Don't take revenge for not hitting it by sound.

And who's this? I don't know you, child.
You've mistaken me. You're someone else's fault.
She's silent. She doesn't eat, doesn't drink.
There's ice shining on her lips.

And who's that? You? You used to love me.
I'm drinking so you'll have enough strength
to seize the little knife among the monstrous guests.
They'll forgive murder —
                                    but not missing.

I drain my criminal goblet like an aggressor
and thief
who, provoking the neighborhood,
produced a natural selection!

The beasts sensed my farewell,
inhaling the parting and the pine needles.
And tears rolled down their bristles,
and they drank to Bruderschaft.

I came to, evidently, in immortality.
We carried our burden up a hill.
Legs lashed to a long pole,
his guts already tossed in a tin pail,
my host swung back and forth at the feast.

And along the road where we made our way
blood coagulated in little dustballs.

translated by F. D. Reeve

IV

Selected Prose

I AM FOURTEEN

"It's Pasternak on the telephone. For you!"

My dumbfounded parents stared at me. When I was still a schoolboy, without a word to anyone, I wrote to him and sent my poems. This first decisive action was to shape my life. And now he had responded and invited me to come see him at two o'clock on Sunday.

It was December. I arrived at the gray house on Lavrushinsky Alley, it goes without saying, an hour early. I waited, and then took the elevator up to the dark eighth-floor landing. There was still a minute to go before two. But they must have heard the elevator. The apartment door opened.

He stood in the doorway.

Everything swam before my eyes. The surprised, elongated dusky flame of his face looked out at me. A wax-yellow sweater clung to his sturdy torso. A breeze ruffled the hair on his forehead. His later choice of a burning candle for his self-portrait was not haphazard. He stood in the door's draft.

The dry, strong hand of a pianist.

I was astonished by the asceticism, the impoverished expanse of his unheated study. A square photo of Mayakovsky and a dagger on the wall. Müller's English-Russian dictionary — he was chained to his translations then. My school copybook cowered on the desk — probably prepared for the conversation. A wave of horror and adoration passed over me. But it was too late to flee.

He launched right into the middle of things.

His cheekbones quivered, like the triangular skeletons of wings, pressed tight before beating. I worshiped him. He had magnetism, strength, and a heavenly unworldliness. When he spoke he tugged his chin upward, as if he wanted to escape from his collar and his body.

I quickly felt comfortable with him. I observed him on the sly.

His short nose, starting from the depression above the bridge, rising to a hump, and then continuing straight, resembled a dark miniature rifle butt. The lips of a Sphinx. Short gray hair. But most important — that floating, smoking wave of magnetism. "He, who compared himself to a horse's eye."

Two hours later I left, carrying a pile of his manuscripts to read and, most precious, an emerald-green notebook of his new poems, held together by a crimson silk cord. Impatiently I opened it as I walked, gulping down the breathless lines:

All the Christmas trees in the world, all the childhood dreams.
The flicker of lighted candles, all the chains...

The poems contained the sensations of a schoolboy in prerevolutionary Moscow; childhood — the most serious of Pasternak's mysteries — cast its spell.

The flicker of lighted candles, all the chains...

The poems preserved the late crystal state of his soul. I came upon his autumn. Autumn is clear to the point of clairvoyance. And the land of his childhood came closer.

...All the apples, all the golden balls...

From that day on my life took on a magical meaning and a sense of destiny: his new poetry, telephone conversations, Sunday chats at his house from two to four, walks—years of happiness and childish adoration.

Why did he get in touch with me?

He was lonely in those years, tired from many troubles; he wanted sincerity, an honest relationship, he wanted to break out of the encirclement—but it was more than that. Perhaps this strange relationship with an adolescent, a schoolboy, this friendship that was not quite a friendship, explains something about him. It was not friendship between a lion and a dog, it was more like that of a lion and a puppy.

Perhaps what he liked in me was himself, who had run to Scriabin as a schoolboy.

He was drawn to his childhood. The call of childhood never died in him.

He did not like to be called—he did the telephoning. He would call several times during a week. And then there would be a painful silence. He never gave his Christian name and patronymic to my stunned family, only his last name.

He spoke passionately, recklessly. And then he would break off in mid-gallop. He never complained, no matter what clouds hung over him.

"The artist," he used to say, "is by nature optimistic. The very essence of creative activity is optimistic. Even when you write tragic works, you must write powerfully; despair and whining do not create works of strength." His speech flowed in an uninterrupted, breathless monologue. There was more music than grammar in it. His speech was not divided into sentences or the sentences into words— everything flowed in a stream of consciousness, a thought was uttered, only to return and enchant. His poetry had the same kind of flow.

When he moved to Peredelkino for good, the phone calls became rarer. He did not have a telephone at the dacha. He had to go to the watchman's office to call. The night was filled with the echo of his voice from the window, he addressed the stars. I lived from phone call to phone call. He often invited me to his dacha when he read his latest works.

His dacha resembled a wooden version of a Scottish tower. Like an old chess castle it stood in a row of other dachas on the edge of the enormous square Peredelkino field, lined with furrows. From the other side of the field, beyond the cemetery, like figures from a different chess set, the sixteenth-century church and bell tower shone, like a carved king and queen, painted toys, dwarf relatives of St. Basil's.

The line of dachas huddled together under the deadly aim of the cemetery cupolas. Only a few of the residents from those days are around now.

The readings took place in his semicircular bay-windowed study on the second floor.

People gathered. Chairs were brought up from downstairs. Usually there were about twenty guests. This time we were waiting for the Livanovs.

Through the wall of windows one could see the September woods. The trees were ablaze. A car raced toward the cemetery. A cobweb reached from the window. On the other side of the field, beyond the cemetery, the church peeked sideways as motley as a rooster, asking whom to peck. The air over the field shimmered. And the same agitated trembling was in the air of the study. It vibrated with anticipation.

In order to shorten the wait, D. N. Zhuravlyov, the great reciter of Chekhov and tone-setter of the Old Arbat elite, demonstrated how people used to sit at society receptions — backs arched and shoulder blades barely touching the chairs. That was his tactful way of reprimanding me! I could feel myself blush. But embarrassment and stubbornness made me slouch and rest on my elbows all the more.

At last the latecomers arrived. She — shy, nervously graceful — explained that they had had trouble finding flowers. He was an enormous man, who waved his arms about and rolled his eyes in mock horror: a star, shaker of the boards of the Moscow Art Theater, a Homeric portrayer of Nozdryov and Potemkin, and a hail-fellow-well-met.

We quieted down. Pasternak took his place at the table. He wore a light, silvery jacket, of a military cut now popular again. That time he read from *Dr. Zhivago*, and the poems — "White Night," "Nightingale," "Fairy Tale," his whole notebook of that period. "Hamlet" came at the end. As he read, he stared at something above our heads, visible to him alone. His face grew longer and thinner. And his jacket was a reflection of the white night.

> I see a distant time,
> The house on the Petersburg side,
> Daughter of a poor steppe landowner,
> You're taking courses, you're from Kursk.

The readings usually lasted about two hours. Sometimes, when he had to explain something to his listeners, he would address me, as if to explain: "Andryusha, here in 'Fairy Tale' I wanted to strike the emblem of emotion as if on a medal: the warrior-savior and the maiden on his saddle." That was our private game. I knew all those poems by heart, in them he had perfected his method of naming actions, objects, and states. Hoofbeats rang through the poems. He asked them in turn which poems they liked best. Most replied: "All of them." He expressed dismay at the evasiveness of the reply. Then they singled out "White Night." Livanov chose "Hamlet." The unperformed *Hamlet* was his tragedy, and he covered up the pain with buffoonery and swagger.

> The din subsides. I have come out on the stage,
> leaning on the doorframe. . . .

Livanov blew his nose. The swollen bags under his eyes seemed more prominent. But a minute later he was laughing again, because everyone was invited downstairs, to the table.

We went down. To the blue fireworks of the misty nudes that had come from the brush of his father, probably the only Russian Impressionist.

O, those Peredelkino mealtimes! Not enough chairs. Stools were dragged out. Pasternak sat at the head of the table, enjoying the festive Georgian ritual. He was a warm host. He embarrassed departing guests, personally helping each one with his coat.

Who were they, the poet's guests?

Squinting in the dry glow of his mind was the tiny, ever-so-quiet Genrikh Gustavovich Neigauz, Garrik, with his hair like unpolished granite. The distracted Richter, Slava, the youngest at the table, his eyes half-closed, taking in the colors and sounds. "I have a question for Slava! Slava! Tell me, does art exist?" Pasternak would ask, with a sob in his voice. Next to him sat the slender, sad Nina Dorliak, as graphic as black lace.

What is a table without a samovar?

The samovar at these gatherings was Livanov. Once he arrived wearing all his medals. He was as tall as Peter the Great. He was placed at the foot of the table, opposite the host. He made noise and shone. And had a capacity of several buckets.

"I knew Kachalov's Jim. You don't believe me?" He bubbled and boiled. "'Give me your paw, Jim'... Yesenin said. That dog was a mean black devil. Beelzebub! Everyone trembled. He would come in and lie down under the dining room table. No one at the table dared move a toe. Forget about patting the velvety fur. He'd bite your hand off in a wink. How's that for a trick? And he said: 'Give me your paw....' Let's drink to poetry, Boris!"

Next to him, diffidently and humbly, large-eyed Zhuravlyov sat in a brown suit like a June bug. There was Asmus, the critic, musing. Clumsily, bearlike, Vsevolod Ivanov would burst in, shouting: "I've given birth to a son for you, Boris!"

I remember classical Anna Akhmatova, most august of all in her poetry and her age. She was taciturn, in her loose tuniclike robe. Pasternak seated me next to her. And for the rest of my life I will remember her in half-profile.

Hikmet's entrance is sharply etched in my mind. The host proposed a toast in his honor, in honor of the revolutionary dawn over his shoulder. Nazim, responding, bewailed the fact that no one knew Turkish, for he represented not only a dawn but was also a poet and would read his poetry. He read boisterously. He had angina pectoris and breathed heavily. When he left, he stuffed newspapers—Russian and foreign, the dacha was full of them—inside his shirt to protect his chest. I saw him out. On the poet's chest rustled the events and the days of this world.

Pasternak's wife, Zinaida Nikolayevna, her lips pursed in an injured Cupid's bow, wearing a black velvet dress, her black hair bobbed, and looking like an Art Nouveau lady, worried that her son, Stasik Neigauz, had to play in the morning at the Paris Competition though his reflexes were better for evening performances.

Ruben Simonov with sensual bliss and imperiousness read Pushkin and Pasternak. Vertinsky flashed by. To roaring laughter, the marvelous Iraklii Andronikov imitated Marshak.

What a feast for the eye! What a feast for the spirit! Renaissance art, or, rather, the canvases of a Borovikovsky or a Bryullov came alive during these meals.

He generously set before my eyes the splendor of his fellow poets. He and I had an unspoken agreement. Sometimes through the intoxicated monologue of a toast I caught his mocking brown conspiratorial gaze, directed at me, expressing something only we two understood. He seemed to be the only person my age at the table. This secret common age united us. Often delight on his face was replaced by an expression of childish hurt or even stubbornness.

Sometimes he asked me to read my poems to the group. Plunging in as into cold water, in a bad voice, I read and read....

> Stunned, the clouds rest their elbows
> On the trolley bells.

Those were my first public readings.

Sometimes I was jealous of the others. Naturally, I cared much more about our conversations together, without guests, or rather his monologues, addressed not even to me but past me — to eternity, to the meaning of life.

Occasionally my hypersensitivity showed itself. I stood up to my idol. Once he called and said that he liked the type on my typewriter and asked me to retype a cycle of his poems. Naturally! But to my childish pride that seemed insulting — what did he think I was, just a typist! I stupidly refused, pleading an exam the next day, which was true, but not the reason.

Pasternak: the adolescent.

Some artists always seem to be the same age. For instance, Bunin and Nabokov have the clarity of early autumn; they are always forty. But Pasternak is an eternal adolescent, disobedient — "I was created by God to torture myself, my family, all those it is a sin to torture." Only once in his poetry, speaking in his own voice, does he give his age: "I am fourteen." Once and for all.

He was blinded by shyness among strangers, in a crowd, how he bent his neck, bull-like and tense!...

One night he took me to the Vakhtangov Theater for the premiere of *Romeo and Juliet* in his translation. I sat next to him, on his right. My left shoulder, cheek, and ear were numbed by the proximity, as if by anesthetic. I looked at the stage, but I saw him — his glowing profile and the hair falling on his forehead. Sometimes he mumbled the text along with the actors. Onstage dueling with Tybalt was a brilliant Romeo — Yuri Lyubimov, then the young star of the Vakhtangov, not yet thinking of his future theater or of the fact that he would stage *Hamlet* in Pasternak's translation as well as Pasternak's war poems.

Suddenly Lyubimov's sword broke and — O miracle! — its tip, describing a fairy-tale parabola, fell on the arm between our seats. I bent over and picked it up. Pasternak laughed. But soon there came the applause and the audience, meaning it seriously, chanted: "Author! Author!" The embarrassed poet was dragged out onstage.

Feasts were his relaxation. He worked like a galley slave. Two months a year he did translations, his tithe that let him spend the rest of the time working for himself. He translated up to 150 lines a day, saying that less than that was unproductive. He berated Tsvetayeva, who when she did translate, finished only twenty lines a day.

A master of language, he did not like rough speech or profanity. Only once did I hear even an oblique use of a swear word. When some petty puritans attacked a friend of his for publishing in an organ they did not like, Pasternak at the table told a story about the poet Fet. In a similar situation, Fet allegedly replied: "If Schmidt (I think that was the name of the worst hack in Petersburg at the time) put out a filthy leaflet with a four-letter word for the title, I'd publish in it anyway. Poetry purifies."

How cautious and chaste he was! Once he gave me a packet of new poems, which included "Autumn," with the golden stanza, Titian-esque in its purity, imagery, and feeling:

> You discard your dress
> The way a grove discards its leaves,
> When you fall into my embrace
> In a robe with a silk tassel.

(The first version was:

> Your unfastened dress,
> Like leaves discarded by a grove....)

The next morning he called to say: "Perhaps you found it too frank? Zina says that I should not have given it to you, she says that it's too daring...."

His support for me lay in the very fact of his existence, which gave off its radiance next to mine. It never occurred to me to ask him for anything practical—for help to get published or anything like that. I was convinced that you did not enter the world of poetry through connections. When I felt that the time had come to publish my poems, without saying a word to him, I made the rounds like everyone else; without phone calls to smooth the way, I experienced all the prepublication torments. Once my poems reached a member of the editorial board of the journal *Moscow*. He called me into his office. Asked me to sit down—such a friendly hulk. He looked at me lovingly.

"Are you the son?"

"Yes, but. . ."

"No buts. It's all right to mention it now. Don't hide it. He's been rehabilitated, after all. Mistakes were made. What a mind that was! They'll bring us some tea in a minute. And you, as the son. . ."

"Yes, but. . ."

"No buts. We're putting your poems in the next issue. We'll be understood correctly. You have a master's touch, you're particularly good with signs of our atomic age—for instance, you write 'caryatids.'. . . Congratulations."

(As I later realized, he had taken me for the son of N. A. Voznesensky, the former chairman of Gosplan.)

". . . What do you mean, you're not the son? What do you mean, you have the same name? What are you wasting my time for? Bringing in all sorts of garbage. We won't allow it. And I kept wondering—how could such a father. . . well, actually, not a father. . . What do you mean, how about the tea?"

But later I did manage to get published. I brought to Peredelkino the first copy of the *Literary Gazette*, still smelling of ink, with a selection of my poems.

The poet was ill. He was in bed. I remember the sorrowful autumnal silhouette of a woman bent over him, like Vrubel's majolica muse. The poet's dark head dug deep into the white pillow. He was given his glasses. How he glowed; how excited he became; how his face began to quiver! He read the poems aloud. Obviously he was happy for me. "That means that my affairs are not so bad, either," he suddenly said. He liked the poems that were freest in form. "You'll probably be sought out by Aseyev now," he joked.

Aseyev, impulsive Aseyev of the streamlined vertical face that looked like a lancet arch, as fanatical as a Catholic proselytizer, with thin, acid lips, the reformer of rhyme. I never met anyone who loved other people's poetry so selflessly. An artist, an instrument of taste, of smell, like a lean, nervous borzoi hound, he could smell a good line a mile away—he keenly appreciated Sosnora and Yuna Morits. He was respected by Mayakovsky and Mandelstam. Pasternak was his ardent love. I met him long after they had gone their different ways. How difficult are misunderstandings between artists! Aseyev always interrogated me besottedly and jealously—"How's 'your Pasternak' doing?" While Pasternak spoke of him with some distance—"Even Aseyev's last work is rather cold." Once I brought him a book by Aseyev, and he returned it unread.

Aseyev was a catalyst of the atmosphere, the bubbles in the champagne of poetry.

"You mean you are Andrei Andreyevich? Fantastic! We've all been doubles! Mayakovsky was Vladimir Vladimirovich, I'm Nikolai Nikolayevich, Burlyuk's David Davidovich, Kamensky's Vasili Vasilyevich, Kruchenykh's—"

"What about Boris Leonidovich?"

"The exception confirms the rule."

Aseyev invented a nickname for me—Vazhnoshchensky, which means something like "important little dog"—and wrote a poem for me: "Your guitar is a tzigane, Andryusha," and at a difficult time in my life saved me with his article "What Is to Be Done with Voznesensky?" directed against the critics' habit of mindreading. He chivalrously defended young sculptors and painters in the news-papers. In his panorama *Mayakovsky Begins*, in a big circle next to the names of Mayakovsky, Khlebnikov, and Pasternak he placed the name of Aleksei Kruchenykh.

Here my notes begin to smell of mice.

A pointed nose twitches and pokes into my manuscripts. Pasternak tried to protect me from meeting him. He appeared right after my first publication in a newspaper.

He was a junk dealer of literature.

The skin on his cheeks was granular and always covered with gray stubble, which grew in untended clumps, making him look like a poorly plucked chicken. He was short. He dressed in rags. He made Gogol's Plyushkin look like a fashion plate. His sharp nose was always sniffing something out — a manuscript or a photograph — on which he could make some money. He seemed to have existed forever — not a bubble of the earth, no, he was the mildew of time, the werewolf of communal apartment strife, vampire rustles, and cobwebbed corners. What you took for a layer of dust in the corner was him sitting there for the past hour.

He lived on Kirovskaya Street in a small storeroom. It smelled of mice. There was no light. The only window was piled to the ceiling with garbage — rubble, bales, unfinished cans of food, age-old dust — where, like a squirrel with its berries and mushrooms, he stored his treasures — rare books and manuscripts.

For instance, you could ask: "Aleksei Eliseyich, would you have the first edition of Tsvetayeva's *Versts*?" "Turn around," he'd bark. And in the dusty glass of the bookshelves, as if in a mirror, you saw him pull out the precious booklet from under a moth-eaten coat with the agility of a younger man. He charged next to nothing. Maybe he had already gone mad. He swiped books. His arrival anywhere was considered a bad sign.

To live longer, he used to go outside with his mouth full of warm tea and soaked bread. He said nothing until the tea grew cool, or he made noises as he leaped among the puddles. He bought up everything. To turn a profit one day. He pasted his acquisitions in albums and sold them to libraries. He even managed to sell my rough drafts, though I wasn't of museum age then. He was proud when he came across the word *zaumnik* in the dictionary.

In his day he had been the Rimbaud of Russian futurism. Creator of the *zaumny* language, author of "Dyr bul shchyl," he abruptly stopped writing, unable or unwilling to accommodate himself to the ensuing period of classicism. Rimbaud at the same age also abruptly dropped poetry and became a merchant. Kruchenykh had written these lines:

> Forgot to hang myself
> Healing
> America

He had an excellent education and could quote entire pages from Gogol, that fount of futurism.

He sold Khlebnikov's manuscripts. He carefully spread them out on the table first, smoothing them, like a pattern cutter. "How much?" he would ask in a businesslike way. "Thirty." And quickly, like a salesman with a bolt of cloth, he measured out and cut off a piece of manuscript—exactly thirty rubles' worth.

Like a mossy spirit, an insinuating vampire, he made his way quietly into your apartment. Grandmother pursed her lips suspiciously. He whined and begged and, if he deigned, suddenly gave you his "Spring with Refreshments." That work, its words with the *kh*, *shch*, and *yu* sounds so rare in Russian, "bore the mark of spring, when beauty rises out of ugliness."

But first, naturally, he refused, grumbled, pretended, snorted, the faker, rubbed his eyes with an antediluvian handkerchief that resembled the oily rags truck drivers use to wipe their engines.

But once his eyes were cleared, they turned out to be pearl gray, blue even! He tensed, hopped like Pushkin's cockerel, cupped his hand, taut as a cockscomb, to his lips, and began. His voice was high, with a pure unearthly tone, the kind soloists of rock groups now strive for in vain.

He finished, his hand still at his mouth, as if expecting an echo from his youth—erect, the gray-eyed prince once more, once more the bugle of Russian futurism—Aleksei Eliseyevich Kruchenykh.

He may have become a profiteer, petty thief, and speculator. But one thing he did not sell—his poetic voice. He simply stopped writing. Poetry befriended only his youth. And to that period alone he remained pure and honest.

Why do poets die?

Why did World War I begin? Because the archduke was bumped off? What if he hadn't been? What if he had overslept? There'd have been no war? Alas, nothing is random, there are processes called Time and History.

"A genius dies at his chosen time," said his teacher Scriabin, who died because he had picked at a pimple on his lip. Allegedly Stalin said about Pasternak: "Do not touch that holy fool."

Perhaps it is all a question of the biology of the spirit, which in Pasternak coincided with Time and was an indispensable part of it?...

I talked with him about "Blizzard." Do you remember how the line "In the suburb, where no one had stepped" keeps shifting, creating the total illusion of snow snakes, the movement of windblown snow? Behind it moves Time.

He said that working in form is a "stone soup." You forget about it.

But the "stone" is there and you must hack your way through it. You set yourself a problem and it leads on to something else, an energy that achieves not only formal but also spiritual and other goals.

Form is a wind screw, twisting the air, the universe, you can call it spirit, if you like. And the screw has to be strong and precise.

Pasternak has no bad poems. Well, perhaps a dozen that are less successful, but no bad ones. Which makes him so different from the poetasters who sometimes enter literature with one or two worthwhile works in their gray flood of mediocre poems. He was right: why write badly when you can write precisely, that is, well? And here it is not merely a question of the triumph of form, as if life, divinity, and content were not the form of a poem! "A book is a cubic chunk of smoking conscience," he once said. That is particularly noticeable in his *Selected Works*. Some readers are exhausted by the spiritual tension of each poem. It is hard to read, but think how hard it was to write it, to live it! Tsvetayeva gives one the same feeling, such was their pulse.

In his poetry, as in his life, strange combinations rhyme— everything is mixed together.

> Our apartment, like a fruit dish
> Was crammed with products from different spheres,
> A seamstress, a student, an administrator...

When I was a child our family of five lived in a single room. In the other five rooms of the apartment lived another six families—a family of workers who had come from the oil rigs, headed by the talkative Praskovya; the aristocratic, strapping Neklyudov family, consisting of seven people and a German shepherd called Baguira; the family of the engineer Ferapontov; a buxom and friendly daughter of a former merchant; and a divorced husband and wife. Our communal apartment was considered underpopulated.

Sheets hung to dry in the hallway.

By the wood-burning stove, amid the kitchen squabbles, the family heirloom earrings trembled in Musya Neklyudova's ears above the kerosene heater. In the toilet the divorced husband whistled the *Bayadère*, to the indignation of the waiting line. I was born in this world, I was happy, and did not imagine anything else.

Pasternak had himself lived in a communal apartment until 1936, until the duplex apartment in Lavrushinsky Alley. The bathroom had been occupied by a separate family, and at night, when you went to the toilet, you had to step over the sleeping figures.

All this was in his small emerald-green notebook with the red cord. Let's open that notebook. In it childhood wove its magic spell.

> All around it is still night.
> It is so early in the world.
>
> The square lies down like an eternity
> From the intersection to the corner,
> And until dawn and the warmth of day
> There remains a millennium.
>
> But in the city in a small
> Space, as if conferring,
> The trees stare naked
> Through the church railings. . . .

Do you see a boy with a schoolbag, watching the rites of spring, feeling spring coming on? Everything that is happening around him is so much like what is happening inside him.

> And there is horror in their eyes.
> Their anxiety is understandable.
> The gardens are coming out of their fences.
> They are going to bury God.

That early time, that stunned sensation of childhood, the recollection of the student of prerevolutionary Moscow, when everything is full of mystery, when a miracle awaits around every corner, when the trees are animate, and you are in communion with the magical golden boughs. What a sense of the childhood of humanity on the brink of paganism and the anticipation of still other truths!

These poems, written in longhand, he gave me with others, held together by that crimson silk cord. Everything about them was enchanted. At that time autumn reigned in him.

In those days I dreamed of studying at the Architectural Institute. I went to art classes, did watercolors, I was in thrall to the mysteries of painting. The Dresden collection was in Moscow then, exhibited at the Pushkin Museum. Volkhonka Street was jammed. The visitors' favorite was the Sistine *Madonna*.

I remember how dumbfounded I was standing in the crowd in front of those soaring contours. The dark background behind the figure consists of many blended angels, which the viewer does not notice right away. Hundreds of visitors' faces were reflected in the picture's dark glass. You could see the contours of the Madonna, and the cherubs' faces, and the attentive faces of the public overlaying them. The faces of the Muscovites entered the painting, filled it, melted into it, becoming part of the masterpiece.

The Madonna had never seen such crowds. She was strong competition for mass culture.

Moscow was shaken by the spiritual and artistic power of Rembrandt, Cranach, and Vermeer. *The Prodigal Son* and *The Last Supper* became part of everyday life. World art and the spiritual power of its concepts were opened up to hundreds of thousands of Muscovites.

Pasternak's poems from the notebook with its silk cord spoke about the same things, the same eternal themes—humanity, revelation, life, repentance, death, self-sacrifice.

All the thoughts of the ages, all the dreams, all the worlds.
All the future of galleries and museums. . . .

The same eternal questions had tormented Michelangelo, Vrubel, Matisse, and Nesterov, who used the metaphors of the Old and New Testaments for their canvases. Like theirs, his resolutions of the themes in poetry were not modernistic, as, say, Salvador Dali's are. The master worked with the stern brush of the realist, on a classically restrained scale. Like Breughel, whose Christmas vistas are populated with Dutch peasants, the poet filled his frescoes with the life and objects around him.

How Russian, even Muscovite, is his Magdalene, washing the feet of the body she loved with water from a bucket!

I have always pictured his Magdalene as a reddish-blonde with straight hair falling to her elbows. I knew her well. She lived in Chistye Prudy, and I often saw her with Boris Leonidovich.

What a prophetic connoisseur of the feminine heart wrote these lines:

Thou hast flung thine arms to the ends of the crossbeam
To embrace too many.

What agony is in that metaphor! What ecstatic sadness, what pain of parting, what understanding of the human failure to grasp a universal gesture, what pride in the high calling of the beloved and, at the same time, the unconscious expression of the feminine jealousy felt toward one who gives himself to humanity and not just to her, to her alone.

The artist depicts life, depicts the people around him, his family and friends, only through them understanding the meaning of the universe. His sanguine, his bloodred crayon, the material for this depiction, is his own life, his unique existence, his experience and actions—he has no other material.

Of all Pasternak's traits, sources, and mysteries, childhood is the most significant.

Both *My Sister Life* and *Nineteen Five* are first of all a celebration of the heedless primacy of feeling, the confession of childhood, rebellion, the sensing of the world for the first time. In Lermontov, to whom he dedicated his best book, he loved the child who escapes from the supervision of adults.

It is appropriate to speak of the poetic flow of his life. In it, in that poetic flow, what was said once is repeated more than once, taking on a rebirth, his childhood echoes over and over, and through the stern frescoes appear citations from his earlier poems.

I remember a New Year's party in his apartment on Lavrushinsky Alley. Pasternak was glowing. He was Christmas tree and child at the same time. Neigauz' brows met in a coniferous triangle. The elder son, Zhenya, still with military bearing, came, as if mirrored, from the portrait done by his mother, Yevgeniya Pasternak.

The apartment had an exit onto the roof, to the stars. It was a time when he had much to fear; the dagger on the wall was not only for decoration, but also for self-defense, even self-destruction.

He did not acknowledge his birthdays. He considered them days of mourning. He did not permit congratulations. I managed to bring him flowers the day before or the day after—on the ninth or eleventh—without violating the letter of the law. I wanted to offer him some consolation.

I used to give him white and red cyclamens, and sometimes lavender columns of hyacinths. They quivered like lavender crystal goblets etched with *X*'s. When I was at the Institute, I could afford a potted lilac. How happy he was, how Pasternak glowed when he undid the paper and saw the white clusters of the bush. He adored lilacs and forgave me my annual subterfuge.

But then imagine the horror of my parents when, in imitation, I rejected my birthday celebration and the presents, announcing that I considered it a day of mourning for my failed life.

More than once in Pasternak's mature period he turned to the image of the fig tree. There is a sketch he dedicated to Lilya Kharazova, who died of typhus in the twenties. It is part of the collection of the Georgian critic G. Margvelashvili.

"Mediocrity usually implies average, ordinary people. Nevertheless, being ordinary is a living quality that comes from within and in many ways, strange as it may seem, is remotely similar to being gifted. Brilliant people are the most ordinary.... And even more ordinary, breathtakingly ordinary, is nature itself. The only thing that is extraordinary is mediocrity, that is, that category of so-called interesting people. Since antiquity they have shunned work and have lived off genius, seeing it as something *flatteringly exceptional*, whereas in fact genius is extremely and impetuously *ordinary*, heightened only by its unlimited nature." He later repeated this in his speech at the plenum of the board of the Writers' Union in Minsk in 1936.

Did you hear? "Nature is breathtakingly ordinary." He was so ordinary in his life, with that true nightingale-like intelligence as opposed to the sterility, the noncreative merchant-class pretentiousness—he dressed modestly and lived modestly, unnoticed, like a nightingale.

Vulgar people do not understand the life and actions of a poet, for they perceive and explain them in a base and often self-serving way. They impose categories they understand—the desire to become more famous, to get rich, to play a dirty trick on a colleague. Whereas in truth the only thing a poet worries about and begs fate to spare him is losing the ability to write, that is, to feel, the ability to harmonize with the music of the universe. No one can grant it and no one can take it away.

That ability is necessary to the poet not as a source of success or wealth or as a way of moving pen across paper, but as his only tie to the universe, to the world spirit, as it would have been put earlier, the only signal up to it and down from it, an objective sign that his life, its earthly segment, is going correctly.

The path is not always clear to the poet himself. He obeys higher call signs, which determine his route, as they do for the pilot of a plane. I am not trying to explicate anything of the poet's path: I'm simply writing what I saw and how I read what he wrote.

> Part of the pond was hidden by the alder crowns
> But part was visible from here
> Through the nests of rooks and tops of trees.
> As we walked along the millpond...

Well, here's the millpond. We've arrived. And the pond's edge. And the felled fir tree... This is all part of the biography of his wonder working.

You could write a dissertation on rook nests in his work. That is the mark of the master. "Where like charred pears a thousand rooks on the branches..." is from "Beginnings." And how about the graphic brilliance of the war years:

> And the rook nines fly by,
> The black nines of clubs.

And now his beloved rooks of the thickets of broom near Moscow have flown up and over to the brown-black crowns of a classical landscape. And they have woven their Peredelkino nests there.

Did he help me find my voice?

He simply told me what he liked and why. For instance, he spent a long time explaining the meaning of my line: "The epaulets' big hands gripped you by the shoulders." Besides precision of imagery, he wanted poetry to breathe, to have tension, and the added ingredient that he called "force." For a long time none of his contemporaries existed for me. Any sort of gradations among them seemed ridiculous. There was Pasternak—and all the rest.

He himself esteemed Zabolotsky. As a member of the board of the Writers' Union, he saved "Land of Muravia" from severe criticism. He considered Tvardovsky an important poet, thereby ridding me of my schoolboy nihilism.

It was hard to escape his force field.

One fall after college military camp I brought him a notebook of my new poems. He was preparing his *Selected Works* then. He was rewriting poems, turning against his early looser style, selecting only those poems that suited him now.

About my poems he said: "There is facility and imagery here, but they are within acceptable limits. If they were mine, I would include them in my collection."

I beamed.

Pasternak himself would have taken them! But by the time I got home I decided to stop writing. For he would have put them in his collection, and that meant they were his, not mine. I did not write for two years. Then came "Goya" and other poems that were truly mine. "Goya" was severely criticized; there were several articles attacking it. The mildest epithet used was "formalism."

For me "Goya" meant "war."

We had been evacuated to the Urals.

The man who took us in, Konstantin Kharitonovich, a retired locomotive engineer, a dry, quick man who grew shy when he drank, had run off with his brother's wife, the immense Siberian Anna Ivanovna. That was why they lived in the boondocks, never legalizing their union, in fear of the wrathful avenger.

Things were tough. Everything we had brought with us we traded for food. Father was in the siege of Leningrad. They said he had been wounded. Mother used to come home from work and weep. And suddenly Father returned—terribly thin, unshaven, in a black field shirt with a canvas rucksack.

The landlord, solemn and shyer than usual, brought on a tray two pieces of black bread with small white squares of bacon and two glasses of vodka—to toast the "happy survival." Father knocked back the vodka, wiped his mouth with his hand, thanked the landlord, and gave us the bacon.

Then we went to see what he had in his pack. There was a dull yellow can of American pork and beans and a book by a painter named Goya.

I did not know anything about that painter. But in the book partisans were shot, hanged bodies swayed, war grimaced. The black cardboard loudspeaker in the kitchen talked about that every day. Father had flown over the front line with that book. It all rolled up into one horrible name—Goya.

Goya—that was the whistle of the evacuation trains in the great resettlement of the nation. Goya—the moan of the sirens and bombs

before we left Moscow, Goya—the howling of the wolves outside
the village, Goya—the keening of the neighbor when she received a
death notice, Goya...

That music of memory was recorded in poetry, the first poem that
was *mine*.

Because of a broken leg, Pasternak did not fight in the war. But he
traveled to the front as a volunteer and was shaken by the people's
spirit in those years. He wanted to write a play about Zoya
Kosmodemyanskaya, about a schoolgirl, about the nature of war.

> And since my early childhood years
> I have been wounded by woman's lot...

His attitude toward women was both manly and adolescent. He had
the same attitude toward Georgia.

He had gathered material for a novel about Georgia with a heroine
named Nina, from the early Christian period, when the worship of the
moon-god organically evolved into the rites of the new culture.

How sensuous and natural are the Georgian rites! According to
legend, Saint Nina made the first cross by overlapping two shoots of
grapevine and cutting her long hair to bind them together.

In Pasternak himself the pantheistic culture of the early period was
transformed into the severe spirituality of the later culture. As in life,
the two cultures coexisted in him.

Several times, realizing its importance, I tried to keep a journal.
But with my disorganization, each attempt was short-lived. I cannot
forgive myself to this day. The few brief notes I did take disappeared
in the jumble of constant moves. Recently my family, going through
the masses of my papers, found a notebook with a diary of several
days.

In order to convey to some degree the excitement of his voice, the
flow of his lively daily speech, let me quote at random from his
monologues, which I wrote down in my youthful diary, correcting
nothing, merely omitting purely personal details.

Here he is talking on August 18, 1953, on a bench in the little
square near the Tretyakov Gallery. I had just come back from summer
work, and he read me "White Night," "August," "Fairy Tale"—all
the poems in that cycle—for the first time.

"Have you been waiting long? — I came from the other side of town — no taxis — a 'pickup-chik' gave me a ride — I'll tell you about myself — you know I'm out in Peredelkino early — early spring is stormy and strange — the trees don't have leaves yet but they're blooming — the nightingales have begun — it seems banal — but I wanted to tell about it in my own way somehow — and here are a few sketches — of course all this is too dry — as if written with a hard pencil — but then it will have to be rewritten — and Goethe — there were a couple of sclerotic passages I couldn't understand in *Faust* — the blood flows and flows and then hardens — a clot — *kh-kh* — and breaks off — there are eight such places in *Faust* — and suddenly in the summer it all opened up — in a single flow — the way *My Sister Life*, *Second Birth*, and *Safe Conduct* once did — I got up at night — the sensation of strength — even a healthy man would never believe that it's possible to work like that — the poetry came — of course Marina Kazimirovna says that one mustn't after a heart attack — while others say that it's like medicine — well, don't worry — I'll read to you — listen —"

And here's a phone call a week later:

"I had a thought — maybe Pasternak sounds better in translation — what is second rate is destroyed in the translation — *My Sister Life* is a primal scream — as if the roof had been torn off — the stones began to speak — things took on symbolic value — back then not everyone understood the essence of those poems — now things are called by their real names — so, about translations — earlier when I wrote and I had complex rhymes and rhythms — the translations did not work — they were bad — in translation the force of form is not necessary — lightness is — to carry the meaning — the content — why was Kholodkovsky's translation considered weak — because people were used to seeing poor works, both translated and original ones, in that form — my translation is more natural — what a magnificent edition they did of *Faust*! — usually books shout I'm glue! — I'm paper! — I'm thread! — but here it's all ideal — Goncharov's marvelous illustrations — I'll give it to you — the inscription is all prepared — how's your project? — I got a letter from Zavadsky — he wants to stage *Faust* —

"Now tell the truth — is 'Parting' worse than the others? — no? — I deserve your kind words but be direct — but it's the same thing in 'Spektorsky' — it was the same revolution — here's Stasik — he's come with his wife — he's got insomnia and something wrong with his digestion — doesn't 'Fairy Tale' remind you of Chukovsky's 'Crocodile'? —

"I want to write poetry about Russian provincial cities — sort of a persistent refrain of 'city' and 'ballad' — the light from windows on the snow — getting up and so on — rhymes like *'de la rue'* – 'October view' — it'll be very good — I'm writing a lot now — done the whole rough draft — I'll polish later — because at the height of inspiration — getting excited about the beauties of finished sections —"

As far as I know, those poems were never written.

Often in choosing a variant he relied on chance, on random advice. He liked to use Chopin as an example, who when bewildered by an array of variants, would play them for his cook and keep the one she liked. He appealed to chance.

One of his acquaintances was bothered by the double metaphor in the verse:

> And as rafts float down a river...
> Like a caravan of barges for me to judge,
> The centuries come swimming out of darkness.

He changed it to: "The centuries come tirelessly swimming out of darkness."

I asked him to keep the original. Apparently, he preferred it also — he reinstated the line. It was impossible to get him to do anything against his will.

He wrote the poem "Wedding" at Peredelkino. Upstairs in his tower he heard the patter of a *chastushka*, sung in the watchman's lodge. He brought elements from an urban landscape into the poem.

The next day he called me. "So, I explained to Anna Andreyevna [Akhmatova] how poetry is conceived. I was awakened by a wedding celebration. I knew that it was something good, and mentally I joined in, and in the morning, it really was a wedding" (I'm quoting from my diary). He asked what I thought of the poem. It had the splash and freshness of a blue-gray morning and a youthful rhythm. But I, a student in the fifties, found alien and archaic such traditional and old-fashioned words as "matchmaker" and "groomsmen"; "best man" sounded like "busman." Probably I merely confirmed his own doubts. He dictated another version over the telephone. "Now, about your calling it old-fashioned. Write this down. No, wait, we'll get rid of the matchmaker too. And it'll be even better about the groomsmen, because the place will be shown more concretely: 'Crossing the back of the courtyard...'"

Maybe he was improvising on the telephone, maybe he was recalling another draft. This is the version that was published. I remember that the editor was worried by the line: "Life after all is only an instant...only a dream...." Today that seems incredible.

At our first meeting he gave me a ticket to the VTO (the All-Union Theater Organization), where he was going to read his translation of *Faust*. That was his last public reading.

At first he stood in a group, surrounded by dark suits and dresses, his gray one showing through, like an embarrassed glimmer of northern sky through tree trunks. He was given away by his glow.

Then he hurried to the table. Pasternak read sitting down, wearing his glasses. The golden curls of his fans stopped their rapturous bounce. Someone was taking notes. Someone else called out a request for "Witches' Kitchen," which included authentic incantations in the translation. In the archives of Weimar, you can see how Goethe, thinker and freemason, studied works on the cabala, alchemy, and black magic.

Pasternak refused to read "Kitchen." He read only poignant passages. As he read, his face took on more and more the look of his early period. Strength, inspiration, determination, and the will of a master who had driven himself to a new life, which had even brought down Mephistopheles—or what was his name?—"the tsar of darkness, Woland, master of time, lord of mice, flies, and toads."

> And I am shackled by a fantastic force
> To the images that engulfed me from without
> The Aeolian harp has wept
> The beginning of the stanzas born in blackness.

He was also reading about himself, that was why *Faust* had captivated him—he did not translate it only for the money or for fame: he sought the key to this time, to his age, he was writing about himself, he was breaking through to himself, and Marguerite was his, he was tortured by it, he wanted to renew time, the most important part began "when he was Faust."

I think that if he had been offered Faust's choice, he would have begun again not at age twenty, but at fourteen. But then, he never stopped being fourteen.

"That's all," he said, awakening from the spell and putting away the manuscript. There was no discussion. He spread his hands with a helpless look, as if in self-justification, because he was already being dragged off somewhere, downstairs, probably to the club restaurant. The elevator door slammed shut over the light strip of sky.

A few years later, when the complete translation of *Faust* was published, he gave me that heavy cherry-colored volume. He inscribed books without hurrying, with thought, usually on the day after he had presented them. You died of anticipation overnight. And what a generous New Year's gift awaited you the next day, what understanding of another heart, what an advance on your life, on your growth. In January 1947, exactly ten years before giving me the *Faust*, he had given me his first book.

In his last years he was often ill.

I visited him in Botkinskaya Hospital. I brought him *The Forsyte Saga* to read. He read it diligently and joked as he returned it, "In the time it takes to read it, you could write your own book...."

He wrote to me from the hospital: "These cruel illnesses have become too frequent. This one coincided with your entrance into literature, sudden, headlong, stormy. I am terribly glad that I have lived to see it. I have always liked your way of seeing, thinking, expressing yourself. But I did not expect it to be heard and acknowledged so soon. All the more reason for me to be pleased by this unexpected triumph....It is all so dear to me...."

At the same time, while hospitalized, he gave me his photograph: "To Andryusha Voznesensky in the days of my illness and his wild success, the joy of which did not keep me from my suffering...."

What shame engulfed me for my healthy heart, my legs, my skis, my youth, and the horror of being unable to pass it on to another life, the one dearest to me!

> Artists — go off
> without hats, as if into a church,

into the resounding lands
to the birches and the oaks.

I had known him for fourteen years.

How many times his words had uplifted and saved me, and what bitterness and pain lay behind those words.

His late poetry displays a more painterly manner, it smells of paint — ocher, sepia, white lead, sanguine — he is drawn to the odors that had once surrounded him in his father's studio, drawn to the place where

> I am fourteen years old.
> Vkhutemas
> Is still the School of Fine Arts
> In the wing with the workers' faculty
> Upstairs
> Is father's studio....

He mounted his father's works and hung them on the walls of his house, particularly the illustrations of *Resurrection*, and those of Katyusha and Nekhlyudov — he valued so much the idea of starting a new life. He seemed to want to return to childhood, to start afresh, he had decided to rewrite the collection *My Sister Life*, he said that he remembered exactly the feelings that gave rise to each poem, he redid several times works that were thirty years old, he wasn't rewriting his poems, he was trying to redo his life. He never separated poetry from life.

He approved of my decision to enter the Architectural Institute, since he did not think very highly of the literary world. The Architectural Institute was right where the Vkhutemas once stood, and our studio, which later burned down, was located in the wing where the workers' faculty had been, beneath his father's studio....

I told him about the Institute. We were all stunned by the Impressionists and the new painting, which was now displayed after a hiatus of many years in the Pushkin Museum. This coincided with his feelings about the exhibit of the Shchukinsky collection when he was a student. The idol of our youth was Picasso. Little did I know that ten years later I would be reading my poems to Picasso, that I would be in his studio or that there would be a prophecy in his canvases of a crazed bald sphere and the black triangle of elbows raised over it. . . .

"How is your project?" That is Pasternak's question written down in my diary. Asking about my daily life, he carried himself back, to the beginning of everything.

Harking back to his musical compositions as a child, as if recalling what Scriabin had said to him on the dangers of improvisation, he returned to his early "Improvisation."

He grew younger when he spoke of Severyanin. He told me how when he was young, he and Bobrov, I think, went to Severyanin to ask for his autograph. They were asked to wait in his room. A book lay face down on the couch. What was the master reading? They took the risk and turned it over. It was an etiquette book.

Many years later the manager of Caesar's Palace in Las Vegas, a strapping émigré from Estonia who had known Severyanin well, would show me a notebook of his poetry, written in faded violet script, with faltering pressure, so incongruously quivering in an age of ballpoint pens.

> How beautiful, how fresh will be the roses
> My country will throw into my grave!

The blurred, jerked letter *H*, wedged between the pages, had faded and resembled a translucently purple cruciform lilac blossom, pressed there, alas, not the lucky five-petaled one. . . .

The recently published small volume of Severyanin is not very successful. It mixes blatant bad taste with the colorful character and lyricism of the poet, whose work had found a musical echo even in the early Mayakovsky and Pasternak, not to mention Bagritsky and Selvinsky.

In his late period Pasternak worked for purity of style.

He rewrote "Improvisation," now calling it "Improvisation on the Piano." He made it powerful in a new way. And more severe. But it lacked something. Perhaps the artist should not have property rights to the things he creates. What if Michelangelo had kept fussing with his *David* as his taste matured?

Artists often recoil from what they have created, considering their past sinful and mistaken. That speaks of their spiritual strength, but it in no way abrogates their creations. That happened with Tolstoy. Such was the asceticism of the late-period Zabolotsky. Age thirsts for a second birth. In 1889, upon receiving an invitation to participate in an exhibition called "One Hundred Years of French Representational Art," Renoir replied: "I will explain one simple thing to you; everything that I have done up to now I consider bad, and it would be extremely unpleasant for me to see it all exhibited." What he found "bad" included the green-pink *Sa Marie*, and Anna's pearly back, and *The Swing*, that is, all of Renoir—luckily he could no longer destroy them, or repaint them in an Ingres manner or a new reddish-brown style.

Pasternak tried to vanquish the past Pasternak.

I feel irrevocably sad about lines that are lost, just as I do, perhaps stupidly, about certain crooked alleys that have vanished from the Old Arbat. In his work in general, there is much of Moscow with its streets, boulevards, houses, which are always being rebuilt, re-fashioned, always covered by scaffolding.

Pasternak is a very Muscovite poet. In him are the jumble of back streets, the connecting courtyards of Zamoskvorechie and Chistye Prudy, the Vorobyev Hills, the language, the life-style, the transoms, the city lindens, that Moscow way of walking—"as always, coat open and muffler on the chest."

Moscow seems to be drawn freehand, its lines alive, full of slang, a free mixture of styles, Empire alongside Ropet's modern and the archaisms of constructivism (eight hundred years old and still adolescent!), and houses don't seem to be built, but entire sections simply spring up like trees or shrubs.

In contrast to Petersburg, that Palmyra of the North, which is miraculously formed with ruler and compass, with its constant geometry and classicism, Moscow, in its culture and its way of life, is more elemental, broader in scope, coming from a Byzantine ornamentalism and close to the living elemental force of language.

Andrei Bely was his master—a Muscovite in spirit and in artistic thought. He highly prized the collection *Ashes*. He once told me how sorry he was that he had missed meeting Blok, who had lived in Petrograd. However, dividing poets into Petersburg and Moscow groups is somewhat artificial; for instance, Blok's "The Twelve" clearly has "Muscovite" touches. Pasternak's childlike yearning for Blok was evident in his description of him. Pasternak compared him to a Christmas tree glowing through the icy patterns on a window. You can just see a boy staring at the tree from the street through the frosty window.

He and I were walking from the House of Scientists along Lebyazhi across the bridge to Lavrushinsky Alley. Ice was breaking up. He talked the whole way about Tolstoy, about leaving, about Chekhov's depiction of boys, about chance and predestination in life. His fur coat was open, his gray karakul hat was tilted to one side — no, my mistake, it was his father's that was gray, his was black — and he walked along with the light flying stride of an experienced walker, as open and breezy as March in his poem, like all of Moscow around us. The weakness of the melting snow was in the air, the anticipation of change.

Passersby turned to look, thinking he was drunk.

"You have to lose things," he said. "You have to lose so that there is a vacuum in your life. I've only saved a third of what I've done. The rest perished in my moving about. You mustn't regret anything. . . ." I reminded him that in Blok's notes there is a passage about the necessity of loss. It is when the poet speaks of his library that burned down in Shakhmatovo during the revolution. "Really?" he asked in astonishment. "I had no idea. That means I'm doubly right."

We took the connecting courtyards.

Near the entrances crones, cats, and thieves dozed in the sun. They stretched and yawned after a hard night's work. Their foggy, contented gazes followed us.

Ah, those postwar courtyards in the Zamoskvorechie district! If I were asked: "Who brought you up besides your family?" I would reply: "The courtyard and Pasternak."

The Fourth Shchipovsky Alley! O world of twilight, trolley running boards and coupling buffers, games of *zhostochka*, June bugs — such creatures still lived in the world of those days. The rattle of tin cans, which we used for footballs, blended with the screech of "Rio Rita" coming from the windows along with the worn, slippery "Murka," sung by the banned émigré Leshchenko on a bootleg recording done on an old X-ray plate.

The courtyard was a cauldron, a club, a commune, a courtroom, hungry and just. We were the courtyard's small fry, the keepers of its secrets, laws, and its great folklore. We knew everything. Shnobel stood by the entrance. He had that day heroically parboiled his hand with boiling water to get sick leave for a week. This superman merely gritted his teeth, surrounded by admirers, and urinated on the swollen, purple hand. The new yellow boots worn by D.'s gang made it easy to guess who had robbed the store on Mytnaya.

Something or other was always exploding in our courtyard. After the war there were lots of guns, grenades, bullets. We gathered them like the mushrooms collected in the forests near Moscow. In the entrances, the older boys practiced shooting through the linings of their coats.

Where are you now, idols of our courtyard—Fiksa, Volodya, Shka, the carefree knights of the order of the short-peaked cap? Alas...

Sometimes Andrei Tarkovsky, my classmate, came through our courtyard. We knew that he was the son of a writer, but we did not know that he was the son of a marvelous poet and the son of the future father of a famous film director. Their family was poor. He managed somewhere to get his hands on an orange jacket with sleeves that were too short and a broad-rimmed green hat. He was the first fashion rebel (*stilyaga*) in our courtyard and the only spot of color on the drab gray palette of those days.

The elevators didn't work. Our main activity as boys was to open the shaft and slide down from the sixth floor along the steel cable, first wrapping our hands in a rag or old mitten. By holding tight or letting go slightly, we could regulate our speed. The cable was full of steel splinters. By the time we reached the bottom the mitten would be worn through, smoking and melting from the friction. No one ever got hurt.

We had a game called *zhostochka*.

A copper coin was wrapped in a rag, tied with string on top, leaving a protruding collar of cloth—the way a chocolate truffle is wrapped in tissue paper. The *zhostochka* was kicked with the inside of the foot. It landed, filthy weight down. The courtyard champion managed to kick it 160 times without missing. He was bandy-legged and pigeon-toed. We envied him.

O unforgettable *zhostochkas*—the truffles of the wartime era!

The ultimate status symbol among the older boys was a *fiksa*, a gold crown worn over a healthy tooth, and among the even tougher crowd, pearls implanted under the skin of the penis. We small fry settled for homemade tattoos made with pen and ink.

Being taken down to the militia station house for hitching rides on trolley running boards was an everyday event. Our parents were away at work all day. Our clubhouse was the attic and the roof. You could see all of Moscow from there, both good places from which to throw cartridges with nails tied to the detonator caps. When they hit the sidewalk, they exploded. It was up there that my older friend Zhirik brought me my first green volume of Pasternak.

Pasternak listened to my tales of these courtyard adventures with a delighted conspiratorial gleam. He thirsted for life in all its manifestations.

Today the courtyard has changed completely. The communality is gone, and neighbors often do not know one another's names. On a recent visit, I did not recognize Shchipovsky Alley. Our sacred spots — the fence and the garbage dump — were gone. On the bench a group with a guitar was picking out a tune. Could it have been Pasternak's "Candle" burning on the table?

Once, writing in the journal *Foreign Literature* about Pasternak's translations and the unity of cultures, I quoted in full his poem "Hamlet," perhaps the best of his late works. (This was how it first saw print.)

Recently the Tbilisi Museum of Friendship Among Peoples acquired Pasternak's archives. With what excitement, as if meeting an old friend, I found the original draft of "Hamlet," which I had memorized from the emerald-green notebook. In the same archives under an early number I found my schoolboy letter to Pasternak. In some lines of his "Hamlet" there is already a hint of the distant rumble, a presentiment of his fate.

Here I am entire. I have come out onstage,
Leaning against the doorframe.
I try to catch in the distant echo
All that will happen in my time.
That is the sound of the acts being performed in the distance.
I play a part in all five.
I am alone. Everything is drowning in hypocrisy.
To live one's life is not like crossing a field.

The field to be crossed was near where he took his Peredelkino walks.

At a time set aside for poetry and meditation, dressed like a local handyman or railway worker in a gray cap and a dark-blue waterproof gabardine raincoat with the black-and-white-checked lining so popular at the time, and in muddy weather with his trousers tucked into his boots, he would come out of his gate and turn left, past the field, down to the spring, sometimes crossing to the other bank.

At his approach the golden maples near the Afinogenovs' dacha straightened and grew still. They were originally brought over as seedlings from across the ocean and planted along the *allée* by Jenny Afinogenova, who, they say, was a circus star born in San Francisco. Later the trees trembled with the tongues of flame of the ship's fire in which their mistress had perished.

The sensuous field of the brook and the silver willows, the forest thoughts set the tone of his lines. From the other side of the field three pines on the hillside watched his free stride. Through the branches the painted church blazed like a stamped gingerbread cookie. It seemed suspended from a branch like a golden tree ornament. Here the Patriarch of the Russian Orthodox Church had his dacha. Sometimes the mail carrier, misreading "Patriarch" for "Pasternak," brought letters addressed to His Eminence to the poet. Her mistake amused Pasternak and he beamed like a child.

He was buried on June 2.

I remember the feeling of terrible emptiness that engulfed his dacha, filled to overflowing with people. Richter had just finished playing.

Everything swam before my eyes. Life had lost its meaning. I remember only fragments. They say that Paustovsky was there, but I'm writing only of the little that I saw.

He was carried by pallbearers (they had refused to use the hearse), carried from the house, the haven of his life, circling the famous field he loved, carried to the hillside with the three pines, at which he used to stare.

The road was uphill. It was windy. Clouds flew past. Against the background of that unbearably blue sky and white scudding clouds was etched his profile, clothed in bronze, already alien and sunken. He trembled slightly from the unevenness of the road.

The unneeded hearse moved slowly ahead of him. Back down the hill was the grieving nonliterary crowd — locals and out-of-towners, witnesses and neighbors of his days, sobbing students, the heroines of his poems. His features surfaced desperately on the face of his eldest son, Zhenya. Asmus was frozen with grief. Cameras clicked. The trees came out from behind their fences, the melancholy dirt road, which he had taken so often to the station, bitterly threw up dust.

Someone stepped on a red peony, fallen by the roadside.

I did not return to the dacha. He was not there. He was not anywhere anymore.

I remember waiting for him on the other side of the Peredelkino pond by the long wooden bridge, which he had to cross. Usually he came here around six o'clock. You could set your watch by him.

It was a golden autumn. The sun was setting, illuminating the pond, bridge, and shoreline with oblique rays through the woods. The edge of the pond was hidden by the top of an alder.

He came around the turn and moved closer without walking, somehow soaring over the pond. I realized only later what had happened. The poet was dressed in his dark-blue raincoat. Below the coat were pale-beige trousers and light-colored canvas shoes. The freshly cut planks were of the same shade. The poet's legs blended into the boards. Their movement was invisible.

The figure in the raincoat soared without touching the ground and moved toward the shore over the water. There was a childlike smile of puzzlement and delight on his face.

O

Once in the middle of a sultry, stormy day, I had forgotten to shut the hinged windowpane and a black hole flew into my room.

All I remember is the window ballooning out. My pathetic room was the least enviable in the writers' colony. Its cheap ceiling puffed, cracking, as if a huge juicy watermelon were being stuffed into a cardboard box designed for a small transistor radio.

In the middle of the room sat the black hole.

It was spherical, and its dented top pushed through the ceiling, cracking the plaster.

Why could Mayakovsky drink tea with the sun and I not have dinner with a black hole?

Horrified, I cringed in the corner. The atmosphere was oppressive. There was a hot chill in the air. The glass fronts of my paintings on the opposite wall were pulled out of shape, and now resembled bell jars. The plywood veneer of the wardrobe arched like a full sail.

"I am your lost civilization," the black hole said.

Lost already? Really?

What happened to everyone? What happened to my mother? To you? To Natasha? What about my friends? What happened to me? When? Why?

Had we overestimated or underestimated technology? Had we overestimated or underestimated freedom? Or did you destroy yourself?

Fool, you're a liar! See how the June daisies have reached the windowsill. On TV soars the ball of the soccer championships — the world can't miss the finals. I finally got two tickets on a cruise, and there's no way the machinations of world reactionaries or otherworldly powers can wrest them from me!

"I'm not destruction, I'm opportunity."

"Then what the hell are you doing here, you cast-iron eyesore? Go to the kitchen and fry up some potatoes! Why are you bugging me?" I shouted, growing brave with horror. "You've made my only wardrobe buckle. Go back where you came from. A cooper in Hamburg makes moons. Moore makes holes outside London. Get!"

I offered it a Marlboro.

"Thank you. I don't smoke," it said.

Twenty years into this century, your sun, ignoring you, dropped by to see a poet. Why then have you come here today, twenty years before the century's end?

It did not have eyes. It was a gloomy clump of limitless gaze.

"I'm lonely," it said.

It moved in with me.

To maintain that it "said" something would be inaccurate. It could not speak, having no voice. It transmitted thoughts.

Of course, sometimes it emitted a strange sigh that remotely resembled the Russian *O* — sorrowful delight, and regret, and a moan. I called it "O." All I had to do was mentally say "O," and there it was.

Now I think: what had attracted it to my window? My loneliness? I hadn't had a word from you all day. Or was it the pages of this manuscript lying on my desk?

On what was I writing that day?

On the holes of fates? Or again on the architecture I had abandoned? On the five geniuses of the passing age? On the black ring?

Memory, a round-the-clock half-witted telephone operator, plugs in random voices. The holes in the dial spin.

I hear the voice of the informed critic who reads nothing but my chapter headings: "How can a letter, even one like *O*, become a subject? The author himself admits that he is a zero. Heh-heh. That's the title of his opus — 'Andrei Voznesensky — O.'"

Or was I writing on the gaze of Eternity, fixed on us from the frescoes of Rublev, El Greco, and Vrubel? Or on life, which is and was at the same time?

"On the line — long-distance!"

He is sitting on a stool, small glasses perched on his pointed nose, moving his weathered, faded bushy eyebrows, the great English sculptor, looking like a peasant-forester, purring with pleasure, he sits and makes his "Moories," you and me, tiny plaster figures.

I sit in the twilight with Moore.

On the table before him are wire, plaster crumbs, a jawbone, a fragment of Paleolithic bone. His figures resemble multimembered peanuts with wrinkled skin, but white, made of plaster. Some of them stand on the table like toy peanut soldiers. Others lie about like the dried-out skeletons of wasps.

Old Moore creates holes.

An unfinished hole leans against the wall.

He is eighty-three. He has recently hurt his back, he moves with difficulty, and so he forms these mini-models, which assistants later enlarge to gigantic telephone poles. His cubicle is tiny, on the scale of the figures. By the wall, like the chief life model, a white mammoth skull with small eye sockets stands next to a pelvis the size of a washbasin.

"O" turned out to be a rather tame monster. I took it for walks.

It fed on chunks of energy, sucking them out at a distance from cats, thinkers, car batteries, and Alla Pugacheva's fan clubs. We walked, leaving the sidewalk behind us littered with dead cats.

I did not take it anymore to my apartment on Kotelnicheskaya Embankment — it had sucked up all the electric energy from the nearby power plant.

I must tell you that it had a nasty disposition! It was capricious, sulky, always full of some sort of negative charge. Jealous of my human life, it ruined the telephone by plugging into it. The telephone received several lines at a time. The voices tripled. I'd get the Jackson Five, the operator, and a fellow named Pushkin all at the same time. As well as oinks, meows, and hoots — I realized that I was dealing with a complicated creature. In particular, it did not like conversations on architecture.

It told me that it was not yet a hole, but a holette that had broken off from the mass and had gotten lost. I learned that black holes are clots of compressed memory and feeling and not entrances to other dimensions, as people thought. I learned that darkness is not the absence of light but a special dark energy.

They looked for it once. There was something like an eclipse. Chickens moaned. Dogs howled. Cats had hysterics. Corks popped. The engulfing gloom looked everywhere for it.

It hid under the bed and turned itself off so they could not find it. The posse flew past. It spent two days or so there in hiding. What did it like about my place?

My family got used to it. When I went away, I locked it in the pantry.

Once, having locked it up, I went off to the mountains. I was walking along a plateau. Suddenly on the heretofore flat ground a joyous hole flung itself at my feet, and I fell in. Delighted fear resounded. I had broken my collarbone.

It liked to lick the acid electrodes on my transistor radio batteries.

I saw how it brightened up when it was free — it took over the entire colony and the Minsk highway as far as the motel. All the lights went out. But for convenience it could compress itself to the size of an ordinary Newfoundland.

We had a game. I had to leapfrog over it. When I was in the air, it spread out and I would suddenly find myself over the Daryal Ravine, then it would contract instantly, and I would come down on solid ground.

But most of all it liked me to toss it in the air like a volleyball, pushing it with the magnetic force of my hands and fingers. It tumbled and laughed, emitted its sighs, fooled around, jumped on my head, jumped from my shoulders — ah, such happiness, such fun. Then came the immediate downer, the chronic depression. Life with it became intolerable.

In our spats I forgot that it was still a child and totally forgot that it was an entire universe.

Off, out, gone!

It's as if I had chased it away. The January storms were starting then. Living with it was increasingly dangerous. Friends warned me with tales of the animal trainer Berberov's family, devoured by its "pets." Planes headed for Vnukovo Airport were diverted above Peredelkino. The black hole's innocent expression told me that it was responsible for these tricks.

That day all my telephone calls were answered by Pushkin, Julius Caesar, and the steam baths. Someone had drunk up two of my brilliant ideas. Someone had sucked the darkness out of all our water pitchers. It grinned joyfully before me, expecting praise.

"Do something worthwhile! Leave Aeroflot alone. Your peers are in school and building hydroelectric stations. Who licked all the batteries again? If you're bored here, no one's keeping you!"

It was offended.

It gave me an angry, bewildered, and helpless look. It went through the small windowpane and flew off.

"When you're done wandering around—the window's open!"

I worried that it hadn't taken a coat but realized at once that it didn't matter.

It didn't come back the next day or on Wednesday.

It wasn't under the bed, it wasn't in the garden behind the shed, it wasn't in the ditch by the highway, it wasn't on the hill in the cemetery. It wasn't over the hill, either.

I made a megaphone of my hands and called it: "O-o-o-o!"

The echo responded, but it wasn't its "O."

Sometimes I seemed to see its face in the back of a darkened theater, that's why I was drawn to reading my poems. Once in a plane I felt a lonely stab in my chest and I knew it was close by.

Then I forgot about it.

"Oughtn't I to show you my holes?"

Moore jumped down from the stool. You try to support him. He squirms away and, leaning lightly on two canes, jumps out into the street, and there slowly wends his way down the path to the car. His stocky figure is full of strength and lightness, a kind of flight. It seems that if he weren't tied to his two canes, he would fly off into the sky, a cubic balloon. Just as the chrysanthemum plant we pass, wrapped in a plastic bag to protect it from frost, is also tied to a stake and thus cannot fly off.

What a wind today! It ruffles his whitish forelock, it tears out my slippery scarf, which undulates like a snake as it flees down the path and gets caught in the prickly bushes.

A sheep trail leads to one of his sculptures.

That is his *Sheep Arch*. Two marble forms, one tenderly bent over the other — as cuddly as a mother and child. They form an overhang, a marble arch of tenderness, which is a favorite place for sheep to huddle. Feeling the gentleness of the forms, the sheep hide under them from the heat and bad weather. What a feeling for nature you must have to be loved like that by animals!

The fresh black pellets of sheep dung glisten dark blue, like olives.

And here at last are Moore's famous holes. They stand knee deep in the grass and in eternity.

An emotional resonance emanates from the sculpture. There is a lump in my throat. I ask him to stop. We get out.

A two-ovaled silhouette of dark marble with a hole in the middle lies on its side — like Vysotsky's guitar, petrified into a monument.

On Kotelnicheskaya Embankment, we welcomed the New Year 1965 to the guitar playing of Vysotsky.

Come in, find a chair, or sit down on the floor. Grab a steaming potato and some slippery, oily pieces of herring. Drink whatever you can find! There's a scent of pine warmed by candles. Vysotsky and some of his pals dropped the tree off unexpectedly a few days ago.

The guests, having polished off everything on the table — none of us had money in those days — now thirst for spiritual nourishment.

Nostalgic Bulat Okudzhava, the founder of the stringed poetic style, masterfully tunes a strange guitar and, with a look at his Olya, sings his "François Villon." Could he then know that he would one day write "Black Moscow Stork" on the death of Vysotsky?

Here's Oleg Tabakov, with a wicked smile on his spoiled cupid's face, only squinting at his future role in *Oblomov*.

Heavy thoughts, like a sort of plague, weigh down Yuri Trifonov's head, his nostrils and lips pulled down like those of an Assyrian buffalo. Alas, he will not drop in on us again, the chronicler of the life of asphalted Moscow.

Bella Akhmadulina reads. She lifts her crystal chin so high that neither her lips nor her face is visible, her face is in shadow, and all we can see is her defenselessly open neck with the pulsing, unearthly, chilling sound of convulsive breathing.

Chagall is here, too. White, translucent, like a frosty pattern on a windowpane, with cheeks as rosy as a sunset. Here he is, shyly looking up from under the delicate brushes of his eyebrows and saying: "Oh! I haven't had borscht like this in ages. Just half a bowl more, may I?"

Maya Plisetskaya in a tight gold dress leans, as if against a black chair, on the broad, powerful chest of her husband, the composer Rodion Shchedrin.

And they all glow brightly, shaded by the abyss of destiny at their backs.

Through the door of the balcony snowflakes blow in and melt as they touch the bare shoulders of a young woman of head-spinning beauty.

Through the open door the great dark well of the courtyard beckons.

The courtyard sang in Vysotsky's voice.

The suburbs, courtyards, the hurriedly paved-over Russia found expression in him—the same Russian note Yesenin had, not of the peasantry now, but of a new, urban sound. That's why he was beloved by the taxi driver, the general, the actress—the children of a rebuilt country.

Where is it written that natural prodigies are born only near babbling brooks or in deep forests? That only shepherds and herders are the people's elect? People live in cities, too. Vysotsky was a natural prodigy. He became a living legend, the subject of people's talk, the fairy tale of the connecting courtyards. He stole the heart of a French mermaid, putting her up on the yellow double saddle of his guitar.

When he sang, you feared for him. He grew white in a frenzied pallor, beads of sweat broke out on his brow, the veins stood out on his forehead, his throat strained, and the sinews showed on his neck. It seemed that his throat would crack at any moment, stretching out and tearing all its tendons. . . .

Pasternak said of Yesenin: "In life he was a smiling curly-haired prince, but when he started to recite his poems, it became clear that he could stab you." When Vysotsky sang, it was clear that he could stab himself.

What did you see, looking into the impenetrable moon of your guitar?

At age forty-two you publish your first book, at forty-two your second book comes out, and the others also at forty-two, at forty-two they will come to say their farewells to you, at forty-two they will erect a monument to you—all in your eternal forty-two.

Wait, Volodya, don't leave, sing some more, don't go, they'll wait for you, sing some more. . . .

Of what does the hospitable sculptor speak?

"Do you recognize it?" Moore asks, driving the car around two flat forms with a gap between them, like two cymbals brought together the instant before being struck.

It is 1964. I stand insouciantly and confidently on the stage of Albert Hall in London, ready to read my poems. But there is a draft on my neck. Behind my back I feel the coolness of movement—on the spinning, barely spinning stage smoothly revolve two enormous, majestic white plates specially constructed for this evening. Their turning raises the hair on the back of my neck, I feel the cold behind me, white reflections sweep over the faces of the audience, the sixties rumble outside the window.

And the premonition of a spasm grabs my throat.

Alas, ovations are not the only memories of that year.

I was tortured by terrible nausea, which had begun the year before and continued cruelly and ceaselessly. Attacks resembling seasickness or airsickness became more frequent after my readings. Some sort of eclipse with raised fists ran through my fevered brain. Doctors said it was caused by stress, nervous overload, shock, shouting from stages. They even discovered a thinning in the intestinal wall.

The main sensation of that period was the coolness of the washstand pressed against my hot forehead. Oh, vomit-covered chrysanthemums!

Ladies, stand back! I'm even embarrassed in front of you, my love, quickly, quickly, give me a wet towel. Turn yourself inside out, poisoned soul!

I was afraid that people would find out, that they would pity me. Suddenly, without explanation, I would leave gatherings, without finishing a reading, breaking off my performances. I stopped eating. Many of my actions of that period are explained by a fear of those attacks. I began leading a double life—confidence and brazenness in public and tormenting spasms in private. A few years later the illness ceased of its own accord, remaining only in the spasms of my verse.

Oval holes, spaces, where do they come from in Moore's work? What does his name tell us? How does it appear unconsciously in his creations?

Moore is spelled with two *o*'s. May Moore specialists forgive the naïveté of my linguistic method! Yes, I'm convinced that those *o*'s become an unconscious creative autograph for Moore in stone — that's the genesis of those openings, those oval holes. The sculptor is unconsciously outlining in his creations the letters of his own name.

On a pedestal lies an enormous sculpture with two holes, like heavy stone eyeglasses with shattered lenses, left behind by a giant. Music whistles through them as through the windows blown out by war.

I see another pair of eyeglasses, nervous cheeks, and flat nose, like an ivory knife for cutting pages of genius.

Russian music became the main note of the twentieth century — Stravinsky, Prokofiev, Shostakovich.

"On the line — Shostakovich."

He called me in 1975. We had not met until then. He invited me to come see him and to consider working together. He had in mind my translating the sonnets of Michelangelo, the most sculptural of poets.

I came to his piny penates. When he turned to the window, I saw his exhausted profile.

He must have just had a haircut. The short cut had taken away the hair around his temples and most of that on the back of his head. Bangs, curling slightly at the end, gripped his forehead like dark bird claws — an invisible tormenting bird of fate and inspiration.

In a fast, whistling whisper he told me his idea. Nervously, he scratched the bottom of his cheek with his nails, as if plucking an instrument.

The warm air beyond the terrace windows quivered with the same high frequency.

That tremolo is heard in the third movement of his Fourth Symphony, which I love so much, where nothing happens, where you hear only the terrible, oppressive cold of nonbeing, and that icy rustle — *shshshshshsh* — travels like a shiver along your spine.

His wife, Irina Antonovna, resembling a stern high school student, was in and out of the room. So was the young, skinny Maxim. Then Shostakovich played — the keyboard heated up under his hands, like white E's with the black flats in between — he was a passionate pianist!

The two *o*'s in his name, like eyeglasses, merely cover up his essence. He was not round. He had the squareness of harmony. It looked out of place between his oval, questioning ears. The line of his face was filling out, but still the triangle and squares of the cheekbones, nose, and cheeks were visible.

Shostakovich is the most architectural of composers. He thinks in terms of space, he does not get lost in details. Shostakovich is an overpass, a Dostoyevskian shorthand of the spirit. If the theory of the extraterrestrial origin of life is correct, then he was a fragile piece of trembling light that flew into our lives.

Nothing came of the Michelangelo project, although I did the translation. I remember he had Khachaturyan, Shchedrin, practically the whole secretariat of the Union of Composers come to his house, and he made me read for them. He kept scratching nervously, like a cat. He was pleased.

But something didn't come off, or the singer had already memorized the old texts, or the new music didn't work, but anyway at the Leningrad premiere the music was performed with the former text, which he had wanted to replace.

He wrote me a long, Dostoyevskian letter of apology: In it he told me of the plan for a new work, which he had already written in his mind, based on seven of my poems, including "Lament for Two Unborn Poems" and "Pornography of the Mind." But he never wrote down the music.

He was so weak in his last days that his fingers could not hold a sheet of paper. I have a score of his musical setting of my translation, on which in a jerky, cardiogrammatical hand are written the horrifying words: "I feel the end coming."

On hold — childhood!

Evacuation dumped us in a real hole, but that hole was kind!

Quite often the lights went out. And we had to save on kerosene. The inhabitants of our wooden house, all of us, sat on the porch, illuminated by the steady light of the free night sky. We watched the twilight. We did not speak.

The smokers crouched, holding their home-rolled butts between tobacco-stained thumb and index finger, lit end down. When they inhaled, red light cast a glow from below on their lips, nostrils, and creases in their cheeks. The plump lips of our neighbor Murka appeared and vanished in the dark, as if in a round mirror. After each drag, she sucked deeply through her teeth, then spat out rapid-fire. She smelled of floral soap.

She had a suitor, a middle-aged driver from an airborne unit. He brought the car into the yard, right up to the porch. Murka waited for him.

Once he brought her an orange. They must have been distributed to the pilots. The orange was wrapped in special tissue paper. Murka took it off and spread it out on her lap. Her knee showed through the paper just as the orange had. On the paper was printed a round sun with rays and something in Georgian.

"A gift from sunny Georgia," said Potapych. Murka folded up the paper, in quarters, like a hankie, and stuck it in the pocket of her padded jacket.

"Good for tobacco," the landlady said.

Tissue paper's good for playing on a comb, I thought. I knew oranges from May Day demonstrations and New Year's parties.

Murka peeled the orange to the bottom, where the pith forms a white pig's tail. She put the orange peel in her pocket.

She must have taken a half hour to eat that orange. Section after section disappeared in Murka's beautiful, insatiable jaws. When there were two sections left, she said to me, "Here, schoolboy, have a taste." And gave me one. My jaws locked in joy.

The Studebaker engine cooled down near us. The Siberian twilight smelled of gasoline and oranges. That odor was mixed with the scent of the home-grown shag, dog smells, and the milky scent of the plank porch, freshly washed with hot water.

Later they sat, embracing, in the car, illuminated by the red dashboard lights, listening to the radio with the motor running. They rolled the windows down so we could all hear.

We had just had a trainload of evacuees from Leningrad. "Goners," they were pityingly called.

The radio was playing a broadcast from Leningrad. The quiet music was hoarse, piercing, inexplicably frightening and majestic — it made me tremble.

We all listened intensely. Faces lit up and went dark more and more often. The Tobol River glistened. Everything they were listening to was about them, about their fate. They did not understand everything the composer was writing about. But everything that was happening to them, to the country, had become music, frightening and majestic.

Someone stopped by the fence.

"What are they playing?"

"Shostakovich," Murka said after a pause.

"A goner, and what a symphony he wrote!" said Kharitonych.

Open windowpane, rectangular and empty.

Where are you racing now, black hole, tumbleweed, tumblecloud?

See, I've forgotten all about you. Who needs you! See how many white rectangular pages I've written without mentioning you once. I don't remember you in the morning, I don't remember you during the day, I don't remember you at all in the evening.

But you did teach me the art of remembering. "You humans, in order to see a past image, look back at where it had been. But it's not there anymore. You won't see anything that way. To hit a duck, you have to aim three ducks ahead. The past flies in front of you. Look into the now—and you'll see the past."

And so, looking at Moore's works of today, I see yesterday shining through them.

Sometimes you were naughty. Your jokes were stupid. Creeping up from behind, you'd push me into someone else's memory and fate. I'd become Goya, or Basil, the Blessed. And did I get it for clambering into Marilyn Monroe!

Were you jealous?

When women called, they'd get a thunderclap from the receiver. They went deaf. They lost their hair. When my lips touched a cup, you'd shatter it. You were specially jealous of the past. Sensuously you snooped, sniffed out the memory of my friends of long ago. Your face would light up. How angry and beautiful you were! I have the feeling that you could have fallen in love out of jealousy but not vice versa. My unsuspecting acquaintances who had long since forgotten me suddenly blanked out onstage, had car accidents, and carelessly brought matches up to their flimsy robes instead of to the stove, and burned with a blue flame.

Friends criticized me. Seeing us, they began to vibrate. "Come down to earth more frequently," Arno commiserated as he drove past and hurriedly rolled up his window. Aunt Rita called: "Rumors have reached my ears, which I do not believe. But they are horr..."

298

"Horr, horr... horr..." teased the hooligan telephone pixies. It was only then that I realized that Aunt Rita had been dead for a year.

But now even the openings in the sculptures do not remind me of you.

Every night during the war one hundred thousand Londoners hid in the holes of the underground. Moore did a series of drawings. He became the Dante of the Underground. At night, Moore went below. He wandered past sleeping figures, took their measure a few times by eye, and then went off to a corner to make tiny drawings stealthily on an envelope or half-hidden piece of paper — notes for his memory. He did not want to embarrass suffering people by spying. At home he transferred what he saw onto good paper. He worked with pen, India ink, wax pencil, and gouache.

Water drips from the Dantean ceiling of the bomb shelters. Figures are frozen in anticipation. A bare bulb flickers.

My foot is asleep. I want to turn, but it's too crowded. Mother's skirt makes my cheek itch. The concrete vaults of the Serpukhovsky bomb shelter drip — either the breath of hundreds of people is condensing or the pipes are leaking up above.

Next to us my grandmother and sister nod, falling asleep. Grandmother always brought along her small pillow, a *dumka*, as they were called.

As the youngest, I lie on the small mattress we carry along. Something is poking my back. Our poor treasures are sewn into the mattress — silver spoons, grandmother's watch, three gold glass holders. During the evacuation they will be traded for potatoes and flour.

All around, caught unawares by the air-raid signal, people are waving off sleep, rubbing their eyes, fastening their clothes, pinning up their hair. Fragments of dreams float about. Everyone's inflamed with the need of sleep.

These are primarily workers' families. Our house belongs to the Ilyich Factory. Despite the dusty underground, many have hurriedly donned their dress-up best, their most expensive things, just in case they get bombed out. It's late summer, but some are wearing fur coats.

In just this way Renaissance painters of Old and New Testament scenes dress suffering in rich garments.

A tiny infant wails, straining the old man's skin on its face, as

299

wrinkled as a crimson rose. A disheveled madonna with a young sleep-crumpled face and a fox neckpiece askew soothes him, calms him down, whispers to him in a passionate, piercingly tender whisper: "Sleep, my love, my shit maker... Sleep, my little asshole, sleep."

Those rough words sounded as fabulous and tender to me as "tsarevich" or "my little baby bunting."

Chmur, the local thief, suffering from inactivity, lies bored with his head in his wife's lap; she is twice as old and fat as he. "Chmurik, Chmurik," she soothes his soul the way you talk to a sheepdog that suddenly grumbles in its sleep.

In their thoughts they are all up above. Everyone is thinking about the sky. There, in the dark sky crisscrossed by lights, as if by a broad St. Andrew's cross, is an aerial battle that might drop a bomb at any moment, and what can these women do about it?—only wait; their men are in the sky, on the rooftops, at the sandbags, among them were Shostakovich and Pasternak, putting out incendiary bombs, red-hot fragments are flying up there so that we may collect them in the morning, elongated and molten along the edges, like Giacometti figures.

Children of the bomb-shelter underground, we saw so much horror, it crippled our fates and souls and some took the crooked path—but why do I remember those underground places now as radiant chambers?

Mother and I are running along the boundary, past a green field of oats; as I run I pick some stalks and, stumbling, extract the plump milky grain from the long green stems. We're reaching the edge of the forest.

They said, and maybe they were lying, that the Germans had a secret airfield far beyond the forest, from which they flew off to bomb Moscow. The armed militia volunteers combed the forest.

Suddenly in the middle of the day it rose, almost touching the fir crowns, a roaring Messerschmitt with a black cross, it flew limping, so low that I thought I could see the pilot's helmet. It fired a few rounds over the forest and went off toward Malakhovka. Mother shoved my sister and me into a ditch and then, shading her eyes with her hand, stood against the urgent sky in her defenseless blue cotton dress that my grandmother had made.

For what future sensations is the new subway being built? Today, as an architect, I am walking through the underground construction zone of the Nagatinskaya station. The rails already laid down glimmer, and there is a lot of water on the walls and underfoot. Two hard hats are pushing a wagon filled with concrete. One looks back—he has the face of a shepherd. In the trailer, on the table next to the empty kefir bottle covered with cement dust and leaning against the window are two bags of oranges. The strong language coming from the site lets us know that construction of the station is well under way.

Through a gap in the fence the long-haired man with the shepherd's face comes out onto the platform of the commuter train. He's had time to change. He's wearing a cranberry shirt over his trousers. He's carrying the two bags of oranges. He takes a flying leap into the open door, polished by the backs of the riders. One bag tears, and oranges scatter on the platform, like a well-broken pyramid of billiard balls. The car takes off with the cranberry shirttail sticking out between the doors.

One orange sped along the platform, rolled down the steps, along the asphalt of the street, like a ball weaving in and out of the heavy traffic, flew across a dark section, rolled along another sidewalk and right up to the oak door of the Chelsea Hotel.

Only the antibourgeois Chelsea could it have been—probably the most ungainly hotel in the world. It looks like an enormous train station of circa 1910, with cast-iron grillwork—it even seems to have a coal-burning smell. Or that just might come from people smoking illegal substances in their rooms.

Dylan Thomas died of the DTs here. The elevators are always breaking down, they're understaffed and short on conveniences, but that's exactly what people pay for. This is the life-style of an entire social order of people who are concerned with changing the world, their energy attracted toward "white holes," and who have semimilitary bags slung over their shoulders and red Swiss Army knives in their pockets.

At the switchboard sits the owner, Stanley, who looks like a frustrated amateur violinist living in his own world. In his distraction, he constantly connects you with extraterrestrial civilizations.

The elevators carry underground cinema directors, protest stars, a Bakuninite with shaved head in a leather motorcycle jacket, mulatto women in gold lamé pants worn over bare skin. Opals flash on their fingers like the lights on empty taxicabs at night.

Going up in the mirrored elevator, I saw his reflection—the

reflection of a poet who had come here from a harsh, snowy land. He had come to read his work. A famous playwright, away for a month, had lent him his three-room suite at the Chelsea. The tiny hallway led into an enormous living room with a thick gray carpet. Beyond that was the bedroom.

He had begun to be fashionable. Parties were given for him every other day. His head was spinning.

She was one of the results of that head-spinning.

She was a photojournalist. Breaking away from the bourgeois milieu of her father, who I think was an Austrian lumber magnate, she became a groupie of the left elite, the circle of Castro and Cortázar. A magnetic flash underlined her proximity to other elements. She was starlike, slender, ironic, sharp-tongued, with a Western combination of energy and indifference. She flew into destinies like a small sunny whirlwind of delighted and delightful energy, charging you with a current from a field that is not ours. "Storm butterfly" the poet might want to call her.

No sooner had she run into this narrative than sun reflections danced across the pages, the words grew agitated and rushed about. Quick tiny fingers ran up from behind and blindfolded him.

"Storm butterfly!" he shrieked.

It was a heavenly affair.

On assignment for her magazine, she flew in for his performances all over the world. Even though he had a suspicion that she did not always use the services of airplanes. Once in September when the airports were shut down by storms, she managed to fly in somehow and spent half the day drying off.

Her black casual hairdo was convenient for airports, her slanting eyes were constantly squinting at some elusive light, and her cheekbones were a sly reminder that the Huns had really reached Europe. Her thin nose and nostrils, flaring and as nervous as tiny beads, bespoke a capricious and irrational talent, and her slightly puffy lips gave her face a perplexed expression. She wore clothes elegantly cut from cheap fabrics. Orange became her. His secret nickname for her was Orange.

In his harsh snowy land oranges were an exotic import. Besides which, in the orange's bitter smell he imagined a catastrophe, a breakdown in her life, about which she would not tell him and which she forgot when she was with him.

Without knowing the language, what could she understand in his

Russian verse? But she sensed moments of fate behind the frenzy of his performances, and behind his romantic escapades, provincial awkwardness, and pop-star brazenness she saw a bird of a different color.

That day he received his first advance for a book. "I'll show off," he thought as he came back to the hotel. "I'll get a set of wheels. Bring home gifts."

At the hotel there was a telegram waiting. "Coming tonight stop orange."

His heart beat wildly. He lay down on the couch, dozed. Then he went into a vegetable market, one of the many around the Chelsea. They made juice for you from carrots, turnips, oranges, mangoes— the big city's new fad. The oxen-eyed bartender was squeezing oranges.

"I want some oranges to take out."

"How many?" the ox bellowed disdainfully.

"Four thousand."

Clerks in the West are fazed by nothing. The store had fifteen hundred. He went into two other stores.

Smooth-moving blacks in checked shirts huffed and rolled dollies with cardboard crates of oranges into the elevator. They took them up to the tenth floor. The residents of the Chelsea sighed and calmly assumed that a killing had been made in the fruit market. He unplugged his phone and locked his door.

She arrived around 10:00 P.M. Her hair was soaked, and she wore a black slicker. She was squinting.

He opened up for her with his hair mussed and his unbuttoned shirt only half tucked in. His bewildered look let her know that this was a bad time. Her face fell. He could see the cobweb of weariness after her flight. He had someone in there! She was about to turn around and leave.

His heart was pounding. Barely controlling himself, he said softly and casually: "Go into the bedroom, I'll be right there. Don't turn on the light—there's a blackout."

And he fussed with her things in the half-light of the hallway.

So that was it! She still didn't know what she was going to do, but she knew that it would be something horrible. She was going to expose everything right away. She flung open the bedroom door. She tripped. She was stunned.

The floor blazed.

The dark empty room was lit from below by the red hot tiles of the floor.

The floor burned at her feet. She thought she had lost her mind. She floated.

Four thousand oranges were tightly laid out like a fiery cobblestone street. Tongues of flame burst from some of them. In the middle a lone chair bounced, as if its rear end were being toasted and its legs burned. The ceiling swam in red circles.

With bated breath he watched over her shoulder. He hadn't expected such an effect himself. It was as if he had forgotten the four hours of crouching to lay out those devilishly slippery oranges, putting a round orange wax candle in every twentieth place, or lighting the candles, balancing on one leg and using a long taper to keep from squashing them. The flames illuminated the bumpy surfaces, as if they truly were red hot. Maybe it was the oranges burning? And all of them cried out orangely about you.

They danced on your stunned black slicker, they burned like slaps on your cheeks, they were reflected in the tears of horror and repentance, in your shaken life. You burn from head to toe. You have to be put out with a hose.

We're burning, my love, we're burning! There was never anything like this in your life nor will there ever be again. Five, ten, fifteen years from now you will squint like this—and under you will swim blazing your only inextinguishable floor. When you run to another bathroom, it will burn your bare feet. We're burning, my love, we're burning!

We reached the sacred flame. Be still, Nero's petty vanity, blaze, my Hussarlike, pop-art gesture!

In revenge for stolen childhood, blaze, vain years of a belated life. Fly, blazing raft, over blizzards and capitals!

Now we will squash them, frolicking, laughing in their slippery, juicy, sharp-scented mush, making distant candles hiss in the juice.

The room was filled with the bitter, smoky heat of warmed rinds.

She squinted and began to sink. He barely caught her in time.

"You're certifiable," she managed to say. "What are you doing! I adore you...."

A few days later imperturbable workmen laid a new carpet, which resembled an abstract masterpiece of Pollock or Kandinsky; the happy-go-lucky residents of the Chelsea scarfed down the remaining oranges, and Shirley Clark, the underground filmmaker and Chelsea resident, rolled her camera and, with respect for the customs of other nations, intoned: "A Russian design."

On Moore goes, drawing daily. In the morning he works on sculpture, after lunch, he rests, and in the evening, when his hand is tired, he draws.

"I have three reasons for drawing. When you draw, you can take a close look at people, it's a pleasure. Though dangerous. When I was working on my wife's portrait, I looked so closely it was almost grounds for divorce." He winks. "Second. It's an instantaneous sincere impression. Third. It's my poetry."

One who draws catches moments; he quickly stops faces and destinies on paper, saving them from disappearing, seizing them from the encroaching darkness of oblivion. One is saved, and then another. . . .

That is the aim of my hurried notes — I want to retain, to save from accelerated decay the faces of my friends, their living features — one is saved and then another. . . .

My life has been saved many times.

In 1946 an engineer of a state fruit farm in Odoyevo saved me, after I had gone down a second time and lost consciousness in a whirlpool. I clutched his wrist so hard that I left a bruise like a band around it.

My life was saved by the surgeon Dr. Ryabinkin, rosy-cheeked, with a little wedge-shaped sparrow-colored beard.

Olzhas Suleimenov saved my life (and his) by speeding up so that our car flew over a ditch and rolled onto a soft meadow instead.

I was saved by Siberian restaurant companions I had never met before who kept me sitting and talking and made me miss my plane, which crashed with my luggage.

During what were horrible days for me you flew to spend a few hours with me in Novosibirsk, after which you yourself went blind for a month.

I remember everyone who has saved me in the most difficult situations (as is everyone, probably, saved many times in his lifetime), those who saved and forgot about it, I remember your faces, which have become near and dear, and I will spend all my life trying to repay you.

Once my life was saved by the editor of one of our "fat journals," whom I shall call Comrade O.

Unsuccessful suicides are often funny, and this one is too.

My destiny was rushing on with frightening speed. I got all mixed up. No one wanted to publish my programmatic work. I realized that it was time to end it.

Those close to me know that I never complain (except to a sheet of paper), do not whine to acquaintances and girlfriends, do not pour out my soul. It is tactless to force one's problems on others, who most likely have more than enough of their own.

But I had reached the brink. The impenetrable, enticing hole seemed the only way out.

I tried to gather my thoughts. A swollen drowned corpse did not attract me. Neither did a raspy throat in a noose or an accompanying poisoning. I thought about those who would come. As a young poet, I was satisfied only with a bullet through the skull.

I sealed two envelopes and went to a white-haired theoretician who had a German pistol that you could heft sweetly in your hand. "Give it to me for three hours," I explained convincingly. "I'm being blackmailed by a gang. I want to put a scare in them."

Selflessly lying eyes stared through me, comprehended something, and sighed: "Yesterday Lyalya found it and threw it into the pond. Fly down to Tbilisi. You can always buy one there for three hundred rubles."

For two days I borrowed money. The morning of my departure I got a call from O's office: "Old man, we need to raise our circulation. Do you have anything sensational?" I did.

The editors asked me to delete only one line. Eternity stood behind me. I calmly refused. Soloukhin, who was there and who knew the situation, groaned, but said nothing. I remember the good words of Rekemchuk and the other members of the editorial board. They printed the poem as I had written it.

Holding the freshly printed issue of the journal or later swimming in the river that morning, I wondered how I could have been such a cretin—not to see so much, not to learn so many things, not to meet you in the morning, not to write these very lines. How ravishing it is to live!

I rarely see O. We are not close either in life or in literature. When he meets me his gaze dims. But my heart fills with joyful gratitude to him.

Oh, why do Russian winds blow through the windows and cracks of this British country house? What is this nostalgic draft piercing it? Why is it that within these walls I am overwhelmed by memories of home?

Irina, the sculptor's wife, is Russian. They have lived together for over fifty years. When he introduced us, Moore barked at her:

"Well, go ahead, speak Russian to him. He must be tired of expressing himself in a foreign tongue."

Now she cannot accompany us because she is lying upstairs, a tormenting cast on her broken leg. Her pain is transmitted to all the plaster in the studio.

The Russian muse in twentieth-century art is a separate topic. Matisse, Dali, Léger, and Picasso were all inspired by their Russian wives. Tatianas, Galyas, Vavas, Nadyas, redheads from Moscow and Smolensk, there you were soaring over the world abysses, among the Lauras, Delias, and Valkyries!

Only answer me, if nothing else, tell me where you are now, my sad tumbleweed, my tumblecloud?

Off for good. It got all lathered up and went off.

I repeat, it had a disgusting character.

Once my battery went dead and I plugged the black hole into it. We regained consciousness outside Zhitomir.

In rare moments of kindliness it demonstrated visions to me of witches, Russian history, and images from my childhood that I had not remembered.

"Show me what awaits me."

"Oh, for that you have to meet a white hole."

And another explosion of aggression.

Once I brought it to dine at the Writers' Union. It sucked up all the unwashed thoughts of the entire restaurant. Then it was sick for a long time. I had not noticed that a stale, rotten critic had been sitting in the corner.

You never noticed it. It may not have liked you, but it never touched you. When you were out, it tried on your dresses. It disdainfully sprayed itself with your perfume, and the sprays froze on it in the air, like the fluff of an enormous dandelion.

There was no controlling it. Once, angrily, I struck it. The black hole did not know what that was. A smile glowed all over it. It took the blow for a new game. My shoe got stuck in it. When I pulled it out, the shoe was covered with opalescent laughing dust. After that, it understood a bit and withdrew.

And how curious it was! In a word—a female. It feasted on news. Absorbed tons of it. And curiosity was its downfall. It was stolen in the fall. Lured and kidnapped. Two days later, frazzled by the electricity, they brought it back in a sack. I suggested they bury themselves in the ground, to let the current leak off. They still haven't been dug out—apparently, the current hasn't run off.

I liked it when it invited guests. Usually it invited Boris Godunov, the Makarochkins, Napoleon's nose, and Pavlova's foot—it didn't remember the rest of them. Boris Godunov sang well, but was very frightened of cars. The nose perched on his shoulder like a parrot and sang along. Pavlova's foot sat severe and erect at the table, slightly nodding a ballet slipper worn as tight as a shower cap. It fed them roast veal and salmon, which they remembered from the still lifes at the Hermitage Museum.

Once I betrayed it. But I couldn't drag it around with me all the time! It had eternity, while my life was short.

I told it I was going to the office, locked it in, and drove off to visit friends. As I was getting out, I saw a taxicab parked across the street with the meter turned on and the driver tuned out. In the darkness of the car I recognized its vengeful gaze. At home, it met me without a word, but the phone did not work for a week.

Sometimes it disappeared on its mysterious female business. First I used to worry, searched for it, afraid that it would be devoured by other elements or fields. I would leave the hinged windowpane open, and it would come back. I would know by the dead telephone.

The phone is working fine. To tell the truth I'm glad to be rid of it. Excited ripe cats safely soak up the sun. Planes roar over Peredelkino. No one is ruining my mood.

But there is an emptiness gnawing at me, a hole sucking at me. Could there be something inside me, a darkness, a Karamazovism that turns me into a black hole?

I attribute this to my abandoned architecture.

Don't get yourself a second profession, a second passion, a second family. You'll be sucked by a vacuum. At night, you'll get names confused. You'll start messing around with stained-glass windows. You can fumigate the house, but you'll still be drawn to it.

I am told that a poet friend of mine dreams that I'll go back to architecture. My mother would like that too, though for different reasons. She wants me to have steady hours and a roof over my head. I have architectural dreams.

People take up architecture not only for utilitarian reasons, but also to fill up the void, to overcome the space of nonbeing, the black holes and abysses that surround this life. Overcome them with the compressed future, the white columns of the Parthenon, the belfry of Ivan the Great, the "white holes" of stadiums.

I dream of a white marble crown.

Over to one side where he called me with a weak smile, as if to answer a call of nature, Moore led me behind a vertical marble slab.

"I know what you're interested in, it isn't here." He passed his hand over the sun-warmed slab. "It was here. Here's its place in the rock. It belongs to the breed of wandering black holes. They fly off." A shadow crossed his face. "It was my favorite creation. Ask at Picasso's. He might have lured it over. He devours holes."

He did not, of course, say any of this out loud, in words, but transmitted his thoughts to me. This is more complicated than it looks, I thought.

But Moore gave me a wink and a second later had turned back into the classic Moore, his forget-me-not eyes chilled and hidden under the moss of his eyebrows.

O for the sleep of genius!

Have you ever slept in Picasso's bed?

Don't despair if you haven't. You'd toss and turn all night long, you'd never shut your eyes. A square, low bed in the right corner, it fills half of an equally square room. To the left is the door to the bathroom. On the floor is a runner he had designed. Under the bedside table is an album of his graceful erotic graphics. The bed does not want to yield to you; it remembers how it used to make a hollow for him.

Have you been lying a long time in the same position face down, shuddering with waves of nausea?

There's no heat. The maestro's plaster walls give off a chill. The icy, prickly sheets dig into your back and into the calves of your legs.

The bed is very wide.

Picasso was not tall. What did he do, roll on it from corner to corner to warm up like a mad round loaf loose in an oven?

You run several times to take a hot shower to warm up. How scary to put your bare feet into his slippery, trampled, stained slippers. The impenetrable, tipsy night sleeps next to you, tossing, darkening, breathing, while sprawled out there, the heavens, the depths, the Paris that belonged to him sleep on.

Suddenly you see the empty slippers hop and scuffle to the bathroom on their own. A light shows under the door. Water runs.

You push the light switch on the table lamp, but the button goes in an instant before that and the light goes on an instant before you press it. Your teeth chatter, you're feverish and chilled, and you try to convince yourself that it's only from the cold.

On the glass shelf a flock of little silver swans shivers.

It's so quiet that you can hear the shelf of dishes downstairs shiver in the same way. As on a train.

He made those swans from the aluminum bottle caps on mineral water. The bottle caps of French mineral water, like the caps on vodka in Moscow, have tiny tongues. Pulling and stretching out the tongue, he obtained the head and neck of the swans. Then he bent the cap in half and raised the sides to make the wings.

The silver swans slide along the glass. The long shelf opens out into a boundless oval lake. I hear Tchaikovsky, Tchaikovsky. . . .

But not *Swan Lake*, no, I hear the First Concerto, with which Picasso greeted me in 1963.

> Remembering empty concert halls,
> I followed my tall dark friend with her Afro
> hairdo like a black balloon
> while Tchaikovsky grew louder under the doors.

The room is hot. It feels as if the resin will ooze out of the high black backs of the Spanish chairs. Either they had the heat on or he had warmed up the entire house himself with the heat of his stovelike, blazing body.

Picasso was half-naked, in a net T-shirt, like a tanned yellow billiard ball spinning in the pocket.

His face had already started being pulled downward, a bitter, haggard shadow had appeared, making his bulging, wide-set eyes even more prominent. Picasso had a theory according to which the wider apart a person's eyes, the more talented he was.

His eyes rolled out, bulging from his forehead, it seemed as if his intellect were pushing his eyes out from inside.

"Jacqueline, Jacqueline, look who's come!" he shouted with a clown's mocking horror, rolling his dragonfly eyes. And teasing, added with a dig at his guest: "Come on, turn on the TV. He must be on there by now. Look at the snow he brought with him."

In came sun-tanned Jacqueline in a tight green dress. Kabul, a white hound with a mysterious shark's smile, followed, froze, and then leaped up to lick me.

And it began. He exuberantly showed me green-lit canvases, and Jacqueline and the dog were everywhere. He impetuously dragged me to the cellar, where in the smoke of a demonic netherworld lay his sculpture studio, with an orangutan made of scrap metal, its head a Chevrolet hood. Languid white women bathers played with a ball, the same bathers who had influenced the early Moore. Everything showed the wild rush of life, of passion, everything was illuminated by the happiness of his last love, the last fervid attempt at life. The house smelled of love. Objects had halos.

To use astronomical classifications, Picasso was a "white hole." These are strong personalities in whom clots of the future are compressed, whose memories reach not into the past but into the future. Usually they are builders, optimists, fighters of the good fight. Often their sign is Taurus.

In contrast to nostalgic black holes, they are triumphant in form, but sometimes yield to them in their susceptibility to emotion. It is not a question of the size but of the quality of talent. Blok, Lermontov, Chopin were classic black holes; Shakespeare and Eisenstein were white ones. I have never met a more quintessentially white hole than Picasso.

Picasso could do anything. He had overcome gravity. He had crossed the border of the possible. He had stepped over the abyss. Perhaps that was his tragedy.

He did not give me time to catch my breath. He dragged me around, deafened me with questions, to keep me from breaking through to the main question that was on the tip of my tongue. I had almost begun: "Maestro, have you seen—"

But he cut me off, asked me to read Goya in Russian, understood it

without a translation and repeated, laughing, like an echo: "Go. . .
go. . .go. . .ho. . .ho. . .ho. . .!"

Then he stuffed himself on holes.

Tilting his head and squinting, with a juicy slurp, clicking his
tongue, he sucked out holes from purple-black mussels. Around him
on the table lay piles of their crushed shells with microscopic ridges,
like buckled fragments of records on which the sea had been
recorded. He swallowed up sections of golden aromatic cantaloupe
holes. Then, emptying a jar and picking out a hole, he smeared the
holes of black caviar in a thin layer on a piece of white bread, so that
the bread resembled a small sieve. And finally, with a wink, he
sucked out an aromatic hole from the dark neck of a big-bellied flask
swathed in straw, like a basket.

When he came near, holes whisked themselves off to hide.
"Shhh!" came their awed rustle. "Here comes the ogre, the devourer
of holes."

Picasso was the most famous of all living artists. He did not have
posthumous fame. That he knew in his own lifetime. Thus he
overcame death.

Picasso thirsted to know everything.

Everything heard and seen disappeared into Picasso's belly.
Rumbling, he absorbed information on Moscow's artistic life, which
he knew only by hearsay, having trouble with the unfamiliar and long
Russian names — more! more! — thirsting to take in all the energy of
the age, whose culture he had helped build.

This century has eliminated many boundaries. A new community
of people is forming — of aristocreators, as Khlebnikov called them
at the dawn of the century.

The aristocreator of Kurgan in the Urals, who resembled a
mustachioed general of 1812, Gavrila Ilizarov, the Moore of our
bones, grows new ankles, feet, and hands, like magical tulips and
lilies of the valley. Nerve bundles blossom like orchids. For one lucky
woman he sculpted a new Rubensian hip. Now he's growing a
backbone like bamboo.

The heretic Ilizarov had a lot of difficulty overcoming people's
boneheadedness. He did not conform to theory. But his hands and feet
grew rapidly.

I attended first grade in Kurgan. Since then, perhaps not without
his magic, the wooden one-storied town has grown into a nine-story

regional center with a clinic that gives the stunned world lessons in magical materialism.

The essence of his method lies in piercing the bone with Ilizarov needles in a special apparatus that resembles a space helmet. They grow, reaching out toward other dimensions. When the Elysium of shade looms forth, Ilizarov is at work.

The Smolensk aristocreator poet Tvardovsky, with a face as swollen as a teardrop, sang in his high-pitched voice his native song for all Europe to hear: "There even in the morning it rains and rains. . . ."

Naturally he did not like my poems. But he printed two of them in *New World* to support me at difficult times.

Let there be an end to disputes among aristocreators! Who can save the world? Only those in whom the aristocreator spirit lives.

The sleepless envious eyes of vampires watch the aristocreators. At night in a deserted cemetery a coffin lid trembles. A green hand slips through the crack like a lizard and opens the coffin.

Ashes escape from the mouths of urns. Once upon a time the remains of the False Dmitri flew out. But now false poets, false heroes, false leaders materialize. You can recognize a vampire by its stale gaze. One glance sours milk and withers young poets. It appears energetic, carves out its career, tries to be charming. But people don't like it, instinctively sensing that the sour alcoholic smell hides the sweet reek of death. People are cold toward its "creations." It cannot build or create anything, and that makes it hate those who can and do.

Pale-spotted, scarcely discernible portraits of the great vampires hang in Empire frames — those who tasted the blood of Pushkin, who hung the noose around Yesenin's open throat, who drilled a hole in Mayakovsky's chest, who sucked at length their immortal blood. They look down scornfully at the portraits of their victims' descendants. Today's vampires are a sorry lot. Puny, slimy, like bats with childish fingers. Envious. Slandering, intriguing, vile. Now our notorious critic, poking his head through a hole like a dog from a doghouse, declares, "It's all plumbing, nothing but toilet bowls. The classics are down the drain!" Agitated, he exits to weak applause. "Where are you going?" they ask suspiciously. "To warm up my Volga's engine. There's a blizzard out there. And to check my burglar alarm." A half hour later comes the rush of a flushing toilet. The vampire didn't have the purity of his convictions.

Disgusting tiny eyes peer at you with hostility and fear, slimy bat-fingers reach out in your direction.

The chase begins. Away, get away from me!

Oh, the sky is falling.

I brought snow to Antibes.

The dark green groves nestle in astonishment, as if sprinkled with sea salt.

We came out on the icy terrace. At last we were alone. His words were enveloped in steam. Steam came not only from his lips and nostrils, but from every pore of his hot body, the angry column of his life; his whole body was a plume of steam in the cold.

In the same way under a dazzling blue sky, gradually recovering from the surprise of the snow, the earth steamed. Vapor rose from wet benches, the wet branches of the laurel and orange trees, showered first by snow and then by sun, steamed and gave off a sharp, spicy smell. The wooden washtub on the hillside also steamed. A joyous dog raced along the pink paths, like a clump of steaming white soap suds.

People are frank in a steam bath. I would ask him now.

Unsuspecting that they were posing for him, below, down the hill, like women with rivulets between their shoulder blades, rested the walls of a pink limestone house. This was all a great steam bath. And far below, barely discernible in the fog, lay the sea, smoking like Waterloo in an ancient engraving, the bottomless riddle of existence and of history.

And above all this there on my left was the elated, chuckling bather and genius steaming with life, an even row of what looked like white foam circling his tanned throat. He was enveloped in steam, and sometimes only his merry and boisterous eye peeped out through the white clouds.

I turned to watch a car speed away and skid on the road below.

When I turned back toward him, there was a column of steam next to me. The steam dissipated. Picasso was gone.

I had turned back twenty years later.

An open black hole had pulled him in, had it really pulled him in as well?

Out it comes, that I've been preparing all my life to meet you. You couldn't have loaded the deck of my memory with all those circles, could you?

In his Vladimir garden my grandfather had two beehives. A golden hum circled swarming above them. On the riverbank, Grandfather taught me to weave baskets from reeds—bent into arcs, the foundations of the baskets stood like oval frames, the slippery white reed frames of a river landscape.

We would hitch a ride on a truck along the famous Vladimir highway to the city with the white kremlin walls on the hill.

The white stone opening of the arch of the brilliant Golden Gate took on the shape of an O, waist-deep in the ground.

Omnipresent vision!

Overbearing, inflated, honeyed image that pursues me.

Off with you! I will glue you to this page so that you leave me alone.

I've never met a perfectly round idiot, like a round number, but there are plenty of oval ones. You go to the office of this particular editor. He has perfect taste, perfect pitch. His beady eyes narrow as they find your best line. "Genius," he moans voluptuously and crosses it out. The poet Ventiliansky has collected all the lines this man has crossed out in the work of various poets. It makes an entire anthology.

Ovals of Antonov apples weighed down the tree. Grandfather propped up the limbs with forked branches.

The apple tree stood in back of the house, facing the rising sun. Every morning its silhouette was illuminated from behind. Shafts of light sliced obliquely through its branches like the lines in a schoolboy's notebook. The contours of the apples were outlined in glowing rims, like capital O's made with gentle pressure, as if the early morning were giving penmanship lessons.

A tiny worm, like a yet unknown "O," slithered out from under an apple.

My first writing teacher! Thousands of years ago in another garden the first teacher slyly offered a glowing oval letter from which the human race began.

The tree of language filled out. In the beginning was the word that had no form. Sacredly and sinfully man created form for the word, inventing the alphabet, drawing, and sculpture.

I dream, oh, how I dream of the golden tree of language. It grows through me, sucking up my juices, it grows through my life, rustling its crown above me.

The crown of language is my idée fixe. I want to erect in some square a monument to language. This will be a monument to the great lost words and an eternal flame of the living word. It will blend poetry and architecture. Like bells, golden *A*'s will sway, *E*'s will tinkle like earrings, *B*'s will beat their fat drums, wine-grape clusters of *O*'s will ripen — the crown must be gold, and tremble slightly in warmed air, in light, and in human breath.

I've christened it Poetarch. It is a metallic golden sphere. It symbolizes human culture, the sphere of language. It is supported, as if on columns, by four streams of air expelled by compressors, one in the center, the others at angles around it. The air stream, circling the sphere, lifts vibrating cables with the resonant letters from the world's languages.

The sphere's diameter is twenty-five meters, that is, as big as a six- or seven-story house. Its proportions are comparable to those of the globe. Our eye instinctively seeks correlations with the earth's dimensions.

The monument would travel from city to city, country to country, ritually symbolizing the peaceful unity of human culture.

The construction of the sphere is simple — based on Fuller's geodesic dome. Inside there would be a hall for poetry readings and concerts. A sphere is the ideal shape for a hall. The lower part would serve as an amphitheater, the upper, as a dome.

Overwhelmed by the vain struggles of my incorrigible life, I shake the dust from my shoes and as the prodigal son of architecture come to the apartment door marked "L. N. Pavlov."

Years long past will open for me. They will not ask about anything. Nor will I tell.

You haven't aged at all, Leonid Nikolayevich. Solid shoulders encased in a cotton shirt dotted with black horseshoes. A snowy mop of hair, tossed back, resembles a white falcon lowering one wing before taking off — Leonid Nikolayevich, my idol, the artistic conscience of my architectural youth!

His gaze envelops me in regret and forgiveness.

Then I understood how lost I was, and what torture I was exposing myself to by butting in here. But the Supreme Conscience had already taken my coat.

With voluptuous sadism he lingers over architectural terms like "Florentine mosaic" and "volume" while watching me closely. The Supreme Conscience is really saying to me: "How could you give it up, let yourself be seduced, take off after an illusion, I believed in you then.... But now you finally feel ashamed, you're still drawn to it, you've come crawling to confess.... Well, go ahead, punish yourself...."

The Supreme Conscience leads me to a bonfire. On one of his canvases, like tongues of flame, sway narrow triangles of red, gold, and black. A triangle is rebellion, rupture, all that is anti-oval.

The black and red swaying tongues murmur: "You rush around the world without a base, an eternal student, what tempted you—great fame? I'm not so primitive as to think that you were seduced by money, but there is that temptation to become the voice of the people—and then, perhaps, the voice of God. There is the temptation to suffer, to become a black hole. An architect dies in each of his works, remains in eternity, and that, you must agree, is vanity of a higher order, a strategic one, so to speak...."

I try to defend myself, I brag that my drawings have been bought by the Museum of Modern Art in New York, I weep like a coward on his shoulder, complaining that in the workshops I had been assigned nothing but stairway landings and sanitary facilities, while in poetry I continue architectural principles; I can hear my thought rise to a shrill pitch: what about the other renegades of architecture? Why are they allowed? What about the singer Arkhipova? What about the filmmaker Daneliya? What...

I decide on a low blow; I think: Well, fine, those are all nice ideas and plans and dreams, but what have you done in real life, my conscience and dreamer, provider of ideas, the Andrei Bely of our national architecture? What have you accomplished on the prefabricated grid of reality?

Pavlov suddenly brightens up.

"This is my favorite thing—in the world."

That's the way one speaks of a woman. He takes out a precious photo. It's a very frank photo. A building site in the heat of construction. There is in the rhythm of construction the haste of a human embrace. The Supreme Conscience is worried, wheezing jealously. I'm embarrassed to look. Finally the scaffolding is taken down—and two peaceful, enormous, flat squares remain to soar in the air.

Muscovites know that flat building as the windbreak blocking Lomonosov Avenue. That building is an Ear. In the center, as if on a plastic panel, is hung a sculptural-mosaic ear with an enormous hole. Pushkin's genius gave life to a chopped-off head. Gogol cut off a nose, and Pavlov has erected a monument to the Ear. It faces the Cheremushinsky Market. There reigns the chaos of boisterous speech, crunching vegetables, colorful words, motley and disorganized forms and passions, elemental forces gone wild, where the East of melons meets the North of berries, where bulbs of garlic protect from flu and vampires, where new potatoes in late May cost twelve rubles a kilo and veal costs ten, where in the right-hand corner the best roses in Moscow are sold, where rages a bacchanalia of profit. In contrast, the two elegant squares of the Computer Center are a reminder of eternity and harmony.

When the Ear captures particularly juicy expressions it reddens mosaically, the way a music freak's ears redden at the conservatory (if you've ever noticed sitting behind one) when they capture a note of genius.

"It's no ear, it's a Möbius strip," Pavlov maintains. "It's a sculptural-philosophical eight that speaks of the infinity of space, with an almost Mooreian hole in the middle. That is an eye into the belly of Mother Nature. I made its dimension one-millionth of the earth's diameter. That is the magic module of my work. All the details are multiples of that number. That's why you are drawn to the proportions of that square—instinctively man feels a correspondence with the earth."

Pavlov is an adherent of the golden section in architecture. Let us drink to gold! Pavlov is a great home brewer. From a decanter he pours vodka in which flecks of gold leaf have been steeped. I can feel my gullet and intestines being coated like Armstrong's horn by hot gilt plating.

I keep wanting to tell him about my project for the Poetarch, but no amount of drink or torture will loosen my tongue.

But Pavlov seems to know all about it. He calmly says, apropos of nothing: "It's a completely realistic idea—to place an architectural volume on a cushion of air. But you have to develop the direction of air flow. After all, water spray in a fountain holds up glass balls. As for the material, I think it should be brass. Brass is more serious and mighty. Though compressed light is easier to use and less expensive."

Pavlov suddenly pushes me into the water.

Overboard!

I flounder in what I was wearing, trousers, heavy shoes. The trousers stick coldly to my body, restricting my movements. The water of sadness and bewilderment fills my ears. My pockets are stuffed with dense water.

Pavlov swims next to me, snorting. He does the crawl. He pushed me into the idea of his water theater. The cotton shirt sticking to him has grown transparent, and the dark horseshoes of the fabric stick like tattoos to his shoulders and body.

"My plan is for twelve thousand seats!" he shouts, swimming closer. "It's being built in Izmailov. A theater for water ballet."

The water smells not of chlorine but of bitterness and separation. Just like this, in clinging trousers, I swam with you last summer. Only the brass buttons stayed dry. You swim over. "Hey you, in the gray pants, work those legs, those legs!" a coach who looks like half-naked Picasso shouts into a megaphone from the other shore.

Pavlov is comfortable in the water now. He floats, as if on a mattress, on his own sturdy radiance. His hair has dried and is loose and fluffy. Does he use a blue rinse?

"A swimming theater is a new idea. A child of sport and art. A muse for the millions. The audience can watch the action from below through windows in the belly of the pool. When you dive, you see the spectators' faces."

I dive. In green light I see faces under glass, like color photos on the walls — I see Moore, Picasso, Murka, you, all watching our lives. I need air and I surface.

Our journey must continue. Moore's house is ninety minutes from London.

What do I think about, as I ride along? A poet is the most national of creatures, completely involved with his own language, and yet at the same time connected to world culture. Pushkin, the Russian genius, felt an affinity with Byron. Even now, at a moment of world discord, poets join in a common circle. The most Russian of letters,

O, is equally at home in all European languages. And Americans form an O with thumb and index finger as a sign of approval. Poets recognize one another at a glance.

The brakes recall me from my Russian reverie. Returning me, so to speak, to reality, to the prose of life.

"We're here!"

We flex our stiffened legs. Before us is Moore's white house. We have come full circle.

Mumbling something, Moore gives me a drawing. And packs it for me himself. As if to say, you'll open it at home and understand. He wraps it in cellophane, backs it with a cardboard. Not finding a second piece, he tears off the cover from a sketch pad. Then he neatly tapes the whole thing.

On the line now with yourself—honestly, why didn't you stop here then?

"Have a full life, find new forms, be daring," Pavlov told me. "But don't lose yourself, don't step over the edge of the abyss, don't drop into a black hole."

The black hole stands in the middle of my room. Its gaze is open and expectant.

I went into the black hole.

Dante was wrong in describing it as a hopeless, dank, low corridor. His hell is memory. He was forced to forget what he had seen and have it replaced by false information.

There is no time there nor space. Everything is filled with a boundless inner voice.

The only indication of the place where I went in was my body, suspended as from a peg, worn, with a moth-eaten head and an unfashionable nose that had seen better days. I regretted parting with it. It grew smaller as it moved away.

I moved along, avoiding air pockets. Clumps of swept-up energy languished in them. They were the martyrs of memory. That's how Eastern despots tortured people, by making them sit on a pail with a rat in it. The poor creature, in order to get out, ate away the person's entrails.

To one side an exceptionally gifted student struck his mother's skull with a hammer for the umpteenth time. The victim, with upturned bloody face, begged: "Leave him alone, it's not his fault, I hit myself."

A tired teenager turned to me, panting, and asked: "New guy, what's up on earth nowadays? They've knocked my memory out completely down here."

I reminded him. He nodded, the way people thank a stranger for a light, and went back to his business.

A fading Peter the Great kissed the lopped-off head of his mistress. An exhausted painter was being tortured by birds with female faces and breasts. Here my vision was turned off.

I had only sound now. But this was only the ante-hole. It was filled with a question.

Actually, there were two voices. They posed questions. "What's more important—faith or the object of faith? The meaning of life or the life of meaning? Freedom or the path to freedom? Limitless thought or limited natural resources?"

Between the questions energy flowed. It created cities. Above it civilizations dawned and died away. Between the questions wars erupted.

I was asked: "Do you want to know the Only Answer?" I did. "But you saw those who tried to have it, who have gone beyond it. The answer is paid for with one's life."

"People pay with their lives for a pound of sausage."

"What if once you learn it, you damn yourself? What if according to the Only Answer your dream turns out to be a toad? The princess a slimy frog? And some bastard turns out to be 'more majestic than Leo Tolstoy'? What if with your hang-up you don't understand the Answer and listen only to the chimera of your pathetic comprehension? (The way for centuries people have been praying according to an improperly abstracted New Testament.) Eh? And what if once you've learned it, you immediately forget it?"

I stepped into the Only Answer.

The clarity of the Only Answer astounded me. It fit into a single word. That creating Word pierced my entire being with joy. I understood that my life had been realized, it had succeeded, but it no longer had any significance. It blended into the Only Answer. I dissolved into the Word.

Years, centuries?—I don't know.

But somehow, happily dissolved and swimming in historical space, moving off to the edge, I felt a certain pull as if from a hiding place whose presence is revealed by tapping on a wall or by a secret passage. I had noted that place to myself a long time ago. It was the hiding place of the black hole, of confused memory, there where it remembered what it had been keeping from itself.

I saw a pathetic little room with a scruffy wardrobe. The owner's lopsided self-portrait pressed down on the peeling wallpaper. The light had not been turned off. A half-blind lamp bent down as if over the fingers on a stretched canvas with a dusty sketch of some golden sphere.

The hinged windowpane was hopelessly open.

I turned and not far away outside I discovered my hanging and rather well-preserved body. I began pulling it on with difficulty. It had shrunk and shriveled; it did not recognize me. My feet pinched. No problem, I'd loosen them up with walking.

I opened the creaking windowpane and jumped into the room.

"O-o-o-o," abandoned and boundless came the sound behind me. "O-O-O-O . . ."

The world rushed at me—hot, brown, forget-me-not blue, red-blond, babbling, alive!

The self-portrait, not recognizing me, reeled back and sank into the wall. "Why are you bugging me?" it said, trembling with fear. The first to recognize me was the rickety table. It leaped at me yelping and poked like a dog at my belly. From atop the tilted wardrobe a vase you had once given me jumped onto my shoulder and wept all over my shirt. I barely managed to catch it. Shaggy daisies began banging at the window, licking the glass. Strips of the flooring mewed, arched their backs, and rubbed themselves against my feet.

"My dear ones, I've brought you the Only Answer! Now you will know everything!"

But then I realized that I had forgotten the Only Answer.

I forgot, I forgot it all.

I live, and every day I try to remember the Answer. The portrait does not recognize me. What torture—to try to recall something and not be able to! Perhaps the Word will take form from the letters of a gathering cloud? Perhaps the Only Answer should not be received from the heavens, but built up by oneself, and that may be the whole meaning of the Only Answer.

On to the end. I bid you farewell, my dark novella! You will soon fly off around the world scattering your thousands of letters, like beads from a broken necklace, but in each little *o* from now on there will be a reflection of your warmth.

It's getting on toward evening. I am writing in Peredelkino at the garden table. The white window frames seem to recede in the twilight. The white sheet of paper is covered by the darkness of my words, as they disappear beneath the lines.

It is completely dark now. The paper, the pen, my hand are now invisible, blending into your darkness. Farewell. I spent so many days with you. I forgot friends and work for you. How you tortured me! Thank you for finding me.

The tin sky on the drawing Moore gave me is done in neutral gray. The twilight is agitated, the sky is upset, looking for you. There is a gap in the dark clouds, like an open windowpane.

The hurried oval of a lake. Four trees on the other side.

Three graces stand on a dark pedestal. Judging by the black fin, they rest on the back of a dolphin, a grampus, or the Loch Ness monster.

You can see the artist's brush hurrying along: the stroke rushes, color splashes, you can see how excited he was, preparing his paint in a jar, mixing in with his anguish Prussian blue and burnt sienna. The brush hurries and spatters water, paint, life. The century hurries, the century is ending. It hurries to communicate something important that has happened to it.

But what is this? Is it a flaw in the paper? No, and it's obviously not a splotch.

In the center of the sky is suspended a dark, sad spot about to fly off. Its gaze is fixed. It looks at the lake, at the white column, at you and me. Hurry! It's about to fly away.

Moore's hand unconsciously captured what was happening to him at the very moment of your departure. That is your only real portrait.

"On the line, excellent connection...08? Is that you, Sculptor? Greetings! What?! They approved our project at the artistic council!? Repeat that.... It can't be! Hurray! What about Omletov, who opposed it? He didn't show?... What do you mean—he fell? He was walking down the avenue and fell into a hole? But there were no holes there! Well, maybe there was some construction work. That'll teach him to dig holes for others—he ended up in one himself...."

The receiver was filled with the voices of Moore and Pavlov. You and all the others were shouting and congratulating me.

Why did I suddenly turn around?

I can recognize that gaze out of thousands. From one corner, hunched up, my black hole eyed me rapturously. It was back!

Ah, why didn't I shut the window immediately?

It rushed there and stood for a moment in the opening. Hesitated. Swayed. And then turned sadly away.

I never saw it again.

Notes

This volume of Voznesensky's selected poetry and prose includes material from the two previous American editions, *Antiworlds and the Fifth Ace* and *Nostalgia for the Present,* translations of new poems, and two prose essays specially revised for this edition.

I ANTIWORLDS

Most of the material in these notes is drawn from *Antiworlds and the Fifth Ace,* edited by Patricia Blake and Max Hayward (New York: Basic Books, 1966, 1967; Anchor Books, 1967).

I Am Goya
First published in *Mozaika* (Vladimir, 1960). A good example of his use of assonance, it is one of the poet's favorites.

My Achilles Heart
First published in *Yunost'* (No. 6, 1965). The "crack shots" must refer to those who took part in the 1963 campaign against Voznesensky and to whom he refers in later poems also. See the Introduction and the Note to "Winter at the Track."

Wall of Death
First published in *Znamya* (No. 4, 1962). The text is from *Antimiry* (Moscow, 1964). The spelling of "Singichants" shows the name is

Armenian; it probably refers to a trainer in the Moscow Circus, which has a "Wall of Death." In public readings, Voznesensky identifies Androsova as a "Master of Sport of the Soviet Union," a highly coveted title.

Hunting a Hare

First published in *Antimiry* (Moscow, 1964). The poem is dedicated to the writer Yuri Kazakov, the Yuri of the poem.

The character named Bukáshkin, here rendered as Buggins, appears in several other Voznesensky poems, including "Antiworlds" and "The Nose." Bukáshkin is the poet's image of the traditional, downtrodden clerk—a kind of Soviet Walter Mitty whose humdrum, haunted existence is relieved only by fantasies and excursions such as described in this poem. Like the name of Gogol's Akaki Akakievich Bashmachkin (Akaki "Shoe") in "The Overcoat," the name is comically in tune with his personality: derived from *bukashka* ("a little insect"), it corresponds to the English Buggins.

The jalopy (*gazik*) is the classic car made at the Gorky Auto Works (GAZ). The word has come to stand for any old car.

"Tallyho!" is the translator's rendering of *trali-vali,* a similar expression used by sailors. It is also the title of a short story by Kazakov.

The Skull Ballad

First published in *Znamya* (No. 4, 1962). The text here is from *Antimiry* (Moscow, 1964).

In its first version, the poem was titled "A Digression into March, 1719. The Skull Ballad." Slightly altered for the 1962 collection *Treugol'naya grusha,* two years later it was simplified to its present form.

Stanley Kunitz's translation is rather free; it gives approximate equivalents for expressions and concepts that might be meaningless for a person not brought up in the Soviet Union. For example, "dirty foreigner" stands for "Anglo-Swedish-German-Greek spy"; in 1937–38, many Russians were falsely accused of being multiple agents of this kind.

The woman executed by Peter the Great in *Lobnoye mesto* on Red Square is Anna Mons, who was for a time his favorite in the late seventeenth century. An invidious attempt to decipher the poem was made by the critic V. Nazarenko in *Zvezda* (No. 6, 1962), who suggested that Voznesensky deliberately invented the beheading of Anna Mons (she actually died a natural death), inserted "motorbike" and other anachronisms, and used typically Soviet terminology (such as *stroitel'stvo,* "construction," as in "Socialist construction") in order to "express certain ideas of universal application." "We have here, in allegorical form," Nazarenko wrote, "gloomy reflections on the allegedly tragic fate of the individual supposedly crushed by social laws. . .on an eternal and universal scale. The message of *The Triangular Pear* [the collection in which the poem appeared] is that the world is immutable and that everything will remain as it always was—that man is eternal and the tragedy of the individual is eternal."

In his preface to that collection, Voznesensky wrote: "Poems have a life and character of their own. Occasionally, against the author's will, they balk at grammar. This is sometimes the result of the fantastic nature of the theme. For instance, a severed head begins to speak. No time for punctuation here!"

Someone Is Beating a Woman

First published in *Znamya* (No. 4, 1962). The text here is from *Antimiry* (Moscow, 1964).

The Cashier

First published in *Mozaika* (Vladimir, 1960). The text here is from *Scrivo come amo* (*Pishetsya kak lyubitsya*) (Milan: Feltrinelli, 1962).

In the 1966 collection *Akhillesovo serdtse*, it was titled "V magazine" ("In a Store"). The setting is a large Soviet grocery store where the woman cashier usually sits in a separate glass booth, rather like an American movie-theater cashier but inside the store. When the cashier holds a bill up to the light, she is looking for the watermark of Lenin's head, which appears on Soviet bank notes.

Autumn in Sigulda

First published in *Znamya* (No. 4, 1962); variants appear in subsequent editions; this text is from *Treugol'naya grusha* (Moscow, 1962).

The most important variant appears in the first published version, in which the final line, omitted in all later versions, is: "Hold her back" (*Ee uderzhite*), which would give the impression that the previous line, the literal meaning of which is "Save!" (*Spasite!*), is a call to save the woman and not a personal cry for help.

The sixth stanza was not in the original publication nor in the 1964 *Antimiry*.

Sigulda is a summer resort in Latvia.

"Let us sit here a bit" (line 22) has a double significance. It is both an expression of the poet's concern for his weary mother and an allusion to the Russian custom, as depicted in *The Cherry Orchard*, of sitting down together for a moment before leaving a place where one has lived.

"Good-bye" (line 24) is in English in the original. Like many other foreign expressions, "good-bye" is a commonplace in Russian colloquial speech, especially among teenagers.

"In cold stone" (line 42) renders *bul'dik,* a slang word for stone.

"Some old underworld song" (line 53) refers to the extremely popular type of song (there is no Western equivalent) that rose out of the Odessa underworld. Such songs were sung in Russian *cafés chantants* before and immediately after the Revolution. They were suppressed as decadent under Stalin but after his death became current again.

Dead Still

First published in *Znamya* (No. 6, 1965). The poem was written after major attacks on Voznesensky in 1963. See the Introduction and the note to "Winter at the Track."

First Frost

First published in *Parabola* (Moscow, 1960). In the collection *Akhillesovo serdtse* there are five additional lines at the end: *Poskol'znyoshsya. Ved' vy pervy raz. / B'yot po radio pozdni chas. / Ekh, raz, / Yeshcho raz, / Yeshcho mnogo, mnogo raz.* ("You will slip. It is the first time. / A late hour strikes on the radio. / Eh, once more, / Once more, / Many many times more.") The last three lines are the refrain of the popular song "The Two Guitars."

Striptease

First published in *Znamya* (No. 4, 1962). The text here is from *Antimiry* (Moscow, 1964).

Based on images or impressions derived from Voznesensky's 1961 visit to the United States, the poem expresses his search for an American essence. The last line of the Russian calls for martini and absinthe mixed (*absent* rhyming with *aktsent*), unfeasible in translation; accordingly, the translator has substituted a double martini.

Antiworlds

First published in *Znamya* (No. 4, 1962). There are two substantial variants: Subsequent collections have as line 20 *No sokhnet sokol bez zmei* ("The falcon withers without the snake") instead of the original *No sokhnet Solntse bez Zemli* ("The Sun dries up without the Earth"). In the third line from the end, the collections also have *Naverno, prav nauchny khmyr!* ("Perhaps he's right, that learned bore!") instead of the original *V yacheikakh gorodskikh kvartir* ("My apartment cell won't hold me").

For "Bukáshkin" see the note on "Hunting a Hare."

The deserts referred to in line 15 are the Kara-Kum or Black Sands of Central Asia.

In the fifth line from the end, "total loss" is a translation of *mura,* a slang word for something boring and meaningless.

Parabolic Ballad

First published in *Mozaika* (Vladimir, 1960). Our version is from *Scrivo come amo* (*Pishetsya kak lyubitsya*) (Milan: Feltrinelli, 1962), which differs in the important respect that the third line from the end reads: "He is leaving tonight for Siberia." The originally published version had "Galoshes sink in the Siberian spring."

Fire in the Architectural Institute

First published in *Scrivo come amo* (*Pishetsya kak lyubitsya*) (Milan: Feltrinelli, 1962) and *Treugol'naya grusha* (Moscow, 1962). The Italian edition omits the fourth stanza and has *sberkassy* (savings banks) instead of *raikluby* (rec halls) in the sixth. The latter stanza refers ironically to the architecture of the Stalin era, when public buildings were designed in incongruous, monolithic styles.

There was a fire at the Moscow Architectural Institute when Voznesensky was a student. It consumed his designs and ended his architectural career.

Ballad of the Full Stop

First published in *Mozaika* (Vladimir, 1960).

Poets' untimely deaths are a well-known feature of Russian literary history. Among poets "punctuated" by bullets were Pushkin and Lermontov (in duels) and Mayakovsky (by suicide).

New York Bird

First published in *Znamya* (No. 4, 1962). Our version comes from *Antimiry* (Moscow, 1964).

"In Chicago" renders *na Michigane* ("on Lake Michigan"), meaning, by extension, in Chicago, which Voznesensky visited in 1961. In the last stanza, the poet's companion seems to be Yevgeny Yevtushenko, who visited the United States with Voznesensky in 1961.

Italian Garage

First published in *Yunost'* (No. 1, 1963); the text here is from the slightly different version in *Antimiry* (Moscow, 1964). In *Yunost'* lines 25 and 26 of the revised version have been transposed with lines 27 and 28.

Bella Akhmadulina, the Russian poet to whom the poem is dedicated, was for a while Yevtushenko's wife.

The Nose

First published in *Antimiry* (Moscow, 1964). The Russian title is *Ballada-dissertatsiya* ("Ballad-Dissertation"). For Buggins/Bukáshkin, see the note on "Hunting a Hare."

Does a High Wind Make Me Reel?

First published in *Molodaya gvardiya* (No. 10, 1964) but omitted in *Akhillesovo serdtse* and the three-volume *Collected Works* published in 1983. This poem about Stalin, from the fourth section of "Oza," was the first satirical treatment of the subject to appear in print in the Soviet Union. The line "Of Stalin do not sing" echoes Pushkin's "Do not sing, my beauty, / Songs of sad Georgia" (*Ne poi, krasavitsa, pri mne / Ty pesen' Gruzii pechal'noi*).

Her Shoes

First published in *Molodaya gvardiya* (No. 10, 1964), Section VIII of "Oza." The text is from *Antimiry* (Moscow, 1964).

At Hotel Berlin

First published in *Molodaya gvardiya* (No. 10, 1964) as Section X of "Oza," revised for this edition.

The birthday party takes place in Moscow's Hotel Berlin, formerly the Savoy, which has a banquet room with a mirror on the ceiling. The "I" is Voznesensky himself, introduced in the role of buffoon for a serious purpose, much as Alexander Blok introduced himself as Harlequin in his verse play *The Puppet Show*.

Lament for Two Unborn Poems

First published in *Akhillesovo serdtse* (Moscow, 1966) and *Den' poezii, 1966*. This text is from *Akhillesovo serdtse*.

"To hell with it!": In the original, "To Charon's!" In Greek mythology, Charon ferries the souls of the dead across the Styx to Hades.

Ostankino is a park on the outskirts of Moscow.

In the original, Pasternak is referred to only by his first name and patronymic, Boris Leonidovich.

Rasul Gamzatov (b. 1923) is a poet from Daghestan in the Caucasus who has also been a Presidium member of the Supreme Soviet. Lev Landau (b. 1908) is the famous Soviet physicist.

"Eternal Memory!" is said and sung in the Russian Orthodox funeral service.

Boris Livanov (b. 1904) is a well-known actor of the Moscow Art Theater who boldly sought to stage *Hamlet* but was prevented by Stalin, who personally outlawed the play.

The Call of the Lake

First published in *Akhillesovo serdtse* (Moscow, 1966) and *Den' poezii, 1966*. This text is from *Akhillesovo serdtse*.

This poem is about a place that, like Babi Yar, was the site of a massacre by the Nazis in World War II. The names—some Jewish, some non-Jewish—preceding the poem and at the end are those of a few of the victims. The poem makes clear that this mass grave is now covered by a lake where people go boating and fishing.

Volodka is the diminutive of Vladimir. Moishe is a Yiddish form of Moses.

"He's been on a three-day binge": In the original, "he" is identified as Kostrov, who is obviously the Volodka of the earlier stanzas.

"A Jewfish ... The Genius of the Lake!": In the original *chudo-yudo*, a giant fish of Russian folklore. *Yudo* is an onomatopoeic echo of *chudo*, here meaning a fabulous creature, and, in the context, suggests Judea.

Riva (diminutive, Rivka) is a Jewish first name phonetically close to *ryba* (fish). *Zolotaya Riva* (Golden Riva) is a play on *zolotaya ryba*, the miraculous golden fish of Russian folklore, which appears in Pushkin's "*Skazka o rybake i rybke*" ("Tale of the Fisherman and the Fish"). Voznesensky's line *Nichego ne otvechayet ryba* ("The fish answers nothing") is a paraphrase of Pushkin's "*Otvechayet zolotaya rybka*" ("The golden fish answers").

II NOSTALGIA FOR THE PRESENT

Much of the material for these notes is drawn from Part V of *Nostalgia for the Present*, edited by Vera Dunham and Max Hayward (New York: Doubleday, 1978).

Nostalgia for the Present

First published in *Literaturnaya gazeta* (April 7, 1976). This text is from the collection *Vitrazhnykh del master* (Moscow, 1976).

In Russian the word *nastoyashchee* means both "present" (time) and "genuine" or "real."

Family Graveyard

Written in Dumbarton, Massachusetts, at Robert Lowell's grave soon after Voznesensky's arrival in the United States in 1977 and first published in English translation in *The New York Times* of October 15, 1977.

In the summer of 1977, a few months before his death, Lowell had visited Pasternak's house and grave in Peredelkino, near Moscow, and also the little wooden house in Kolomenskoye, on the outskirts of the city, where Peter the Great once lived.

In the first stanza there is a reference to Lowell's habit of holding his head shyly to one side, suggestive of a violinist holding his violin.

At Lowell's grave, Voznesensky laid a branch he had cut from a rowan tree by Pasternak's house. In Russia, the rowan, or mountain ash, with its bright orange-red berries, symbolizes life-in-death, or resurrection, as in Chapter 12 of *Doctor Zhivago*.

Saga

First published in *Literaturnaya gazeta* (May 25, 1977), from which this text comes.

Chagall's Cornflowers

Written in 1973, at the time of Chagall's first return to Russia after his emigration in 1922, the poem was first published in *Sovetskaya Molodezh'* (Riga; July 8, 1973), and also in *Yunost'* (No. 9, 1973). The text here is from the collection *Dubovy list violonchelny* (Moscow, 1975).

At his poetry readings, Voznesensky describes how tears came to Chagall's eyes when, during a visit to Peredelkino, he received a bouquet of cornflowers. The flowers reminded Chagall of his childhood in Vitebsk.

Voznesensky has been severely criticized in the Soviet press for this poem. Yuri Seleznev in *Almanakh poezii* for 1977 mentioned in a footnote that Chagall had decorated the ceiling of the Knesset in Jerusalem, thereby implying the impropriety of Voznesensky's praising an artist with "Zionist" sympathies. Chagall did an illustration for "The Call of the Lake" (see above).

"Man lives by sky alone": The biblical allusion is even clearer in the original, for *nebom* ("by sky") rhymes with *khlebom* ("by bread").

"Your canvases rolled up in a tube": An allusion to the fact that very little of Chagall's work is exhibited in the Soviet Union. Most of his paintings there, such as those in the Russian Museum in Leningrad, are "rolled up in a tube" and stored out of sight.

Provincial Scene

First published in *Yunost'* (No. 7, 1977), from which this text comes.

"A sweet southern town" (*siropny gorod*) refers to Simferopol, a Crimean resort town, where in 1977 with much local publicity a schoolboy was tried for murdering his mother, a waitress named Indulskaya, whose body he threw into an outhouse.

"Bubbles from the earth" echoes *Macbeth,* Act I, Scene 3: "The earth hath bubbles . . ."

Aleksei Gavrilovich Venetsianov (1780–1847) was a Russian painter famous for his portraits of peasant women.

The Interment of Nikolai Vasilich Gogol

First published in *Novy Mir* (No. 1, 1974); the text is from *Dubovy list violonchelny* (Moscow, 1975), revised by the author.

According to an old story, when Gogol's coffin was opened to transfer his remains, he was found to be lying on his side.

In January 1976, Igor Zlatousky in *Zvezda* attacked this poem as a "libel" on Russian history and literature, but Boris Slutsky in *Yunost'* and Vladimir Soloukhin in *Literaturnaya gazeta* defended it.

Phone Booth

First published in *Kurortnaya gazeta* (Yalta; September 28, 1971), and also in *Novy Mir* (1973); the text here is from *Dubovy list violonchelny* (Moscow, 1975).

An Arrow in the Wall

First published in *Den poezii* (1969); the text here is from *Dubovy list violonchelny* (Moscow, 1975).

Old Song

First published in Bulgarian translation in the Sofia newspaper *Literaturen front* (September 1968), with a dedication to the Bulgarian poet Georgi Dzhagarov; the text is from *Dubovy list violonchelny* (Moscow, 1975).

On the Death of Shukshin

First published in *Yunost'* (No. 4, 1976); the text is from *Vitrazhnykh del master* (Moscow, 1976).

Vasili Makarovich Shukshin (1929-1974) was an actor and a popular prose writer known for a bold, candid approach. His most celebrated film was *Kalina krasnaya,* in which he played the lead, a man who returns from prison and is dramatically stabbed to death. In another film, *The Lake,* he played a man joining the fight to save Lake Baikal from pollution, an issue of great public concern and controversy a dozen years ago because of a proposal to build a paper factory on the lake shore. Shukshin's premature death from a heart attack while at work on a new film caused widespread grief. His grave in Moscow's Novodevichi Monastery attracts a constant flow of visitors.

An Ironical Elegy . . .

First published in *Novy Mir* (No. 7, 1969); the text is taken from *Dubovy list violonchelny* (Moscow, 1975).

Winter at the Track

First published in *Literaturnaya rossiya* (March 24, 1977); the text is from *Dubovy list violonchelny* (Moscow, 1975).

The poem is dedicated to Voznesensky's friend, the novelist and playwright Vasili Pavlovich Aksyonov (b. 1932), who now lives in the United States. Aksyonov and Voznesensky were together on March 7, 1963, when, at a crowded meeting between members of the government and representatives of the intelligentsia in the Sverdlov Hall of the Kremlin, Khrushchev lost his temper and berated the young writers present in violent language. For half an hour Khrushchev shook his fist at Voznesensky, angrily accusing him of "formalism," and of wanting to bring about a "Hungarian Revolution" in Russia. Finally, addressing the poet as "Mister Voznesensky," Khrushchev said, "Clear out of my country—I will tell Shelepin here to give you a passport." At this point, Shelepin, then the deputy prime minister, got up and shouted at Voznesensky, "How dare you come to the Kremlin without a white shirt, dressed in a sweater like a beatnik?!" When Voznesensky tried to reply, saying that he was a Russian poet and would not leave the country, many of those present in the hall chanted in chorus, "Shame! Down with him!" For a long time after this incident Voznesensky was not allowed to publish anything.

There are several slang terms in the poem: *vynyukhat konyushnyu* means "get a hot tip," and *khanurik* is a current word for an alcoholic.

Do Not Forget

Written in 1975 and taken from the collection *Vitrazhnykh del master* (Moscow, 1976). "COUNTRY FIRST" is an adaptation of the Russian, which reads *GTO,* the letters on the button standing for *Gotov k Trudu i Oborone* ("Ready for Labor and Defense"), a slogan of Soviet youth organizations.

A Chorus of Nymphs

Written in 1974, included in *Dubovy list violonchelny* (Moscow, 1975); this is a section of a long poem entitled "The Queen of Clubs," with the addition of extra lines in this version.

Maya Plisetskaya is the world-famous ballerina. "Taganka" refers to the theater on the Taganka founded by Yuri Lyubimov and noted for its bold, avant-garde productions—such as the stage version of Voznesensky's *Antiworlds,* which has been put on many times. (Another Voznesensky production, *Save Your Faces,* was banned after the second performance.)

"Rimskaya becomes Korsakova": This double name, more familiar to Westerners, has been substituted for the original Borisov-Musatov, the painter. The two parts of the name have been separated and put in the feminine form in allusion to the custom of exchanging places while standing in line.

Ilya Glazunov is a fashionable Moscow portrait painter.

The Madonna: The Gioconda had recently been brought to Moscow, where it was exhibited for a brief period—those who stood in line to see it were allowed to look only for a few moments.

Technology

First published in the Byelorussian journal *Neman,* the text is from *Dubovy list violonchelny* (Moscow, 1975).

"A hockey game on TV": The original names two popular stars of Soviet hockey, Kharlamov and Petrov.

"The basis of the family, private property, and the state" alludes to Engels's famous work, which is required reading in Soviet courses on Marxism.

"Synthetic caviar": In the early '70s, Soviet scientists announced the discovery of a process for making a caviar substitute, the natural product having become scarce because of dam construction on the Volga, pollution, overfishing, and for other reasons.

The Eternal Question

Taken from *Dubovy list violonchelny* (Moscow, 1975).

June '68

First published in *Komsomolskaya Pravda* (June 16, 1968), included in *Vitrazhnykh del master* (Moscow, 1976).

Sergei Yesenin (1895–1925), the famous poet, in one well-known photograph bears a striking resemblance to John F. Kennedy. In Voznesensky's play *Save Your Faces,* the actors at one point carry portraits of both Kennedy and Yesenin.

Striptease on Strike

A 1966 poem, first published in *Literaturnaya gazeta* (March 22, 1967), taken from *Dubovy list violonchelny* (Moscow, 1975).

American Buttons

First published in *Komsomolskaya Pravda* (June 16, 1968); the text is from *Vitrazhnykh del master* (Moscow, 1976).

Silent Tingling

Included in *Vitrazhnykh del master* (Moscow, 1976), but the translation here is from the original version written in Australia in March 1972.

Pornography of the Mind

Taken from *Dubovy list violonchelny* (Moscow, 1975), this 1974 poem, like the 1971 "Sources" written during the poet's visit to Berkeley, is a reply to Soviet critics' accusations of "pornography."

"Short-order cook": The Russian word *stryapukha* must remind Russian readers of a play of that title by Anatoli Sofronov (1911-1970), editor of the popular illustrated weekly *Ogonek* and a conservative writer who played a part in the anti-Semitic campaign of the late Stalin years.

"Secret millionaires" refers to people who have amassed fortunes from black-marketeering or embezzlement.

Darkmotherscream

First published in *Yunost'* (No. 1, 1972), taken from *Dubovy list violonchelny* (Moscow, 1975).

Skrymtymnym is a word used by folk singers in the Omsk region of Siberia, whose inhabitants are called *omichi*. The word, chanted as a refrain, is of obscure, perhaps shamanistic origin and has no precisely definable meaning, but it has a number of phonetic associations with words such as those for "hidden," "darkness," "prison." Yelabuga is a town on the Kama River where, in 1941, Marina Tsvetayeva hanged herself. "Shagadam" and "magadam" are shamanistic words. Shamans, here, are Siberian witch doctors. "Magadam" evokes the name Magadan, a town at the very end of Eastern Siberia notorious in Stalin's time for the forced-labor camps and mines where countless prisoners died of cold and hunger.

III "RELEASE THE CRANES"

Book Boom

Written in 1977, it was first published in the collection *Nostalgia for the Present* (New York, 1978).

The first line of the second stanza—*I mnogie ne potomu li* (And isn't that why many)—is a revision of the original *Kto nekogda eyo rugnuli,* which has been retained in the translation. In the years between World War II and Stalin's death, Anna Akhmatova (1889–1966) was persecuted and her work was banned. Collections of her poetry are now published in editions of two and three hundred thousand but sell out immediately, so popular and admired is her work, by young readers as well as old.

"Monolithic published hacks" is an adaptation of the fictitious Russian name Massivy Muravlev, itself probably suggested by the word for crane— *zhuravl'* —and by the name of a poet called Zhuravlev.

The Great Confrontation

First published in *Yunost'* (No. 6, 1978); text from *Sobranie sochinenii* (Moscow, 1983).

Introducing this poem at his readings, Voznesensky recounts what the critic Victor Shklovsky told him: In the 1920s, insulted for some reason, perhaps because of a poem Khlebnikov had written, Osip Mandelstam challenged Velimir Khlebnikov to a duel. Shklovsky agreed to be Mandelstam's second. They decided to approach Pavel Filonov to be Khlebnikov's second. Filonov was not only a very great painter but also a poet, an admirer and somewhat a follower of Khlebnikov. When they came to his unheated studio, they found him seated against a wall staring across at the opposite wall, where there was one of his paintings. When they explained why they had come, Filonov replied, "What're you talking about? I'm gathering my energy to command that painting to hang on the wall without a nail. I did it once. It hung for a second. Now I'm going to do it again." The embarrassed poets retreated, and the affair dissipated. Poets are always jealous of one another, Voznesensky adds, quoting Blok's phrase "they greet each other with a haughty smile," whether in Russia or America.

Voznesensky included the poem in a dialogue with William Jay Smith in *Literaturnaya gazeta* (No. 18; April 29, 1981) and in his introduction to the collection of William Jay Smith's poems in Russian, *Shto Za Poezd Priidyot?* (Moscow, 1984), which he edited.

In *Nash sovremennik* (No. 2, 1985) Kunayev viciously attacked the poem and the poet, linking the poem with the work of such "dissidents" as Andrei Tarkovsky and Vasili Aksyonov and, in an ad hominem charge, the poet with putative antidemocratic Georgian rebels. The same Kunayev, with the same sort of reasoning, had argued that because Chagall had cornflowers and cornflowers are blue and blue is the color of Israel, Voznesensky was a Zionist.

Autolithography

Written in 1977 in conjunction with artwork by Robert Rauschenberg and printed at Tatyana Grossman's Long Island workshop; it was included in a "book" with a glass cover inside of which were grains of Long Island sand; the sand falls back and forth as in an hourglass.

"OM—OM—REHT": An example of the poet's adaptation of concrete poetry, this occurs originally in Part IV of *Nostalgia for the Present,* the words for "mother" (*mat'*) and "darkness" (*t'ma*) eliding: *t'mat'mat'mat' mat'mat'*. It was used as a visual presentation preceding the Taganka Theater production of *Save Your Faces.*

"I came each Saturday": Resident at the Kennan Institute in Washington for two months to study Ezra Pound, Voznesensky flew up to Long Island each weekend to work on the lithograph.

"Above Petrozavodsk": There were scandalizing reports of a UFO at Petrozavodsk.

"Houston": The Russian playwright Roshchin underwent heart surgery in Houston.

The "flight from Spain" refers to Tatyana Grossman's flight from Germany through France and Spain to the United States.

"Watermark": In the original, *uzor Gosznaka,* referring to the unalterable mark in notes printed by the official government office.

"Gonzago": The well-known draftsman whose architectural fantasies from the old Italian masters influenced Voznesensky's drawing at the Architectural Institute.

Mother

Written in 1978, first published in *Literaturnaya gazeta* (March 22, 1967) and included in *Treugol'naya grusha*; the text is from *Sobranie sochinenii* (Moscow, 1983–84).

"Sirin": Vladimir Nabokov's pen name under which he published his first poetry and other early work.

"'Don't go, they'll kill you'" alludes not only to the image of gangster-filled America but also to Soviet critics and politicians who attack artists for their foreign connections and inclinations.

Elegy for My Mother

Written in 1983, first published in *Novy Mir* (No. 5, 1983), and included in the group of poems *Maly zal.* The text here is from *Sobranie sochinenii,* vol. 3 (Moscow, 1984).

Voznesensky was on a reading tour in France and Italy when his mother died. Relatives notified him; he returned immediately, on the day she was to be cremated. He stopped the cremation, arranged for her burial beside her husband in Novodevichi Cemetery.

"Catherine's birch tree": Catherine birches are birches planted on orders of Catherine the Great.

"the backbone of a tragedienne": A reference to the grand style of the great actress Ermolova.

"wineglass ...": It's a Russian Orthodox custom to set out a small glass of vodka and a piece of bread for forty days for the spirit of the departed.

The Driver

Written in 1978, published in *Treugol'naya grusha* and in *Sobranie sochinenii* (Moscow, 1983–84) from which the text comes, the title slightly altered.

In recent years, Stalin's portrait has appeared on truck windshields in Georgia.

"Hail to thee!": Roman gladiators, some on their way to death, traditionally hailed Caesar before the contest.

"Hand-raisers": In a meeting, one votes by raising one's hand. In Russia hitchhikers hail a ride by raising a hand the way one votes in a meeting. And autumn trees' bare limbs seem to do so, too.

Voznesensky continues to be an outspoken critic of social and political abuses.

The Singer

First published in *Yunost'* (No. 11, 1985), from which this text is taken.

Though the theme is the popular one of loneliness, the central figure is clearly Vladimir Vysotsky.

"In up to the light bulb" translates the Russian *do lampochki,* a euphemism for *nasrat' do lampochki* ("to shit on it up to the light bulb").

Epitaph for Vysotsky

At one time an underground actor, later a public idol, Vysotsky was a close friend of Voznesensky's. The first great success at The Theater on the Taganka was Vysotsky's presentation of Voznesensky's *Antiworlds,* which had 800 performances.

Despite the insertion of a subcutaneous toxin, Vysotsky continued to drink and suffered clinical death, but was saved. Voznesensky's response was to write his poem "Requiem," the only poem to Vysotsky published during his life, originally titled *"Vladimiru Semyonovu, shofyoru i gitaristu"* ("To Vladimir Semyonov, chauffeur and guitarist"), Vysotsky's first name and patronymic being Vladimir Semyonovich. Not until a few years later could Vysotsky's last name be used. People who hear or read the poem now think that it was written after Vysotsky's death, but, in fact, it was written ten years before.

"Epitaph for Vysotsky" was written in 1980 on the day Vysotsky died; it was carved on a marble slab that stood over his grave for several years. It is now the sixth stanza of a poem *"Pamyati Vladimira Vysotskogo"* included in *Sobranie sochinenii* (Moscow, 1983–84).

Applefall

Written in 1981 after visiting Picasso's house, invited by Picasso's widow; the text is from *Sobranie sochinenii* (Moscow, 1983–84).

Accompanied by a pretty young Santo Domingan woman with an Afro hairdo, the poet entered the house and soon heard some of Tchaikovsky's music. In the room from which it came they found Jacqueline Picasso seated, surrounded, as if by mirrors, by Picasso's portraits of her.

"The idea that preceded creation": Like God's idea of the world before He created it, the central thing, something expressed in the Tchaikovsky piano music interpreted by Rozhdestvensky, a record that Picasso had earlier put on for Voznesensky and which his widow put on in the morning to wake them up. Voznesensky and his companion slept in Picasso's old room, which was very cold and frightening.

In this metaphysical world, the idea of the missing rung of a stepladder is the rib out of which God created Eve.

"Try taking a shower": Picasso was heavier than Voznesensky, who had the feeling that even the shower water was following Picasso's figure, not his. All the objects in the house recalled Picasso.

"Tchaikovsky got turned over": A reference not only to the record that was being played but also to Tchaikovsky's homosexuality.

"The balloon rubbed against ...": The woman's Afro suggested a balloon, all the more because she was taller than Voznesensky.

"The black elbowing of the triangles": Voznesensky asserts his belief that Picasso foretold the encounter between Khrushchev and Voznesensky in 1963, the balloon and triangle of Picasso's painting repeated in Khrushchev's bald head and raised elbows.

"And there sat a woman in a man's shirt": On one level, the poet asserts he created a woman out of apples; on another, he refers to what he calls all women's pleasure in putting on their lover's shirt the morning after making love.

"Tear off the shirt": The woman the poet created out of apples took off her shirt to make love—that is, held out an apple, like Eve, but undressed, like a contemporary, sexual woman—and all the apples rolled away; she disappeared.

"Coauthor of creation": The artist and God.

"The garden in Tarusa": The poet Marina Tsvetayeva's.

Dialogue

A dialogue between the poet and God, or between the poet and his alter ego, written in 1967 about a "poet of the sixties"; the text is from *Sobranie sochinenii* (Moscow, 1983–84).

"Monarchal favor": An ironic reference to the attacks on Voznesensky begun by Khrushchev in 1963.

"Dadaists": A pun on (a) the art movement and (b) the Russian word for "yes" (*da*).

"Ask me": The poet deliberately varies Christ's reply to Pilate's question about what is truth (Christ: "Truth is God") because he insists that any "answer" is static.

The More You Tear Off, the More You Keep

A selection by the author of sections of Part 3 and Part 11 of his 1977 poem "*Vechnoe myaso*" from the collection *Soblazn* (Moscow, 1979), as found in *Sobranie sochinenii* (Moscow, 1983–84).

Based on the finding of mammoth flesh and hide in Siberia, frozen for millions of years but still edible; indeed, dogs ate it. The idea is that immortality comes from self-sacrifice, of which Yesenin and Mayakovsky are held to be examples.

Portrait

First published in *Yunost'* (No. 11, 1985), from which the text is taken.

A Conversation in Rome

First published in *Yunost'* (No. 11, 1985), from which this text is taken.

In March 1985, Voznesensky was received by Pope John Paul II in the Vatican library, where Vyacheslav Ivanov, the Symbolist poet, who emigrated and converted to Catholicism, had been curator. The conversation turned on Russian religious philosophy and Russian poetry.

"A Petersburg spirit" refers to Ivanov, and the "river of knowledge" somewhat obscurely combines the author's response to knowing that the library contains the manuscript of Pushkin's *Rusalka* and to the attempt on the Pope's life.

"Pasolini": The madness of the contemporary world is exemplified by Pasolini's life-style, combining fine poetry, intense homosexuality, and communistic Christianity—his film of the Gospel of St. Matthew includes old Russian Revolutionary songs.

"Who'll we return the ticket to?": Citation of Ivan's question in *The Brothers Karamazov*.

"Bach went blind": Bach, of course, was blind toward the end of his life. Voznesensky considers that mathematical principles were involved in Bach's fugues composed on the notes B, A, and C, and that Leibnitz's theory of monads, published in Weimar in 1714, ties in with Bach's work through the concept of "seed." He likes to quote Leibnitz: "Mathematics is the poetry of harmony that can work out its own calculations but not express itself to the soul."

"Primus": A fictitious, anecdotal name to signify a vulgar rock group.

"Pazzi Chapel": The fenestration under the dome suggested a UFO.

Two Poems

First published in *Metropol'* (Moscow, 1979), a mimeographed anthology of prose and verse compiled by Aksyonov, Bitov, Erofeyev, Iskander, and Yevgeni Popov, with contributions by Akhmadulina, Rein, Bakhtin, Sapgir, Kublanovsky, Lisnyanskaya, Rakitin, and other "subversive" writers. The collection of original and somewhat experimental work, including a first translation of a chapter from John Updike's novel *The Coup*, was quickly declared anti-Soviet and savagely attacked as decadent and obscene. Several writers who published in it were subsequently exiled. Ardis Publishers reprinted the entire anthology (Ann Arbor, 1979); Voznesensky's poems may be found there on pages 377 and 379.

At Ford's Theater

Written on November 11, 1985, by Voznesensky for his reading at Washington's Ford's Theater. This is its first publication.

When voice levels were tested in the late afternoon, an echo came through the loudspeakers as if, Voznesensky thought, it were Lincoln's ghost.

A Man Is Changing His Skin

Originally published as *Chelovek* ("*A Man*") because of a printer's error. The title *Chekolek* is a deliberate scrambling. The text is from *Proraby dukha* (Moscow: Sovetskii pisatel', 1984).

"Poor man entrapped, poor century": In the original, "poor Lokis," a reference to Prosper Mérimée's tale *Lokis* about a creature that is half man, half bear.

A Dream

First published in *Yunost'* (No. 11, 1985), from which this text is taken. In the magazine there is an epigraph: "An ironic poem."

The government's fight against alcoholism is well known; because of alcoholism in the Soviet Union, more than 300,000 children have been born mentally retarded.

"Zhvanetsky": A new popular comedian and artist whose prose stories and anecdotes have made him a celebrity.

"While wiping his nose": The Russian custom is to eat something while drinking; alcoholics, winos, and others cynically sniff their cuffs or their sleeves.

"Chaikas": A luxury car, rather like an old-model Buick, available only to the especially privileged.

"To salt the Dnestr": It happened that some drunken manager, not knowing what to do with several carloads of salt, dumped them in the Dnestr River and killed all the fish.

"Sokolniki department store": The uncovering of a diamond smuggling ring, involving officials at the highest level, caused a scandal a few years back.

An Evening at the Society for the Blind

The text for the 1974 poem comes from *Sobranie sochinenii* (Moscow, 1983–84), with revision by the author.

"Paganini": Niccolò, the violinist.

Silvana Pompanini is a popular movie actress.

The Candle Sculptor

The text of this poem, written in 1977, is from *Sobranie sochinenii* (Moscow, 1983–84).

"Did Calder ever melt . . .": In the original, "Did Konyonkov ever burn . . . ," a reference to the modernist sculptor who worked in wood, who emigrated but returned after World War II.

"A dark time": Our present period.

"'I thank you . . .'": The two stanzas in quotation marks may be read either as the candle addressing the poet or as the poet addressing God.

The Schoolboy

Written after Pasternak's death in 1960 and rewritten in 1977, this poem ties in closely with the essay "I Am Fourteen." The text is from *Sobranie sochinenii* (Moscow, 1983–84). The description in the essay may serve as a gloss on the poem.

"Tolstoy blouse": The belted, collared blouse in which the famous writer was often shown.

The Thief of Memories

First published in *Oktyabr'* (No. 11, 1985), the text of which is reprinted here.

"Empire cornice": The style of the Stalin period.

"Hot-shit publisher's": In the original "Soviet Writer," a Moscow publishing house, *Sovpis,* which sounds mildly improper.

"Simeiz": A Crimean resort.

A Saint Bernard of a Man

First published in *Yunost'* (No. 11, 1985), from which this text is taken, this is the title poem of Voznesensky's next book.

Voznesensky reports that when he was in Georgia he learned about a Saint Bernard named Beko in the mountain village of Bakuriani that had jumped to its master trapped in the snow and, though its leg was broken, for two days kept him alive with the warmth of its body.

"A man everyone knows as Christ": A characterization taken from a French play, *The Man Called Christ*.

The Boar Hunt

A 1970 poem from the volume *Ten' zvuka*; from *Sobranie sochinenii* (Moscow, 1983–84).

"The center of literary gravity": A reference to the most bureaucratic member of the Soviet Writers' Union.

"Bring the ceremonial cups together": Imitation, in parody, of the Orthodox marriage ritual.

"Pugachev": The leader of the so-called peasant rebellion of 1775.

"The Peterhof nymph": A gilt statue in a fountain by the former royal palace at Peterhof.

"Fet": A. A. Fet, Russian lyric poet (1820–1892).

"Alla Verde": With vegetable garnish.

IV SELECTED PROSE

I Am Fourteen

Written in 1980, included in *Sobranie sochinenii* (Moscow, 1983–84), the text has been substantially and specially revised for this edition.

O

Written in 1982–83 and included in *Sobranie sochinenii* (Moscow, 1983–84); the text is from there but has been condensed for this edition with the approval of the author. The woman in question is an Italian publisher.